THE GREAT WAR, 1914–18

THE GREAT WAR, 1914–18

Essays on the Military, Political and Social History of the First World War

Edited by
R. J. Q. ADAMS

Texas A&M University Press
College Station

Published in Great Britain by THE MACMILLAN PRESS LTD.

Printed in Hong Kong

Library of Congress Cataloging-in-Publication Data
The Great War, 1914–18: essays on the military, political and social history of the First World War/edited by R. J. Q. Adams. – 1st ed. p. cm. – (Texas A&M University military history series; 17)
Versions of papers read before a symposium of the Military Studies Institute of Texas A&M University, 4–5 April 1988.
Includes bibliographical references.
ISBN 0–89096–431–9 (alk. paper)
1. World War, 1914–1918 – Congresses. I. Adams, R. J. Q. (Ralph James Q.), 1943– . II. Texas A&M University. Military Studies Institute. III. Series.
D504.G74 1990 89–20363
940.3–dc20 CIP

For Ian

Contents

List of Plates

Acknowledgements

The Military Studies Institute is an autonomous interdisciplinary study and research organization within the Texas A & M University. I would like to express my thanks to the members of its Board, which I have the honor to chair, for their support and assistance in conducting the symposium which brought together the scholars whose essays follow. The members include Professors James Burk, Alex Mintz and John Robertson. Also members of the Board are Dr Frank E. Vandiver, President of the University, 1982–88, and Dr Larry D. Hill, Head of the Department of History. Both were generous with their support of the Institute and this project.

Among my University colleagues I am pleased to thank Professors Betty M. Unterberger and Roger A. Beaumont for their useful assistance during the symposium.

There would be few books if there were not people who can translate rough and battered manuscripts into tidy and readable texts. I herewith acknowledge my great debt to Mrs Deborah Callihan and her staff in the Department of History – their cooperation and patience are a wonder of the age.

I am delighted to single out for special thanks Professor Joseph G. Dawson, Director of the Institute and my close associate, who proved a good and constant friend both in need and indeed as we brought a vague idea to fruition.

R. J. Q. Adams
Bryan, Texas

Notes on the Contributors

Edward M. Coffman is Professor of History at the University of Wisconsin, Madison. A former President of the American Military Institute, Professor Coffman's major works include *The Hilt of the Sword: The Career of Peyton C. March* (1966), *The War To End All Wars: The American Military Experience in World War I* (1986) and *The Old Army: A Portrait of the American Army in Peacetime, 1784–1898* (1986).

Paolo E. Coletta retired in 1983 as Distinguished Meritorious Professor at the United States Naval Academy at Annapolis. His many books include the three-volume *William Jennings Bryan* (1964–69), *Admiral Bradley A. Fiske and the American Navy* (1978) and *A Survey of U.S. Naval Affairs, 1865–1917* (1987).

Joseph G. Dawson is Associate Professor of History at Texas A & M University and is Director of the Military Studies Institute. He is the author of *Army Generals and Reconstruction: Louisiana, 1862–1877* (1982) and is Associate Editor of *The Dictionary of American Military Biography* (1984).

Alfred Gollin is Professor of History at the University of California, Santa Barbara. Formerly the Official Historian of the *Observer* newspaper, he is a Fellow of both the Royal Historical Society and the Royal Society of Literature. His many works include *The Observer and J. L. Garvin* (1960), *Proconsul in Politics: Lord Milner in Opposition and in Power* (1964) and *No Longer an Island: Britain and the Wright Brothers, 1902–1909* (1984).

Thomas C. Kennedy is Professor and Chairman of the Department of History at the University of Arkansas. A Former President of the Western Conference on British Studies, in addition to many historical articles in *The Historian*, *The Journal of British Studies*, *The Canadian Journal of History* and other journals, he is the author of *The Hound of Conscience: A History of the No-Conscription Fellowship* (1981).

Martin Kitchen is Professor of History at Simon Fraser University. He is a Fellow of the Royal Historical Society and the Royal Society of

Canada. His many books include *The German Officer Corps, 1890–1914* (1968), *A Military History of Germany: From the Eighteenth Century to the Present Day* (1975) and *British Policy Towards the Soviet Union, 1939–1945* (1986).

Desmond Morton is Professor of History and Principal of the University of Toronto in Mississauga. A former President of the Canadian Historical Association and a Fellow of the Royal Society of Canada, his many publications include *Ministers and Generals: Politics and the Canadian Militia, 1867–1904* (1970), *Canada and War: A Military and Political History* (1981) and *A Peculiar Kind of Politics: Command and Control of the C.E.F.* (1985).

Charles R. Schrader retired from the United States Army in 1987 as a Lieutenant Colonel, after 23 years of service. Dr Shrader has taught military history at the United States Military Academy at West Point, the US Army Command and General Staff College and the US Army War college and is now a writer and historical consultant. The author of many articles, he is also editor of *Proceedings of the 1982 International Military History Symposium* (1984).

T. H. E. Travers is Associate Professor and Chairman of the Department of History at the University of Calgary. His books include *Men at War: Politics, Technology and Innovation in the 20th Century* (1982), *The Killing Ground: The British Army, the Western Front and the Emergence of Modern Warfare, 1900–1918* (1987) and *Samuel Smiles and the Victorian Work Ethic* (1987).

Trevor Wilson is Professor of History at the University of Adelaide. He is a Fellow of the Royal Historical Society and of the Australian Academy of the Humanities. Among his works are *The Downfall of the Liberal Party* (1966), *The Political Diaries of C. P. Scott* (1970) and *The Myriad Faces of War: Britain and the Great War, 1914–1918* (1986).

Introduction

The conflict of 1914–18, even before the armistice on the eleventh hour of the eleventh day, was known by many – at least in the West – as the Great War. Soon thereafter, probably due to the inventiveness of a British war correspondent, it came to be called by some the First World War.[1] It is highly unlikely that Charles Repington expected the gigantic bloodletting to be the first in a series; what he meant was that there had never been another conflict – a *world* war – quite like it. How frighteningly correct he was.

The sheer weight of destruction of the four years' struggle remains startling: William L. Langer has estimated the direct costs of the War to be $180 trillion and the indirect costs another $150 trillion.[2] The cost in blood surpassed that of treasure[3]: the British Empire lost more than three million dead and wounded, the French 2.4 million, the Italians 1.5 million, Germany's losses totalled more than six million, those of Austria-Hungary almost five million; Turkey, all told, lost more than two million. The United States suffered the least severe losses of the major belligerents, with a total of somewhat more than 300 000, while Russia exceeded the totals of the others with losses estimated at close to seven million. These figures, numbing as they are, refer to uniformed losses only – how many civilians were injured or killed in the conflict? No one knows, and estimates vary wildly.

These were not the only deaths and grievous injuries, of course. Four of the world's great imperial dynasties were doomed by the Great War: the Hohenzollerns, the Habsburgs, the Romanovs and the Osmanlis all passed into history – some more comfortably than others, it should be noted. With them, passed their empires, some young, like the German, some ancient like that of their neighbors, Austria-Hungary. Monarchy survived the War, but it was never the same.

There were many then and now who rejoiced that many key elements of that smug, self-assured, imperial and very European world passed away. Despite its grievous faults, and compared with what preceded and immediately followed it, it was a confident, progressive, enlightened and peaceful world in which disease, ignorance and brutal governancy were under the most severe attack they had ever suffered. The Great War destroyed much of that good with the bad.

If the War destroyed, so did it create. Republics sprang up like May flowers – these, the so-called successor states as well as certain of the restructured defeated powers, almost all failed. One by one they fell into the hands of autocrats who frequently made the rulers of pre-1914 days seem almost liberal in comparison. But it is a seldom-disputed fact that without the War there would have been no Czechoslovakia, no Yugoslavia, certainly no Union of Soviet Socialist Republics – at least not by 1918.

So, too, did the War cause a readjustment among the Great Powers, and the major beneficiary was the United States of America. With the fewest losses; with the accumulated treasure and promissory notes of the other victors (collected largely from the sale of war *matérial*); with the sheer moral horsepower of Thomas Woodrow Wilson, the American republic now took her place – first place – among her elder and exhausted sister powers. As in the case of the new-found enthusiasm for democracy in central and southern Europe, this also was short-lived. Elections came to count for little among the people of the Balkans, and world leadership frightened and repelled them in Nebraska and Indiana; and America fought shy of its new role as world leader.

Perhaps the best known of the War's creations lie in the realm of technology: airplanes, tanks and submarines, but also trenchcoats, wristwatches and surgical techniques – all grew and matured under the pressure of fighting the Great War. Women's roles changed; so, too, did the relations between the generations. Gender demography altered significantly. And, one must also recall the massive dislocation done to the world economy. Surely one should not forget that while this was not destined to be a war to end war, it was surely a conflict which changed the science and practice of warfare forever. When civilians said 'never again' they meant no more war, period. When strategists said the same, they meant the next war, great or small, could not be fought in this dogged and murderous fashion – ever again.

The conflict of 1914–18 was, in fact, the Great War. It changed in some way the lives and futures of every man and woman on the planet. It was, perhaps, the first phase of a new Thirty Years War. It made likely – if not inevitable – a long armed peace followed by a further violent conflict which produced terrors overshadowing any before its time.[4] The last act was inconceivable without the first; its causes, its characteristics and its effects are a meaningless puzzle without an understanding of 1914–18. There would be no Hitler without a Ludendorff, no Churchill without a Lloyd George, no Roosevelt without a Wilson. Even more interesting, perhaps, to those interested in the science of war, there could be no Pétain (in his 1940 guise, that is) without Joffre, no Eisenhower without a Pershing, and no Montgomery without a Haig. Most assuredly there would have been no Stalin without a Nicholas Romanov (or a Grand Duke Michael).

The Great War has touched us – not, of course, by making us precisely what we are but by playing a massive role in making the world which we have inherited and, after making our marks, which we shall pass along to our children. It is in many ways, regardless of competitors for the dubious honor, the seminal event of our century.

The chapters which follow are versions of papers read before a symposium of the Military Studies Institute of Texas A & M University on 4–5 April 1988. The theme of the symposium was simply stated as *The Great War*, but in fact papers were commissioned which touched on issues large and small which have either been overlooked or underemphasised even in the massive literature on the conflict. The resulting papers range widely across the scope of First World War studies. Though it was clearly impossible to touch on all – or even most – of the many elements in which the planners of this volume sense an interest among readers, the following offer insights broad and narrow into several significant elements of the military, political and social history of the First World War.

Part I of the collection is the paper which was the plenary address of the conference: 'The Significance of the First World War in Modern History', in which Professor Trevor Wilson examines the relevance of World War scholarship not only to the study of modern history but to modern times themselves. In this brilliant and wide-ranging essay, myths fall like autumn leaves.

Part II deals with aspects of the war experience of the great European antagonists, Britain and Germany and begins with a chapter by Professor Alfred Gollin discussing the little-known machinations of the making of British air policy in the years immediately before and during the War, and revealing inter-service rivalries and the poverty of civilian leadership during the Asquith years. Professor Martin Kitchen's chapter demonstrates the growth of German military influence over civilian government during the war years. It does much to clarify both the personalities involved and the flaws in the German constitutional system which could allow such a disaster to occur. Comments on the two chapters are provided by Professor Thomas C. Kennedy.

Part III features essays dealing with elements of the war for America and Canada which are too seldom studied outside of relatively confined circles. Professor Desmond Morton discusses the Canadian Military experience in the War, with particular attention paid both to the evolution of the Canadian Army and the effect of the War experience on the development of Canadian national identity. One of the most significant elements of each individual soldier's war is too often ignored by scholars; this is, of course, logistics. Dr Charles R. Shrader reveals much about the real-world experience of the AEF as it passed in record time from peace-time to fighting force, largely under the logistical tutelage of the British Army. It is a remarkably informative and sometimes amusing story. Comment on these contributions is by Professor T. H. E. Travers.

Part IV includes two chapters on the education for total war of the United States Army and Navy. Professor Edward M. Coffman discusses the military instruction of professional officers who came to reach high command during the War. Professor Paolo E. Coletta interprets the little-known story of the struggle between the political and uniformed leaders at the Navy Department in the years before American entry into the conflict, over the proper conduct of the great neutral power. Comment on these chapters is offered by Professor Joseph G. Dawson.

NOTES

1. Charles à Court Repington, *The First World War, 1914–1918* (London: Constable, 1920).
2. William L. Langer, *The Encyclopedia of World History* (New York: Houghton Mifflin, 4th edn, 1974), p. 976.
3. For these estimates, see C. R. M. F. Crutwell, *A History of the Great War* (London: Oxford University Press, 1964), pp. 630–2.
4. See Rene Albrecht-Carrie, *The Meaning of the First World War* (New York: Prentice-Hall, 1965), pp. 167–72.

Part I

The German Offensive: A British Soldier in the Ruins of Arras Cathedral. The Imperial War Museum. Popperfoto

1 The Significance of the First World War in Modern History

Trevor Wilson

I

I take it to be indicative of the significance of the Great War in modern history that one hardly needs to go looking for it. The Great War is an event which keeps presenting itself to us, sometimes on occasions when we are least expecting it.

Let me give a couple of examples. A while back I was prevailed upon by a young friend to accompany him to an open-air concert by a rock star. There, to my considerable astonishment, I encountered for the first time a song called *Children's Crusade*. Its subject is young Englishmen in 1914 going off to the fighting fields of Belgium and France and dying there straddled upon barbed wire or fallen face down in mud. The image which encapsulates them is the crimson poppy which grew so prolifically in Flanders Fields.

These lines might be the work of one of the lesser poets who perished in the trench struggles of 1916 and 1917, or of one of the survivors of these struggles seeking through the medium of verse to say goodbye to all that. As I have indicated, this is not the case. The author of the song has had no experience of the bloodshed – or the poppies – of Flanders Fields. Yet his indignation against the bloodletting of 1914–18 is plainly great.

What is yet more significant, this is not a song whose main thrust is a protest against war. As we learn only from its terrible last stanza, its focal-point is a desperately contemporary phenomenon: the destruction of young lives by the scourge of hard drugs. The poppy remains the focal image, but now it is the opium poppy, not the Flanders poppy.

What we are observing is a poet-songwriter of today seeking after the paradigmatic image for the squandering of young life, and finding it in the First World War. If some are inclined to doubt Paul Fussell's claim that the Great War has burned deep into the modern memory, they would do well to note these lines from a multi-million selling rock album of the mid-1980s (Sting, *The Dream of the Blue Turtles*).

II

Let me offer a second example of how the First World War sometimes forces itself on our attention when we are not expecting it. A recent BBC television program on the career of Lord Baden-Powell and the Boy Scout movement made it clear that Baden-Powell spent a great deal of the 1920s and 1930s portraying his movement as a crusade for peace. Here was the hero of Mafeking wishing to stress his role in promoting the world brotherhood of boys. So at the coming-of-age jamboree in 1929, where 30 000 scouts represented 42 nations and a movement two million strong, Baden-Powell announced: 'We alone have the universal ear of the young. Let us set about teaching that the highest virtues are friendliness and good-will. And there will be no more war'.[1]

Yet the original text of *Scouting for Boys*, which first appeared in 1908, seemed to be conveying a different message. It had much to say about the fall of empires, which sprang from 'the decline of good citizenship and the want of energetic patriotism'. Each empire, it warned, had become 'blind to the fact that other nations were gradually pushing up to destroy it'. Before it was too late, Britain must see 'that our Empire also be not undermined by these defects', for which purpose it should 'turn the rising generation in the right road for good citizenship'.

In a section of the book called 'Our Empire' Baden-Powell had further pressed home a message of something less than universal brotherhood. He explained how the forebears of the present generation had 'fought for and won' Britain's colonies. For example: 'In South Africa we had to drive out the Dutch and then fight the natives for our foothold, which once gained we never let go – and though it cost us thousands of lives . . . we have got it now'. His conclusion was a call for national and imperial defense. 'Peace cannot be certain unless we show that we are always fully prepared to defend ourselves in England . . . The surest way to keep peace is to be prepared for war.'

Entirely in keeping with this message, newsreel film from before 1914 reveals boy scouts parading in military fashion with sticks at their shoulders in lieu of rifles; very much as many of Kitchener's early recruits trained in the opening months of the Great War, there being initially an insufficiency of rifles.

These bellicose aspects of the pre-war scouting movement make all the more noteworthy the manner in which the onset of the Great War changed the thrust of Baden-Powell's orations, from social Darwinism and the armed retention of empire to international brotherhood and the breaking down of barriers. The extent of the transformation must not be exaggerated. At those post-war jamborees he was still laying down as the supreme duty of scouts reverence towards God and loyalty to the King: a message which, if received by the youthful subjects of the Emperor Hirohito or the Duce or the Fuhrer, would set their feet on the path of duty leading directly to such catastrophes as Guadalcanal or Libya or Stalingrad. Yet even so, the transition from Mafeking to Passchendaele had wrought a great change in how Baden-Powell and others of his persuasion perceived war. Too many recent boy scouts had gone to premature graves between 1914 and 1918 to make war seem anything but a national misfortune.

III

My opening point, then, is almost painfully obvious. At least as far as the English-speaking peoples were concerned, it had become extremely difficult after 1918 to think about war in the same way as it had often enough been portrayed in the past – as being fundamentally a character-building, nation-enhancing undertaking that raised moral fiber and (if well conducted) returned a comfortable profit. The slaughter now inherent in war – and not least, the slaughter of middle-class lads, the brightest and the best – had rendered international conflict a perilous proceeding.

This was a substantial change. War in the nineteenth century had sometimes proved a long-drawn-out agony, as in the case of the European-wide conflict which ended in 1815. And the merits of particular wars might be challenged even by some on the winning side, as when a prominent English figure, by way of anagram, had rendered the war in the Crimea 'a crime'. Yet few drew the conclusion that wars were always a futile or an unrewarding experience. For the British, as for the Russians, the Napoleonic War was deemed a great and worthwhile endeavor. Perhaps more astonishing, even the losing power was soon looking back on the Napoleonic era with veneration and no spirit of debunking. Indeed it would become one of the principal laments of the French during the First World War that the nation had failed on this occasion to bring forth a Bonaparte; as if the architect of the hare-brained expeditions to Egypt and Moscow was just what the unfortunate *poilu* needed in 1916 or 1917.

As for the wars which befell Europe in the century between Waterloo and Sarajevo, they were often demonstrably cost-effective for the side enjoying the victory. Most manifestly was this the case with the wars which Prussia waged from 1864 to 1871. In the course of three relatively abbreviated conflicts, the rulers of Prussia secured a threatened political hierarchy against liberal challenges from within, solved the problem of Austria's place in a potentially unified Germany by denying it any place whatever, overcame the resistance of the South German states to the political hegemony of Prussia, routed the great power and traditional enemy on Germany's western border, and thereby converted what had been little more than a geographical expression into the mightiest power on the continent of Europe.

The Great War, as Baden-Powell promptly deduced and as poets, novelists, playwrights, film-makers, and even an occasional rock star have been proclaiming ever since, was different. As Sting tells us in another of his songs, admittedly in the context of Soviet-American rivalry and nuclear weaponry, there is no such thing as a 'winnable' war; that 'lie' has ceased to be believed.

The Great War, in short, had no winners. All of humankind was on the losing side.

IV

On the face of it, this is a compelling assertion.

There were, first of all, the traditional losers: that is, the participants who went down to defeat and had to accept whatever terms they could get. The most evident losers were the empires of the Sultan and the Habsburgs. Having entered the war under severe internal difficulties, they had withstood the shock of battle and retained internal coherence for longer than many observers had deemed possible. But when their powers of resistance and the support of their major ally finally failed, collapse was total. Turkey managed to rescue something from the wreck, becoming in the early 1920s a decidedly minor but self-respecting state under a dynamic leadership. The small republics of Austria and Hungary which emerged from the ruins of the Habsburg empire fared less happily. Austria found itself a capital without a heartland. According to the Chancellor of the Austrian republic, when presenting the draft peace settlement to the Austrian assembly: 'We have been abandoned by all the States we have ruled and we are unprepared for nationalism after six hundred years at the heart of a mighty Empire with many languages'. One possible solution, union with Germany, was proposed in the three-sentence document which proclaimed the Austrian republic in November 1918. But it was not acceptable to the rulers of France, who had no wish to confront in the precarious post-war world a Germany strengthened in this way.

In the case of Hungary, it underwent a brief spell under Communist control which was brought forcibly to an end by Rumanian intervention, in the aftermath of which the peace settlement ceded to Rumania large sections of territory populated by Hungarians. As for Bulgaria, the principal ally of the Habsburgs in the Balkans, it was forced to experience for the second time in six years the underdog status and lost territory as a defeated power.

Two other great empires found themselves on the losing side: the empires of the Kaiser and the Tsar. Being more securely founded at the outset, neither Germany nor Russia underwent the disintegration or the loss of major power status sustained by the Austrians and the Ottomans. But each was forced to relinquish territory secured in wars dating back at least to the eighteenth century. And each underwent political upheaval and a measure – be it profound or less-than-profound – of social upheaval.

Some at least of the consequences were tragic. The regimes of the Kaiser and the Tsar fell in circumstances which provided no opportunity for the substitution on a secure basis of liberal systems. Constitutional government in Russia crumbled within months, to be replaced by a one-party dictatorship consisting of political ideologues with a desperately limited social base. Constitutional government in Germany survived only as long as the victor powers, at whose behest it had been formed, insisted that it survive. When their will failed, it vanished. Russia and Germany then passed under dictatorships capable of deeds of barbarism on a massive scale such as had lain beyond the imaginings of European man before 1914.

In saying this, I realize I am trespassing into controversies that have long engaged the attention of serious experts in German and Russian history – something that I decidedly am not. Yet they are controversies which the non-expert is bound to follow, and about which he and she must endeavor to make a judgment. To what extent were the regimes of Hitler and Lenin – even, perhaps, of Hitler and Stalin – attributable to the Great War?

In the case of Germany, it appears to me evident that the First World War, and more specifically the inability of the Kaiser's regime to prosecute it to victory, occupies a central place in the terrible progression from the merely despicable regime of Wilhelm II to the diabolical system of Adolf Hitler. In concluding thus I must add a qualification. In no sense am I saying that, had the course of the war gone otherwise and Britain and France emerged as the losers, either would have sought to reverse its defeat by pursuing such a course.

As far as Russia is concerned, it appears to me that the weight of the argument belongs with those whom Arthur Mendel classifies as optimists: that is, those who feel that 'it is difficult to imagine a Bolshevik victory apart from the cataclysmic impact of the war experience', and who regard as 'unreasonably speculative' the 'attempt to derive a victorious Bolshevik revolution from prewar conditions'.[2] In sum, the war terminated opportunities for Germany and Russia to soften their existing autocracies into something more humane. And it opened the way to the establishment of new and hideous forms of dictatorship.

To say this, of course, does not end the matter. There is an issue which has much exercised German historians in recent years. In the view of one noteworthy group, resort to war was a course which the Kaiser's regime was always prepared to embrace if that was the only means whereby it could prevent a liberalization of the system. And given the pressures from within which the German autocracy was experiencing, speculation about how German history might have gone had not the Great War intervened is quite beside the point. There *had* to be a war, given the nature of the system and the internal challenges it was confronting. The only alternatives facing the historian are either a war in which Germany was victorious, thereby enhancing all the militaristic and autocratic and expansionist tendencies of the regime, or a war in which Germany went down to defeat, so leaving it seeking after an Adolf Hitler to reverse this setback.

Let at least part of this argument be admitted. There were strong internal pressures thrusting against the Kaiser's regime, and these helped to stimulate a bellicose attitude on its part in the international sphere. Yet it is hard to see the objective circumstances within Germany in July 1914 which compelled the Kaiser and his advisers to hurl Europe into war as the price of their survival internally. Granted that they did initiate and persist in a course of events which brought Europe to catastrophe, employing as justification the painfully inadequate ground of events in Bosnia, it is still less than evident that they *had* to follow this course to avoid collapsing before their own liberalizing forces. Unless one deems that all history is a succession of inevitabilities, in which case the subject of this chapter vanishes into nothingness, then it is plain that some very large events may contain an element of choice. The outbreak of the First World War appears such an event. Admittedly over several decades a number of European rulers, and particularly the autocrats of Germany, had acted in ways to destabilize the peace of Europe. But the decision remained open in mid-1914 whether any would commit the irrevocable deed. It is therefore legitimate to characterize the Great War as a discrete event, with a substantial role in causing major political events occurring during and after it. High among them was the collapse of the Kaiser's regime in circumstances inimical to the establishment of a secure constitutional system and susceptible to the emergence of a new, more malevolent, form of autocracy.

Clearly the political upheavals in Germany and Russia as a result of the war were not of significance only to themselves. Russia's resort to Bolshevism would have serious political consequences, in greater or lesser degrees, for all European states: for example, the disruption of the French Left and its emasculation as a potential force in government, and the movement of several Balkan states from potentially constitutional forms of government to right-wing autocracies. As for Germany's ultimate resort to Hitlerism, it would have the most profound – and deeply injurious – effects on almost every part of Europe, including those powers which had triumphed over Germany in 1918.

To say this is to indicate just one of the ways in which this war evaded the nineteenth century's usually distinct separation between losers and winners: that the winners also found themselves looking out on a world bleak or precarious or unrewarding. This is evident enough in the case of Italy, which gained so much less than it thought its due from the share-out of 1919 that it adopted thereafter the discontents and the demeanor of a defeated power. It is even more evident in the case of Greece, which participated on the winning side but only at the cost of enduring profound humiliation at the hands of France and Britain, and only as a prelude to suffering a savage defeat at the hands of renascent Turkey.

At an altogether further remove, China's experience was somewhat akin to that of Greece. China entered the war on the side of the victorious Allies, but only after undergoing a severe episode of Japanese expansionist pressure (the 'Twenty-one Demands') followed by political disruption internally, both of them developments which might have been warded off had not the muscle and the money of the European powers been engaged elsewhere. And at the peace settlement the Chinese delegates, dismayed at the manner in which the disposition of former German territory on the Chinese mainland appeared to favor Japan, refused to sign the treaty.

Here are instances of countries on the winning side who became, to all intents and purposes, losers: in fact or in their own estimation. Is it also the case with the major victor powers – those who bore the heat and burden of the day and, at the last, drove their adversaries from the field of battle? Were they more truly disadvantaged than advantaged by their involvement in the war?

The burden of disadvantage with which each emerged from the war was indeed heavy. France, admittedly, had regained the lost provinces of Alsace-Lorraine and acquired booty overseas in the shape of former Turkish territories. Britain also had some cause for satisfaction. The German navy, nestling at the bottom of Scapa Flow, no longer threatened its lifelines. And it too had taken a share of the old Turkish Empire. Indeed the post-war years have been characterized, in a distinguished work on the matter, as *Britain's Moment in the Middle East.*

Yet this was poor stuff, in terms of what had been expended to achieve it and in terms of what it promised for the future. For one thing, Britain's adoption of a direct role in the Middle East was a consequence of the unwelcome collapse of the Turkish Empire, which Britain had spent much of the nineteenth century propping up in order that the route to India might be secure without Britain's direct intervention along the way. And anyway, imperial gains were of slight consequence in terms of what had been at stake between 1914 and 1918. For Britain and France, the Great War had not been about empire. It had been about Europe, and about the preservation of their great power status and liberal parliamentary systems in face of the challenge emanating from the greatest of Europe's military autocracies. The terrible exertions of the war could only be considered adequately rewarded if this threat from the power which bestrode central Europe confronted them no longer. Manifestly, this was not remotely the case.

Indeed, France faced the anomaly in the post-war years that its situation *vis-à-vis* Germany was inherently less secure than it had been before 1914. Certainly, France had secured the paraphernalia of enforced German disarmament, a temporarily occupied Rhineland, and reparations. But these were insubstantial guarantors of Germany's momentary status as defeated power. The crucial fact about Germany's situation after 1919 was that the internal upheaval at the end of the war and the territorial settlement which followed it had brought about neither the social dislocation which had befallen Russia nor the dismemberment which had overtaken the Habsburg and Ottoman regimes. Germany remained the greatest power on the Continent. It overshadowed France, as before, in terms of population and economic development. So, potentially, it overshadowed France in war-making capacity.

In truth, not only had the war failed to alter the fundamental imbalance between France and Germany in the former's favor, in important respects it had moved the balance yet further to Germany's advantage. The apparent restoration of France's status in Europe which had developed after 1890 was fatally undermined by events beginning in 1917. After all, the Franco-Russian alliance had from 1894 confronted Germany with a potent deterrent to war-making – the menace of a war on two fronts. If, despite its potency, that deterrent had failed in effect in 1914, how much more threatening was the situation confronted by France after 1919, with no major power on Germany's eastern frontier on whom France could rely for assistance. That is, the withdrawal of Russia from a clear-cut, regular place in the European power alignment following the Bolshevik seizure of power had introduced a fatal element of instability into European affairs such as had not existed prior to 1914 – itself not an era of surpassing stability. Should a regime arise in Germany tempted to seek a replay of the endeavors of 1914–18, the circumstances of the post-war years were altogether more menacing for supposedly victorious France.

That was not only because Russia had ceased to function as a brake on German expansionism. In 1904 and again in 1917, France had acquired further sources of support. It is idle to pretend that the French, despite their devoted sacrifices, would have emerged victorious in 1918 had they lacked the assistance in terms of manpower, seapower, finance, and industrial resources provided by Great Britain, supplemented as the war proceeded by the manufacturing capacity, credit facilities, and even some fighting men from the USA. (Equally, let it be added, it is difficult to see how Britain would have managed to rid Western Europe of its German conquerors had France in 1914 gone the way of France in 1940.) Yet at the outset of the 1920s France was confronted with the spectacle of the USA repudiating a peace treaty which its representatives had played a considerable part in shaping and rejecting the role of guarantor of French security which they had adopted. And in the ensuing decade France also found Britain a less than reliable supporter in preserving the balance on the Continent. It might be the case that if the victor powers did not enforce those safeguards against German revanchism embodied in the peace settlement then they were in effect abandoning their victory. But it was also the case that Britain, having declined to become a considerable military power before 1914, was not remotely inclined after 1919 to maintain the military muscle which – in Russia's absence – was plainly required even to preserve such security as the Western powers had enjoyed prior to the Great War.

Britain's circumstances in the aftermath of war were scarcely happier than France's. It too confronted an insecure world apparently requiring a high level of military preparedness. Except at sea, this was something that Britons even in times of economic buoyancy had never been happy to undertake. The years after 1919 were not economically buoyant. Britain was now required to fund a heavy overseas debt. And within two years of the war's ending, it encountered a severe downturn in its export industries. The workshop of the world was confronting painful problems of readjustment. What was more, as a direct outcome of the war the British government had undertaken heavy commitments towards supporting not only its war victims (that is, maimed ex-servicemen and dependents of the fallen) but also its unemployed – without ever guessing that not just temporary unemployment during the transition from war to peace but long-term, structural unemployment awaited it. Two things seemed manifest. One was that Britain could not afford the cost of enforcing the peace settlement, let alone – as Woodrow Wilson's version of the League of Nations appeared to require – the peace of the world. The other was that victorious war, far from enhancing Britain's position in the world, constituted a burden which its economy could not sustain.

There was, as my introductory remarks have indicated, a further respect in which Frenchmen and Britons could only look back with dismay on the accomplishment of victory. There was a widespread and growing feeling that many episodes of the war – and perhaps the war as a whole – had not been well conducted: names like the Champagne and Verdun and the Nivelle offensive, or Gallipoli and the Somme and Passchendaele, suggested not inspired command but stubborn adherence to inappropriate methods resulting in grievous loss of life for little reward. And it was an undoubted fact that, whether on account of military mismanagement or the nature of the struggle, the blood cost of the war had shaken these nations to their foundations. This gave rise to a fundamental question: could any outcome of war, favorable or unfavorable, warrant such blood-letting?

The hideous cost of the war weighed particularly heavily upon the French. After all, in the course of the conflict they had suffered far more grievously than Germany in terms of loss. A wealthy segment of their territory had been overrun, held captive for four years, and only relinquished after much devastation. Germany had endured no such intrusions. Worse still for the French, in terms of casualties per head of population France had fared much worse than its principal enemy. The rural population of France had borne a disproportionate share of this toll; and rural France, if only in order to withstand the effects of France's inheritance laws, was already recognized as a land of only sons.

In comparison with the loss of life endured by the French, Britain with its larger population and late involvement in the war's major episodes suffered less heavily. But judged absolutely rather than comparatively, it too spent its young lives prodigally. Moreover, such grim losses lay quite outside the British experience. Wars had been a small part of British history over preceding centuries. And at least since the civil war of the seventeenth century, there had been no occurence of war levying its toll not upon the usual sources of cannon-fodder ('the mere scum of the earth' was how the Duke of Wellington had described his army) but upon the nation's soberest and most industrious citizens, its devoted upholders of diligence and loyalty and being prepared and performing one good deed a day. One social observer of Britain, writing in 1922, described how the hard-working middle-class which, like the French peasantry, had limited the size of its family so as to secure its economic status, had willingly sent to the war probably the only son it had permitted itself.

> He went out [this observer tells us] – in the great majority of cases – a volunteer. Every spare farthing had been spent on his upbringing from babyhood. He was to be the pride and assistance of his parents when they attained old age. Then from all the terraces and villas which occupy the hills round great cities came the news that no blood sprinkled on lintel or doorpost had been of any avail against the Angel of Death. A house had been left henceforth for ever desolate.[3]

In a world where mortality among children and young adults had been steadily declining, this onset of death and maiming among males often barely out of school constituted a brutal interruption of one of the modern world's most hopeful trends. And in a wider sense, the

First World War proved a terrible blow to what the liberal democracies were beginning to see as Western man's irresistible progress towards a better life. Up until 1914 Western Europe had experienced the phenomenon of rapid industrial and technological advancement in its mainly benevolent forms. Certainly there were grim aspects accompanying the industrial revolution, as school children of earlier generations were required to memorize. Yet, as was very evident by the opening of the twentieth century, industrialization with all its negative features was proving a wonderfully beneficent force. Western nations were now confronting a splendid prospect without precedent in human history: the prospect of tolerable living standards – adequate nourishment, adequate shelter, adequate clothing – not just for the few but for the many. It was not a case of redividing the cake. The cake was growing larger and larger. Without even a social upheaval, everyone might expect a greater – and in time even a sufficient – slice.

Between 1914 and 1918 Western man was obliged to confront the darker side of industrial advancement. Material improvement had not softened human nature. The will of one human community to inflict harm on a neighboring community, and the determination of its neighbor to resist such infliction, had not abated on account of rising living standards. Secondly, industrial and technological development had bestowed on the advanced nations a terrible capacity to inflict destruction one upon another.

One anticipation of war between industrialized states had been that it would certainly be brief, because if it persisted for any length of time it would engender economic collapse. The experience of 1914–18 revealed this to be a miscalculation. Industrial states proved to be blessed with a large capacity for responding to the strains of war. For one thing, the dramatic rise in living standards in the preceding half-century meant that, as long as the spirit of the nation was willing, the flesh could withstand a lowering of standards without losing its capacity to fight or work. For another, the highly-developed practices of the industrial state made it possible to borrow on the future, from within one's own population or from benevolent and astute neutrals. Hence the money did not run out at the anticipated date. And industrialization was anyway the process of producing if not something out of nothing then something out of very much less. The war witnessed the advanced industrialized nations doing just this: producing, in prodigious numbers, new versions of existing weapons along with altogether new weapons. Of course, these feats of production could not go on indefinitely. Eventually, on one side or the other, the using up and wearing out of resources, human and material, must end in exhaustion. But what proved amazing about the Great War were the prodigies of production that it accomplished, carrying warfare into a quite unprecedented form of transaction.

These feats of human ingenuity and dedication had all-too-familiar human consequences. Supposedly decisive battles decided nothing. They had to be refought, time and again, with new casts of participants. This was particularly so because, in the state which the technology of warfare had reached by 1914, existing weaponry rendered considerable advantage to the side standing on the defensive over the side delivering the attack. Such a development severely reduced the potentiality of battle to produce a decision: great offensive movements accomplished little beyond a mutual slaughter in which the advantage of numbers often enough rested with the side under attack. Let it be added that, as the war reached its climax, this balance of advantage against the offensive diminished. Once nations reached their productive potential and battle became a matter of delivering high explosive shells with such accuracy and in such numbers that life became barely supportable in the area under attack, then conditions for attacker and defender were just about in balance. The advantage then would rest with whichever side enjoyed superior types or numbers of weapons and superior talent in employing them.

But what was certainly true by 1918 had not been the case for most earlier phases of the war. For much of the period 1914–17 the range of weapons available to the defender exceeded that which the attacking side could employ. Three examples will reveal this: the heavy machine-gun; barbed wire; and the trench. Each was a potent form of support for the side standing on the defensive. The attacking force, by contrast, could not transport the first, and it had no use for the second. As for the third, the infantry seeking to bring matters to a conclusion had no choice but to advance into the open, thereby foregoing the truly effective protection against gunfire which earthwork trenches were affording to those merely standing their ground.

Hence the war between Germany and the Entente Powers took on the character for which it has ever since been remembered: huge offensives for grandiose objectives which accomplished nothing tangible beyond mighty losses of life on both sides. Being the winner of a contest conducted by such means accorded the Western democracies none of the national satisfaction – the sense of a great undertaking well accomplished – that Britons had earlier derived from the battles of Marlborough and Wellington and Frenchmen from so many of the campaigns of Napoleon. They were more inclined, as with Winston Churchill in *The World Crisis*, to ponder upon a victory almost indistinguishable from defeat.

V

The Great War, then, appeared to proclaim only one message for the liberal states of the West. Under the impact of rapid industrialization and technological change, war had ceased to be a fit activity for human beings. Outside the war in the air, it could not even pretend to be a contest between warriors, in which victory went to the ablest and most resourceful. It had become a process of mass slaughter, with death dealt out impersonally by instruments and operatives often far beyond the sight of their victims. If conflict had ever been a process for improving the species by ensuring the survival of the fittest, this was demonstrably not the case any longer. Rather, fit adult males were precisely those with the least chance of survival. And in that flying machines had now, if only to a trivial extent, brought women and children and homes and factories into the war zone, it seemed only a matter of time and further technological development before warfare possessed the capacity to wipe out the human race altogether.

Yet if this was the overpowering lesson of the Great War, it was not the only lesson. Other potent messages emerged from the struggle.

The issue which baffles many students of the Great War is simply why it continued so long. The participants had been promised that it would be over by Christmas, and that it would – in the supposed manner of previous wars – be decided by skill and valor and other worthy human qualities. Why did the fighting men on all sides, on learning that the conflict would not terminate in short order and that it would largely consist of episodes of mass carnage, not pack up and go home? It is generally concluded that a gigantic process of propagandizing and brain-washing kept the soldiers at their task.

This is desperately superficial. Let it be granted that the combatants hoped for a short war fought in a 'soldierlike' fashion (this latter being a favorite expression of Sir Douglas Haig's, usually employed to describe his own proceedings). But they had not gone to war on account of the lure of easy pickings or in a spirit of limited liability. They had been convinced that what was at stake was the fulfillment of their national destiny, or the assertion of their rightful place in the scheme of things, or the defense of their way of life and political values and international standing against a savage onslaught. These were not light matters, and a conflict centered upon them would not be lightly abandoned. Only the exhaustion of resources, human and material, and only the demonstration that a succession of defeats on the battlefield was the harbinger of total ruin, would cause the struggle to cease.

What is more, if it is the case that the war was fought for such objectives, it is also the case that for at least some of the participants their objectives were achieved. Here is the ultimate irony of the Great War. All humankind was the loser, and all nations centrally participating in it suffered heavy loss. Yet some nations or peoples gained a lot from the war, or emerged with an imperilled way of life triumphantly vindicated, or came out of the struggle with a sense of having approached tantalizingly close to the fulfillment of mighty objectives which only fortuitous circumstances had at the last unjustly denied them.

It is this aspect that the popular mythology surrounding the Great War, along with much of the serious writing about it, refuses to admit: the point that however costly the candle, it was far from self-evident that the game had not been worth playing. It is recognized that the war in some instances brought gains for countries engaged only on its peripheries or only very late in the day. The USA and Japan were presented with the opportunity to move into markets which the principal warring powers could not for the moment supply or into territories where the European powers could no longer assert their interests. And, to look once more to the peripheries, the war advanced – with a fine sense of paradox – such causes as Arab nationalism and Zionism, along with – in lesser or greater degrees – Indian nationalism and South American nationalism. That is, a war in which the European states tore each other apart did contribute to their retreat from other parts of the world: in at least some instances to the benefit of those other parts. And even in those areas, such as large sectors of Africa, from which European powers did not retreat, it appears that colonial rule was softened by the chastening experience of the Great War: that thereafter it appeared more concerned with the welfare of the ruled and less with naked exploitation.

But it is one thing to say that the war brought incidental or even direct benefits to those on the peripheries of what was fundamentally a European and not a world conflict. To speak of the war as conveying substantial rewards, or the tangible prospect of such rewards, to the major participants – to those at the center of the conflict – is to fly in the face of received wisdom and popular perception.

Yet it is the case that the Great War, like its nineteenth-century predecessors, did have its share of winners. A most evident case is the man who, on a very superficial view, brought it all about: Gavrilo Princip, who fired the shots at Sarajevo. Of course he paid for his deed, spending the few years of his life remaining to him in a Habsburg prison; but he cannot have expected anything else. The important thing is that he acted to a purpose, which was to rescue South Slavs from foreign rule and open the way to the formation of a South Slav State. That purpose was fulfilled. A South Slav state emerged from the Great War. It exists today, and enjoys an astonishing measure of independence from any great power domination. By what calculation can it be said that the heavy human losses which Serbia endured in accomplishing this result were not worth such an outcome?

Others than Serbs and Croats also secured clear advantages from the war: that is, they escaped, if for a shorter period of time, the experience of living under a foreign yoke. A restored and reunited Poland returned to the map of Europe, Rumania enjoyed a considerable (and in some respects unwarranted) enlargement, an independent Czechoslovakia and an independent Finland came into being. All of these states encountered severe difficulties in the years after 1918, and none would enjoy true independence once the temporarily suppressed great powers – first Germany, then Russia – resumed their great power status and their expansionist tendencies. Yet if hardly winners in the sense that Yugoslavia has been, it seems fair even on the longer view to recognize these peoples as beneficiaries of the First World War.

It is less easy to demonstrate than any of the great powers fully engaged in that struggle – Russia, Germany, France, Britain – ended up decidedly on the credit side of the ledger. Despite heroic exertions among its fighting men and major sections of its industry, the war Russia waged against Germany (whatever may have been the case of its war against the Habsburgs) was an almost unrelieved saga of misfortune. The nation lacked the manufacturing resources, governing class, and administrative structure to do battle succesfully against a power with an advanced industrial base wedded to a powerful military cadre. The consequence for Russia was the collapse of the Tsarist regime, a brief period of unstable constitutional government, and the seizure of power by a Bolshevik party possessing little direct endorsement from the nation but (anyway for the moment) no very active ill-will. There followed submission to a draconian peace settlement (from which it was rescued only by the victory elsewhere of its former allies now turned into distinct but hardly devoted adversaries), and a civil war rendered more ferocious by the Great War's brutalization of

Russian life. Only those will consider the Great War as any sort of boon to Russia who see the Bolshevik system, with its political ruthlessness and enforced industrialization, as a vast improvement not only on what had gone before but on any regime it is permissible to speculate might have succeeded the Tsars.

The case of Germany is really very different. Manifestly, the Germans lost: they lost the battles that ultimately mattered, they lost self-respect and stable government and segments of territory. Yet if all their endeavors and accomplishments and spoilt lives had proved in vain, nevertheless it was the case that at certain stages in the war Germany had appeared within grasping distance of the promised land; or if not Germany, then those elements in Germany which interpreted its destiny as domination over the most productive areas to its east and west and south. Twice in the course of the war the prospects appeared alluringly good. The first time was in its opening weeks, as German forces on the Eastern front crushed the Russian intrusions into Prussia while those in the west swept through Belgium before wheeling south towards Paris. The second time was in March 1918. Russia and Rumania had been forced to surrender and to relinquish huge quantities of territory and wealth, Belgium and the most productive industrial region of France lay under a three-year German occupation, and the British army on the Somme was falling back before Ludendorff's hammer-blows.

In both instances, let it be said, it was a prospect without substance, a castle of expectation built on sand. In the first instance the Germans marching on Paris were placing themselves in a potentially disastrous strategic situation from which it became necessary to withdraw with alacrity. In the second, the enforced retreat of the British did nothing to advance Germany towards victory. The Kaiser's regime possessed neither the industrial resources nor the military skills to outfight the British army: the notion that procession across the wasteland of the old Somme battlefield would drive the British into the English channel was wild delusion.

Yet if Germany had too many adversaries with too much industrial back-up and too much military know-how to win on either occasion, it was fatally easy to embrace the notion that the war had been a close-run thing (a view to which an historian as weighty as W. H. McNeill still subscribes) and that with a rather different scenario the alluring prospects of August 1914 and March 1918 might have become reality. Within 20 years of the war's ending – if not a good deal earlier – the scenario had indeed changed, and very much to Germany's advantage.

Further, the ruling forces in Germany consisted largely of those elements who all along had refused to believe that Germany had been beaten – as against betrayed – in 1918. For them the experiences of the Great War hardly constituted conclusive grounds against embarking upon a second attempt after such glittering prizes.

Compared with Germany's, the circumstances of France and Britain at the end of the war were markedly different. The prospect of a Europe reshaped under the hegemony of either or both of them had never beckoned. Indeed one of the things that had made their war endeavors appear so paradoxical was that they were paying such heavy cost for little more purpose than to restore the Europe of 1914; restore it, let it be added, with one significant exception. It must be a Europe with Germany-as-great-power still there, but with Germany-as-menace removed. How that particular circle was to be squared was never evident, except that inflicting a thorough defeat upon Germany's war lords was expected to inaugurate a substantial transformation.

Yet if the objectives of the Western Allies were hardly tangible, compared say with the purpose of those who imposed the terms of Brest-Litovsk, nevertheless the liberal states of the West also fought for considerable objectives. *Ils ne passeront pas* was not just negation. It was a mighty assertion of the positive: of the right of Britain and France to remain independent major powers practising, and propagating the merits of, the liberal parliamentary system. At the end of the day that assertion was vindicated. The invaders had not passed. Rather, they had been worsted on the field of battle, driven from the territory they had overrun, and forced to sue for an end to fighting. This was the purpose, in its fundamentals, for which the liberal powers had gone to war. From this viewpoint French and British involvement in the Great War, far from being an exercise in waste and futility, had proved an entirely warranted undertaking.

It is necessary to make this point, if only because it gets so habitually written out of the script. It is the fact that the liberal states of Western Europe did better what autocratic states are supposed to do best: wage war. They were more effective in mobilizing resources, they were more successful in amalgamating into a viable relationship the key elements of government, management, and labor, they brought forth a range and volume of weapons which their enemies could not match, and they devised means for their employment on the battlefield which proved more appropriate to the prevailing circumstances than those their enemies chose to employ. 1918 saw all this come to fruition. By the middle of the year the Allied armies, and in particular the British army, were able to carry the war to their enemies in a series of operations conducted with exemplary military skill and massive support from home industry: operations which their enemies, even when falling back on the most thorough-going defensive system devised during the war, simply could not withstand.

Reading many well-regarded works of history one would never divine any of this. Rather, what masquerades as the story of 1918 disregards the Western Allies except as object. The tale is confined to what, at the year's opening, the German high command set out to do, how resourcefully and with what powers of innovation they did it, how agonizingly close they came to success, and why – falling just short of their ultimate goals – they sued for peace.

So in W. H. McNeill's warmly-admired *The Pursuit of Power*, we read:

> On the battlefield intensified mobilization [he is talking of German mobilization] brought the expected results. Russia was defeated and dismembered in 1917, and in March 1918 new tactics of infiltration broke the Allied trench lines in France. The victorious Germans lacked the transport to keep advancing, but without the moral and material support of the American Expeditionary Force, some two million strong by November 1918, the weary British and French armies could scarcely have survived the German spring offensives. Thus until the final weeks victory hovered always just beyond the Germans' grasp.[4]

This is obviously a passage written to deceive gullible Antipodeans, who may well be persuaded that spring in the northern hemisphere falls in November, rather than (as I gather is the case) many months earlier: many months, let it be said, before the appearance of any of those two million Americans whose contribution to saving the British in the spring was precisely nothing. As for victory, at no stage did it lie anywhere approaching the Germans' grasp.

Such misconceptions are not the prerogative of American historians (and they are not present, let it be said, in John Toland's account of the war in 1918). They can be found in a standard *British History Atlas*, whose depiction of the major battles fought by the British on the Western Front opens with 'German gains' at the first battle of Ypres in October 1914 and stops dead with the 'German gains' of March-April 1918; and in a recent history of the British army on the Western Front, which virtually halts amidst the alarms and setbacks suffered by the

British during the German spring offensive. 'Initially successful', the latter tells us, 'the German attacks of 21 March 1918 and those of succeeding months actually led to such difficulties in the German army that an armistice was eventually requested'.[5] In all this the realities of 1918 become buried from sight: namely that battles occurred on the Western Front subsequent to April 1918 in which 'German gains' were not the order of the day, and that the Germans' capitulation sprang from 'difficulties' resulting not from their successes but from an unrelenting succession of defeats to which there could be no termination short of surrender.

Yet if the major element in the story of 1918, namely the great victory of the Entente Powers, has been and continues to be shouted down, that is all that has happened to it. It did occur, and it was not forgotten. When it mattered, it also proved to be a part of modern memory. The Western democracies had withstood a mighty military onslaught; and notwithstanding appalling mistakes on their part along the way, in time they had beaten it into submission. Heartbreaking the cost may have been. Devoutly it might be hoped that such a challenge would never again be confronted. Yet these were not taken as grounds for doubting that, in identical circumstances, the same response must remain the only response appropriate. Even in the most peace-inclined, or anyway war-averse, of liberal states, the War That Will End War had not abolished the will to take up arms to end it again.

Here, I take it, lies the prime significance of the Great War. It had demonstrated that conflicts among major powers for fundamental objectives were simply too costly to victor as well as vanquished ever again to be undertaken. It had also demonstrated contrary things: that, even though at grievous cost, some participants in war could still secure long-lasting benefits, such as national sovereignty or liberation from an oppressor or the establishment of a national home; that some of those participants who had come out of the conflict truly badly might, in different but not unattainable circumstances, have emerged from it much more advantageously; and that, even for somewhat disillusioned victors, the objectives for which they had fought remained sufficiently fundamental to their well-being, and their idea of the good, to justify their vindication on further necessary occasions.

The Great War, in short, delivered conflicting messages and so taught no coherent lesson. If the world seems any nearer resolving its paradoxes, that is principally because – anyway for the moment – the fate of human kind is being decided by a different, and more benevolent, set of participants.

NOTES

1. See Paul Wilkinson, 'English Youth Movements 1908–30', in *Journal of Contemporary History*, Vol. 4, No. 2, April 1969.
2. Arthur Mendel, 'On Interpreting the Fate of Imperial Russia', in Theofanis George Stavrou (ed.), *Russia Under the Last Tsar* (Minneapolis: University of Minnesota Press, 1969).
3. C. F. G. Masterman, *England After War* (London: Hodder & Stoughton, n. d.), p. 79.
4. William H. McNeill, *The Pursuit of Power* (Oxford: Basil Blackwell, 1983), p. 340.
5. Martin Gilbert, *British History Atlas* (London: Weidenfeld & Nicolson, 1968), p. 101; Tim Travers, *The Killing Ground: The British Army, the Western Front and the Emergence of Modern Warfare, 1900–1918* (London: Allen & Unwin, 1987), p. 260.

Part II

Vickers FB5, 1914. The FB5 was designed as an offensive aircraft, occupying the forward position in an uninterrupted field of fire. The Imperial War Museum.

2 A Flawed Strategy: Early British Air Defense Arrangements

Alfred Gollin

In 1940 Britain faced a test that would determine national life or death. In this instance the threat to the nation came from the air. For centuries and ages past, however, the British had defended their island home from invasion or attack by controlling, with their fleets, the far and narrow seas. When vehicles that could fly successfully in the air were developed early in this century it is not surprising that some people in Britain paid very serious attention to them because of the effect they might have upon the safety of the British Isles.

It is not by chance that the official historian of Britain's war in the air in the period 1914–18 wrote: 'It is not extravagant to say that the 17th of December 1903, when the Wright brothers made the first free flight through the air in a power-driven machine marks the beginning of a new era in the history of the world'.[1]

Despite the significance of these developments historians, in my opinion, have not paid enough attention to the early history of Britain's air defenses. It will be my purpose, in this chapter, to look at the pre-1914 origins of these defenses and then at their situation in the early days of the First World War. It is the story of a flawed strategy, from start to finish.

As early as the end of the year 1908, owing to the technical achievements of the Wright brothers, Count Zeppelin, and the French aviation pioneers, H. H. Asquith's Liberal government found it necessary to take up the question of the air defense of Great Britain.[2] However, this government was never able to force the War Office and the Admiralty to cooperate in the creation of an efficient air defense system for the country. These two departments of State followed policies and strategies that were entirely opposed to each other in this new sphere of the national defense.

The key to this terrible situation is revealed in the British official history where it is explained that: 'The determining factor in the shaping of the defensive policy of the British empire has always been the maintenance of sea supremacy by the navy, and the expulsion of any raiding forces which might elude the Fleet and gain a footing on British territory has always been the concern of the army. In accordance with this long-established tradition, if enemy aircraft cross the coast the responsibility for resisting them, whether by anti-aircraft gunfire or by aircraft, would automatically rest with the War Office'.[3]

But I have to stress that in this early period the authorities in the War Office had scarcely any interest at all in the home air defenses. As time passed they worked out a theory for the employment of the aircraft under their control. It became War Office doctrine that all the Army aeroplanes, grouped in a unit known as the Military Wing of the Royal Flying Corps, would be sent to the Continent, immediately upon the outbreak of war, to serve as the reconnaissance arm of the British Expeditionary Force. An official statement, promulgated in 1912, explained: 'The Military Wing of the Flying Corps should consist . . . of eight squadrons . . . The whole of these squadrons are required for use in connection with the Expeditionary Force'.[4]

Despite this conclusion the War Office, in this period, continued to claim 'sole responsibility' for the home air defenses. They refused to surrender a jot of their authority in this sphere to the Admiralty. The rivalry between the two Services was so intense that reason and logic were allowed no place in Britain's air defense arrangements. The military wanted to send all their aeroplanes to the Continent and at the same time to exercise complete and entire control over the home air defenses. It was a bizarre situation.

In 1913 Colonal Frederick Sykes, Commander of the Military Wing of the Royal Flying Corps, was involved in working out the details of its organization. Given the attitude of the War Office with respect to home air defense, which I have just explained, Sykes prepared a document almost impossible to believe. He wrote to the Director General of Military Aeronautics:

> Eventually, I assume, the duties of the Wing will include the provision of an Air Service for Home Defense. . . .
>
> At the present, however, its functions are limited to the provision of an air service for the Expeditionary Force, and as long as its horizon is thus confined, it would appear necessary to design its war and peace organization mainly with the idea of these functions.[5]

This attitude in the War Office did not change until 27 July 1914. At that time the Director-General of Military Aeronautics, Sir David

Henderson, drew up certain proposals for the employment of aeroplanes for 'Home Defence against Aerial Attack'. He then proposed that 162 aeroplanes deployed in six squadrons should be allocated for the purpose. His detailed plan read as follows:[6]

Command	Defended and Vulnerable Points	Allotment of Aircraft	Total aeroplanes available	Peace Stations
Scottish	Cromarty Aberdeen The Tay The Clyde	1 squadron	27	Headquarters at Montrose
	The Forth	1 squadron	27	New Station near The Forth
Northern	The Tyne The Tees The Humber	1 squadron	27	Headquarters at new station near The Humber
Eastern	Harwich Dover Newhaven	1 squadron	27	Headquarters at Dover
	Shoeburyness Thames and Medway	1 squadron	27	Headquarters at Orfordness
Southern	Portsmouth Plymouth	1 squadron	27	Headquarters at Fort Grange
Western	Barrow The Mersey The Severn Milford Haven	It is unlikely that these points could be attacked from the air for some time to come. In case of unforeseen circumstances aircraft could be allotted from one of the other commands.		
Irish	Queenstown Berehaven Lough Swilly Belfast	These ports do not at present appear to offer a sufficiently important objective to induce an enemy to undertake the difficult enterprise of an aerial attack.		
	TOTAL	6 Squadrons	162	

We must be clear, however, that Henderson and his colleagues in the War Office were overtaken by events. No part of this plan was ever put into effect. The war began before the plan could be implemented in any way.

I should explain here that when war came in August 1914 the War Office, despite its high claims about its responsibility for home air defenses, at once dispatched almost all its aeroplanes to France for reconnaissance service with the Expeditionary Force. The Admiralty, shortly after, had to take over much of the burden of the Air Defense of Great Britain by itself.

The First Lord of the Admiralty at that time was Winston Churchill. Years later, in his memoirs, Churchill tried to explain and account for these singular developments. For political reasons which I have no time to go into, Churchill, in his *The World Crisis*, sought to make excuses for the War Office.[7] This was not his *contemporary* opinion, however. In a memorandum dated 22 October 1914 Churchill gave expression to the bitterness which marked out the rivalry between the two services in this sphere. His unpublished paper, entitled 'Aerial Defence', made crystal clear the absolute failure of the War Office and the Admiralty to cooperate in the matter of the home air defenses in the period before the war and at its beginning. He wrote:

> Until more than a month after the war began, the sole responsibility for the defence of all vulnerable points in England by gunfire, sea-planes, or any other method, against aerial attack, rested with the War Office . . . General Robertson, representing the War Office, claimed for the War Office the sole responsibility, not only in regard to everything inland, but in regard to naval ports and vulnerable points of all kinds, even those exclusively of naval interest.
>
> Notwithstanding these views, the War Office had not up to the time of the declaration of war provided any aeroplanes from home defence; they had limited themselves exclusively . . . to the development of the expeditionary squadrons, and, on the outbreak of war, practically all the army aeroplanes were sent abroad. Not only were none available for guarding the vulnerable points, but none could be found even for the temporary purpose of coast-watching during the passage of the army to the Continent.[8]

In the pre-war period the Admiralty followed an entirely different course from the War Office with respect to the home air defenses. The Royal Navy, in order to carry out its various duties, depended upon its several naval magazines, cordite factories, and dockyards. At a meeting held in the Admiralty on 4 January 1910 it was recognized that these vital shore establishments were also static targets now, for the first time, 'vulnerable to overhead attack . . . '[9] The officers involved in this discussion at the Admiralty recognized that the development of aircraft had already in 1910 created serious problems for the Royal Navy, problems not encountered before in the entire history of the naval service. They did not believe their ships at sea would be endangered by aircraft[10] but they were convinced that their large shore establishments now lay open to this menace from the air.

After January 1910 the naval authorities made several attempts to interest the War Office in this novel subject because, as we have already seen, the responsibility for protecting these land-based naval establishments lay with that department. Not much was achieved, however.

A significant change took place in 1911. In that year Winston Churchill became First Lord of the Admiralty. He was very interested in aircraft and in air defense. In particular, he wanted to employ the aeroplanes of the Naval Wing of the Royal Flying Corps, later called the Royal Naval Air Service, to carry out the Air Defense of Great Britain. Although a recent writer, Malcolm Cooper, has stated of the War Office and the Admiralty that 'neither had been keen to hold responsibility for home air defense . . . ,'[11] this was not the case. One of Churchill's great objects as First Lord was to bring about an increase in the Admiralty's responsibilities in the area of home air defense.[12]

He was unable to achieve his goal. However, when the war broke out in August 1914 a remarkable thing happened. The new Secretary of State for War, Lord Kitchener, adopted a novel course of his own. The War Office, as late as July 1914 had continued to demand 'sole responsibility' for the home air defenses.[13] However, early in September Kitchener asked Churchill if he would accept, 'on behalf of the Admiralty, the responsibility for the aerial defence of Great Britain, as the War Office had no means of discharging it'.[14] This new arrangement was sanctioned by the Cabinet on 3 September.[15]

When Kitchener became Secretary of State in August 1914 he was astonished to discover that the War Office, eager to send every military aeroplane that could be spared to the front in France, had made no provision at all for home air defense. After consultations with Lieutenant-Colonel Sefton Brancker, the officer in charge of The Directorate of Military Aeronautics in the War Office, Kitchener could only appeal to Churchill for his help and assistance. Typically, Churchill responded to this new challenge and accepted the added responsibility. He would live to regret his generosity.

It must not be thought that the officers in the War Office were grateful for the help given them by Churchill in this hour of crisis. These military men were powerful personalities. They did not readily accept the opinions of others. This decision of the War Office to surrender its control of the home air defenses in September 1914 was resented. The military authorities continued to hold fast to the old principle that their department; and not the Admiralty, should be in charge of them. They had not abandoned their original outlook in any way. Shortly after the change-over took place, Colonel Brancker prepared a minute for his superiors. In it he argued that if the army had the 'unrestricted use of the aeroplane industry', instead of having to share it with the navy, 'we would even now be prepared to carry out the aerial defence of Great Britain . . . ' He concluded his minute by arguing that the War Office should not accept the new situation 'forever' even though it had to acquiesce, momentarily, in the change.[16]

The bickering between the two departments continued for months thereafter. They fought each other almost as vigorously as they fought the German public enemy in France. It is small wonder that a long time was to pass before the air defense of Great Britain became an efficient organization.

Much of the blame for this failure in interdepartmental planning must fall on the Prime Minister, H. H. Asquith. After all, he bore 'ultimate responsibility for British defense arrangements'.[17] Nor was this an isolated lapse.

At the time of the Agadir crisis in August 1911 it was revealed that the Admiralty and the War Office had worked out their plans for war with Germany in isolation from each other. The war strategies advocated at that time by each of the service departments were mutually exclusive. Historians have blamed Asquith for this situation, which was nothing less than a national scandal.

One historian has written of the famous Committee of Imperial Defence meeting, held at the time of Agadir, on 23 August 1911, as follows: ' . . . the C.I.D. and Asquith shared responsibility for the lack of coordination and cooperation . . . though he was capable of great ruthlessness to friend and foe alike, Asquith had perfected the art of indecision and evasion as a positive political asset. The . . . Prime Minister . . . preferred . . . to postpone decisions . . . Defense problems, which he often never understood, were not immune from this treatment. . . .'[18]

This 'treatment' determined the quality of Britain's Home air defense arrangements in the months after the war began in August 1914. In the period before the outbreak of war and for months after Asquith did nothing to correct this bizarre gap in his country's defense arrangements.

NOTES

1. Sir Walter Raleigh, *The War in The Air* (London: 1969), vol. I, p. 1, hereafter cited as Raleigh, *The War in The Air*.
2. See Cab. 16/7. 'Report and Proceedings of A Sub-Committee of the Committee of Imperial Defence on Aerial Navigation', dated 28 January 1909 and marked *Secret*'. The Terms of Reference or instructions for this sub-Committee were issued by the Prime Minister on 23 October 1918.
3. H. A. Jones, *The War In The Air* (Oxford: 1931), vol. III, p. 71.
4. See Cab. 16/16 C.I.D. 139–B. 'Report and Proceedings of the Standing Sub-Committee of the Committee of Imperial Defence on Aerial Navigation. 1912', dated March 1912 and marked '*Secret*'.
5. Air 1/118/15/40/56. F. H. Sykes to D.G.M.A., War Office, 16 December 1913.
6. Air 1/511/16/3/59. David Henderson, D.G.M.A. to Director of Military Training, dated 27 July 1914.
7. See Winston Churchill, *The World Crisis* (London: n.d.) vol. I, p. 265.
8. Air 1/2/2314/222/6. 'Aerial Defence' by W.S.C., Admiralty, 22 October, 1914.
9. For the meeting see Air 1/654/17/122/491. 'Report of a meeting held on 4th Jan. 1910 to discuss recent progress made by Foreign Governments in aerial navigation . . . ' dated 7 January 1910 and marked 'Confidential'.
10. It was believed that ships were too small to be endangered. The land establishments were so huge it was believed they could be attacked successfully.
11. See Malcolm Cooper, *The Birth of Independent Air Power* (London: 1986), p. 105.
12. Churchill tried to enlarge the role of the Royal Naval Air Service in the area of home air defense in several ways. In particular, he argued for this object at a series of conferences held between authorities from the War Office and the Admiralty in the period August 1913 and May 1914. These conferences were known as the 'High Level Bridge'. See Cab. 18/27. 'Proceedings of Conferences held at the Admiralty and the War Office between August 14th and May 22nd 1914'. 'High Level Bridge Conferences', marked '*Secret*'.
13. See Air 1/2314/222/6. 'Aerial Defence' by W.S.C., Admiralty, 22 October 1914.
14. See Churchill, *The World Crisis*. vol. I, p. 265.
15. See W.O. 32/5260. 'Confidential' Report by Murray F. Sueter, undated.
16. W.O. 32/5260. Minute by Brancker, dated 2 December 1914.
17. Samuel R. Williamson, Jr., *The Politics of Grand Strategy, Britain and France Prepare for War, 1904–1914* (Cambridge, Mass.: 1969), p. 193.
18. Ibid., pp. 192–3.

A Portrait of General Erich Ludendorff. Reproduced courtesy of the National Archives of the United States of America.

3 Civil-Military Relations in Germany During the First World War

Martin Kitchen

When the Austrian Chief of Staff, General Conrad von Hötzendorf, read the telegram that had been sent to him by his Prussian counterpart on 30 July 1914 which announced that Germany was prepared to mobilize in support of Austria, the Foreign Minister, Berchthold, asked the famous rhetorical question: 'Who rules: Moltke or Bethmann?'[1] In terms of the German constitution there was no doubt about the answer. It was not the Chief of the Prussian General Staff nor the Chancellor of the Reich who ruled, only the Kaiser. His powers were exceptional. He exercised ultimate control over the army, the bureaucracy and the conduct of foreign affairs.[2] But in spite of Wilhelm II's early ambition to establish his personal rule, and for all his later frustrated outbursts glorifying his role as Kaiser, his infringements of the constitutional limits to his power, and his exalted view of himself as Supreme Warlord armed with his unlimited extra-constitutional power of command (*Kommandogewalt*) he was essentially a dilettante, incapable of sustained effort and unwilling to use his executive powers to achieve a satisfactory balance between the various branches of government. By 1914 he had become a 'shadow Kaiser', a neurotic, weak and remote figure whose imperial powers were used by others who were able to obtain from him an 'order of the All-Highest'.[3]

Throughout the July crisis of 1914 it was apparent to all observers that, as the Württemberg envoy to Berlin put it, 'the reins are slipping noticeably out of the hands of the diplomats into those of the War Department'.[4] The civilians were trapped by the plans and timetable of a dead man, General von Schlieffen, and von Bethmann Hollweg's prevarications and the Kaiser's uncertainties merely irritated the military authorities. Moltke angrily told Admiral Tirpitz that the objections of mere civilians should be ignored, for the time had come for the military to take charge.[5]

When war broke out, a war which the German military had done so much to bring about, the civilians were soon pushed aside. The Kaiser plunged into a deep depression and did nothing but sleep until midday, eat large quantities of exquisite foods and spend a fortune on the decoration of his quarters. He lived in increasing isolation, he gave the most optimistic gloss to those documents he actually bothered to read and his aides began to fear that he was living in a fantasy world.[6] In spite of occasional sour complaints that he was being ignored, he left the running of the war to the Army High Command (OHL).

Even though the Kaiser was nominally the head of the OHL, Ludendorff, for example, drew a clear distinction between the OHL and the Kaiser, a distinction which was constitutionally inadmissible and which justifiably enraged Wilhelm II.[7] Indeed the 'Supreme Warlord' soon became a rather pathetic figure. On 20 August 1914 he used a rather trivial incident to complain to his Cabinet Chiefs Lyncker and Admiral Müller that he was regarded as an object of such contempt that no one wished even to sit next to him.[8] The prestige of the monarchy declined to such an extent that by 1917 the Military Cabinet reported that they were receiving numerous requests that the Kaiser should be asked to abdicate.[9]

Although it would be a mistake to dismiss von Moltke as a nonentity, and the charges against him made by most of his colleagues that he misunderstood and mismanaged the supposedly infallible Schlieffen plan are absurd, he was somewhat limited both as a soldier and as a man.[10] But he was very close to the Kaiser who shared many of his unattractive prejudices on race, religion and war, and he was the only person in a position of real responsibility who was also a trusted friend of the monarch.[11] After the German defeat at the Battle of the Marne it was obvious that Moltke had to be replaced; and his successor, General Von Falkenhayn, who now combined the offices of War Minister and Chief of the General Staff, remained isolated from the Kaiser and kept him ignorant of the conduct of the war.

The close relationship between the Kaiser and the army, which had eroded since the turn of the century in spite of the bombastic assurances to the contrary, was now irrevocably broken. The declaration of the state of siege, made on 31 July 1914, meant that all of Germany, with the exception of Bavaria, was administered by the local army commanders who were given precedence over all the civilian authorities.[12] The law provided for the suspension of most of the constitutionally-guaranteed liberties including personal freedom, freedom from unlawful search and seizure, the prohibition of summary courts, the freedoms of speech, association and assembly and restrictions on the use of armed force to put down civil disorders. Bethmann Hollweg had argued against the invocation of the law saying that it would have 'disastrous consequences for the solidarity, depth and strength of patriotic feeling, and that any possible military advantages would not compensate for the harm that could be caused in the area of politics or ideals'.[13] The military insisted that the declaration of a state of siege was an essential part of their mobilization plans and the Chancellor promptly gave way.

Until December 1915 any infractions of the law of the state of siege had to be punished with a prison sentence, but now the *Lex Schiffer* provided for fines of up to 1500 marks. Even with this modest improvement the military commanders could use their dictatorial powers against people who had no effective right of appeal. As the war progressed there was hardly any aspect of domestic politics which did not lie within the field of competence of the commanding generals. Apart from censorship and propaganda they dealt with questions of the control of the labor force and of industry. They were determined to crush political dissent, destroy the labor movement and to impose an ultra-conservative orthodoxy. The government was powerless to control their activities. The Kaiser could not be prevailed upon to issue orders to restrain the military commanders who were thus free to rule their fiefdoms without any moderating influence. It was not until October 1918 that the government of the Reich was given some power over the military commanders as part of the process of democratization preparatory to an armistice. The creation of the *Kriegsamt* under General Groener in 1916 subordinated the commanding generals to the War Ministry in economic affairs, but Groener allowed a great deal of discretion to the local branches, depended on the reports of the commanding generals on economic conditions and they were thus still allowed to go their own way. In 1917 censorship was reorganized, the military commanders following the guidelines laid down by the OHL, but this did not result in them becoming mere executive organs of the general staff.

The creation of a War Press office (*Kriegspresseamt*) in October 1915 gave the OHL direct control over censorship, and Hindenburg and Ludendorff blatantly used it to pursue their own political aims. Through these means the OHL mounted a massive press campaign against Bethmann Hollweg, who was unable to counter these attacks. Hindenburg told Bethmann that 'to my regret I am unable to offer censorship measures against purely political remarks, as political censorship is only justified when the interests of the military command have to be protected'.[14] All complaints by the civilians about this flagrant misuse of propaganda and censorship by the army were countered with the bland assertion that politics was no concern of theirs. On the other hand, attacks on the left-wing press, censorship of reports of food shortages, attacks on businessmen, and criticism by the extreme right were deemed to be justified as essential measures to preserve the political truce (*Burgfrieden*) which had been proclaimed at the beginning of the war and which the OHL insisted was essential for its successful conduct.

Propaganda was handled by Major Nicolai of section IIIb of the OHL.[15] Propaganda committees (*Aufklärungsausschüsse*) were established in each district (*Bezirk*). They followed the OHL's policies by attacking the government for its weakness, denouncing the Reichstag majority, warning against a 'feeble peace' and disseminating all manner of extremist claptrap. Almost all areas of German life became matters of 'military necessity' including denunciations of Goethe as a dangerous liberal, attacks on the sale of contraceptives and the demand for a heavy tax on bachelors for failing in their 'natural duties'.[16] Reports of German defeats and casualty figures were so manipulated that they did much to create the illusions which made it impossible for most Germans to face the realities of a lost war.[17] Fritz von Unruh was courtmartialled for publishing a cruelly realistic novel on Verdun.[18] Strikers were denounced for 'treason and fratricide' and the troops were submitted to endless harangues about the evils of social democracy.[19]

The Chancellor, von Bethmann Hollweg, further strengthened the already excessive influence of the military by agreeing that a mere civilian was incapable of understanding the arcana of military science. In this view 'purely military' affairs should be left to the experts, and the soldiers were quick to extend the definition of military affairs to include almost everything that had to do with a nation at war. In such a situation only the Kaiser could have redressed the balance between the civilian and the military, but this he refused to do. Since Wilhelm II would not attend to the affairs of state, his Cabinets – Civil, Military and Naval – were increasingly ineffective. Thus from the outset of the war the civilians were almost powerless against the OHL and the commanding generals.

At the beginning of the war the Chancellor and the Secretary of State for Foreign Affairs were at headquarters (*Grosses Hauptquartier*), but they soon returned to Berlin, making periodic visits to the OHL. The question of the respective fields of competence of the Chancellor and the OHL was never settled, and as Bethmann Hollweg was to point out to Hindenburg, there could be no full and open discussion of this contentious issue because it would only serve to further undermine the position of the Kaiser, whose constitutional function it was to settle such problems.

Falkenhayn, unlike Moltke, was tough and outspoken as well as being an extremely competent commander.[20] He was convinced that the war could be won and that the decisive campaign would have to be fought on the Western front. Having failed to outflank the French in the 'dash for the sea' in October, he tried to punch a hole through the Entente's lines at Ypres in a massive offensive. After an initial failure Falkenhayn ordered a second offensive in November which was a costly failure, although the catastrophic, senseless but heroic attack on Langemarck provided rich material for right-wing mythology. The lesson which the Germans drew from this experience was that frontal assaults against trenches were unlikely to succeed, given the overwhelming superiority of the defense in such warfare.

Falkenhayn was convinced that the war could not be won in one glorious 'battle of annihilation' of which German strategists had dreamt for years. He now believed that the only hope lay in a strategy that would gradually weaken the enemy so that it might then be possible to break through the lines and turn the flank. He therefore proposed to mount a series of operational attacks on the fortress of Verdun that would force the French to pour reserves into its defense turning these fortifications, as Falkenhayn unattractively phrased it, into a 'meat grinder'. When the French were bled white at Verdun it might then be possible to strike at the weakest point on the Western front and the Germans would once again have the strategic initiative.

This strategy was innovative and imaginative, but it suffered from serious weaknesses. Given the relatively greater resources available to the Entente it was unlikely that this *Ermattungsstrategie* would ever be successful. The plan was also highly ambiguous and the local army commanders were determined to seize the fortresses, rather than constantly threaten them. As a result the Verdun campaign rapidly degenerated into a second Ypres. Losses on both sides were terrible, and the German army was unable to mount a second offensive at another point on the front.[21] The Entente's offensive on the Somme presented a serious threat to the Germans who were only able to hold their positions with great difficulty. In the east the Russians mounted a successful offensive against the Austrians and the Italians seized Gorizia. In August Rumania declared war on the Central Powers. In the west there was a bloody stalemate, in the east Austria-Hungary seemed to be on the verge of collapse.

Falkenhayn's position was now untenable. His strategy had failed and he was widely unpopular. He was disliked by the Reichstag majority for his support of the army's excesses in Alsace-Lorraine during the Zabern affair in 1913.[22] He was cold, aloof, snobbish and sarcastic. He was resented in the army largely because when he was appointed Chief of the General Staff at the age of 52 he was younger than any of the commanding generals, and many officers thought that in addition to his youth he was fundamentally weak behind his brusque military exterior.[23] If the left could not forget Zabern, the right resented his inability to create the military conditions essential for the realization of their exotic war aims. He treated the civilian government with a lofty disdain and refused to keep them adequately informed about the military situation. He was an inveterate political meddler, and it was rumored that he had ambitions to become chancellor.[24]

In the summer of 1916 Falkenhayn was under constant attack by both the civilians and the military. It was a bitter irony that the civilians, headed by the Chancellor, believed that the removal of Falkenhayn would put an end to political interference by the military and be a forceful assertion of the rights of the government. Very few realized the dangers involved in the replacement of Falkenhayn by Hindenburg and Ludendorff. Among them was Colonel Marshall of the Military Cabinet who warned of Ludendorff's boundless ambition that might well lead Germany to defeat and ruin.[25] Most important of all, the Kaiser realized that the clamor for the appointment of Hindenburg and Ludendorff represented a serious challenge to his power of command. Falkenhayn had skillfully avoided creating the impression that he was anything other than His Majesty's loyal servant, but Hindenburg and Ludendorff's machinations introduced an element of plebiscitary democracy into the system which would further undermine the Kaiser's dwindling authority. At the same time the Kaiser began to complain that Falkenhayn was not keeping him adequately informed of the military situation and that he learned more from newspaper reports than from the Chief of the General Staff.[26]

Whereas Falkenhayn had failed at Verdun, Hindenburg and Ludendorff were the popular heroes of the victory at Tannenberg. They complained that Falkenhayn refused to send them reinforcements with which they could finish off the job and that had he supported the Austrians properly the disaster of the Brusilov offensive could have been averted. As an interim solution it was suggested that

Hindenburg should be made supreme commander of the forces in the east, but this proposal was rejected by the Austrians who saw it as a deliberate insult. The Kaiser, who distrusted Hindenburg as the 'people's tribune', felt that the request by the Chancellor, the Foreign Office, the Military Cabinet and many of the commanding generals that he be appointed to supreme command over the German troops in the east was tantamount to a request that he himself should abdicate.[27]

Falkenhayn played a skillful game by suggesting that Hindenburg's authority should be extended well beyond limits acceptable to the Austrians so that they would be rejected; but the deterioration of the situation on the Austrian front was such that the Austrian High Command (AOK) was eventually prepared to give way in the hope that the Germans would then release more reserves. Bethmann Hollweg was now convinced that the war would be won in the east. He called for a halt to the attacks on Verdun and the adoption of a defensive strategy in the west so that reserves could be sent east where Hindenburg would bring victory.[28] The Kaiser correctly pointed out that no troops could be spared from the Western front. Hindenburg then demanded a personal interview with the Kaiser and, in an unprecedented step, threatened to resign if this was not granted. Wilhelm II smoothed Hindenburg's ruffled feathers but did not grant an audience. Falkenhayn complained that he was under constant attack by 'laymen, many of them in field grey and some in the highest ranks of the army' and dismissed all talk of a decisive victory as idle chatter. A counter-attack by Colonel Bauer of the OHL, who had mobilized the support of big business for the appointment of Hindenburg, in the form of a memorandum for Bethmann, misfired, for it merely repeated old arguments which had been effectively countered by Falkenhayn.

Just when it seemed that Falkenhayn's position was secure, the Kaiser's habitual evening round of *Skat* was interrupted with the news that Rumania and Italy had declared war on the Central Powers. Throwing down his cards he announced that the war was lost and that Germany should sue for peace.[29] Hindenburg's supporters hurried to headquarters at Pless for the kill. Lyncker and Plessen, the Kaiser's aide-de-camp, informed Wilhelm II that Falkenhayn no longer enjoyed the confidence of the army. Falkenhayn realized that his situation was untenable and offered his resignation, which the Kaiser accepted.[30]

The appointment of Hindenburg and Ludendorff was the result of high-level intrigue and a massive propaganda campaign which had made Hindenburg a popular hero on whom were projected the hopes of the entire nation. The victor of Tannenberg would bring about the victory which would secure Germany's fantastic war aims, and would restore the sense of national unity which had been achieved in August 1914. Hindenburg thus claimed to represent the will of the people in a way which the Chancellor and the other imperial appointees could never do, added to which he could always use the arguments of 'military necessity' to trump the civilians. He was thus both an ersatz Kaiser and a proto-Führer behind whom stood ruthless men, determined to use his exceptional power and authority to the fullest. Bethmann Hollweg, who had imagined that he had redressed the balance between the civilians and the military, was soon to realize that he had made a terrible blunder.

Prompted by the indefatigable Colonel Bauer, Hindenburg and Ludendorff immediately turned their attention to the problems of manpower and industry. The OHL called for the reorganization of industry so that every man who did not possess essential expertise could be released to go to the front. Industries which did not produce goods essential to the war effort should be obliged to take second place and if necessary be closed down. By the spring the production of artillery and machine guns would have to increase threefold, ammunition by 100 per cent. The army was prepared to use the law of the state of siege to make certain that this program was implemented.[31]

Further details of proposed legislation to increase war production were forwarded by the OHL to the Chancellor on 13 September 1916.[32] They demanded drastic measures to control the work force, regardless of the political effects, and the 'maximum exploitation' of all workers. Profiteers, pessimists and grumblers should be ruthlessly prosecuted and childless women 'who only cost the state money' should be forced to work. A labor office (*Arbeitsamt*) should ensure the enforcement of 'the time-honored principle that he who does not work shall not eat' as well as settling all questions relating to wages. This 'Hindenburg Program' was designed to give the OHL full control over 'all matters of war work, food and the production of war materials'.[33] It marked a radical break with earlier attempts to achieve a modicum of cooperation between capital and labor. It was designed to destroy the labor movement and was a death sentence to those companies deemed non-essential to the war effort.

Bethmann Hollweg and his economic advisor Karl Helfferich objected to these proposals on both economic and political grounds. They wished to maintain the maximum degree of freedom and competition in the economy. They believed in cooperation rather than coercion; but most important of all was their resistance to this attempt further to extend the already excessive powers of the OHL.[34] The battle-lines were soon drawn up. The OHL and the industrialists called for the regimentation of labor, a concentration and monopolization of industry, a controlled economy and the maximalization of war production. The Chancellor and the government, supported by the War Ministry, argued that such measures would have a drastic effect on morale, destroy the last remnants of the *Burgfrieden*, and make post-war reconstruction doubly difficult. Economically it was a struggle between monopolistic capitalism and a free market economy, politically a struggle between authoritarian *étatisme* and liberal conservatism; historically it was part of a long struggle between the General Staff and the War Ministry and between the civilians and the military.[35]

In the first round of the battle the OHL secured the dismissal of the War Minister, a widely unpopular and somewhat duplicitous officer. The Cabinet order instructing him of his dismissal was instructive. It read in part: 'At the suggestion of General Field Marshal von Hindenburg, His Majesty is obliged to appoint someone else to the position of Prussian War Minister'.[36] His successor, General von Stein, was an unimaginative ultra-conservative who was temperamentally incapable of standing up to the OHL. General Groener was made deputy War Minister and head of the *Kriegsamt*, which was designed to deal with problems relating to labor, raw materials, arms and munitions. Stein delegated his authority in economic matters over the commanding generals to the *Kriegsamt*, but although the new office was nominally part of the War Ministry it was subjected to the constant interference of the OHL, its power over the commanding generals was never satisfactorily defined and it was the subject of endless criticism from the industrialists. Even the forceful and resourceful leadership of General Groener could not conceal the fact that the *Kriegsamt* was an unsatisfactory compromise: too ill-defined in its field of competence to be effective, too bureaucratically convoluted to appease the economic liberals.

Having won a partial victory over their rivals in the War Ministry the OHL now turned their attention to labor. They proposed that all males between the ages of 16 and 60 should be obliged to do war service for the fatherland and be subjected to military discipline. This 'auxiliary labor bill' (*Hilfsdienstgesetz*) was to be passed by the Reichstag as a demonstration of national determination and solidarity, and to ensure that should the bill prove unsuccessful the civilians rather than the military would take the blame.[37]

Bethmann and Groener felt that the proposed legislation was divisive and provocative and were able to modify the draft to include union representation on arbitration committees whose decisions were to be binding. Union leaders saw this concession as a triumph of 'war socialism', extremist industrialists led by Hugo Stinnes denounced it as a monstrous enhancement of the already excessive powers of the unions, and the militant trade unionists denounced it as a fraudulent gesture.[38] Groener assured the Prussian Ministry of State that their fears that too much had been given away to the unions were unfounded, and that the arbitration committees were merely 'safety valves'. The ministers agreed that it was far better to give way on the issue of arbitration committees than to have the right to form coalitions and the right to strike written into the law as the union leaders had initially demanded.[39]

Although the bill, which was acrimoniously debated in the Reichstag in November 1916, was celebrated by the Social Democrats as a major step towards 'war socialism', the working-class lost more than it gained. 'Auxiliary service' for males between the ages of 17 and 60 was defined in such a way that it applied almost exclusively to the working-class. Workers were forbidden to leave their jobs without the permission of their employers unless they could prove that a 'suitable improvement of working conditions' would result from such a change. Anyone refusing work assigned to them was liable to a heavy fine and a prison sentence of up to one year. The workers' councils, established in any enterprise employing more than 50 workers, could do little but bring forward employees' complaints.

In some instances radicals were able to use the workers' councils as platforms for political agitation, but very few of the councils fell into the hands of activists. For the army the *Hilfsdienstgesetz* was an admirable scapegoat for all Germany's economic problems. They blamed inflation, swollen profits, industrial unrest, wage increases, and all manner of shortages and shortcomings on the failure of the government and the Reichstag to accept the original draft of the bill. As amended it had, according to this interpretation, delivered the country into the hands of an unpatriotic, greedy and irresponsible working-class.

The failure of the OHL's policy could also be used as a stick with which to beat the Chancellor. Was it not his fault that the bill had been so hopelessly watered-down and had it not resulted, in Colonel

Bauer's words, in an alarming decline of 'German fidelity, morals and sense of duty' and in the country being held to ransom by 'the Jewish free-thinking and international fraternity?'[40]

To counteract these supposedly disastrous effects of the law, the commanding generals were urged by the OHL to use their powers to the full against the working-class. The government was appalled at these provocative actions, which were bound to cause further labor unrest and divisive debates in the Reichstag.[41] Bethmann warned Hindenburg that if the law was drastically changed or abrogated, as the OHL and 'certain employers in heavy industry' demanded, the result would be that 'well meaning' labor leaders would lose control over the rank and file and the result would be 'bitterness and excitement'.[42]

A wave of strikes in early 1917, triggered by the shortages of the 'turnip winter', the February revolution in Russia and the Kaiser's Easter message, which promised reform of the Prussian suffrage, convinced the OHL that Bethmann and Groener had gone much too far with their conciliatory policies. Groener regained some of the favor he had lost with the OHL on 27 April 1917 when he issued a decree threatening to use the treason laws against anyone who went on strike and announcing that 'anyone who strikes is a scoundrel (*Hundsfott*)'. Clearly the decree was an encouragement to the commanding generals to use their powers under the state of siege to break the militant workers. The union leaders tended to agree with Groener and made sure that there were no political strikes on 1 May.

The OHL were content to leave things to Groener, but continued their attacks on the Chancellor and the civilians. They complained that the socialists and 'Jewish liberals' were out to destroy the monarchy and the state and had been encouraged by the feeble handling of the *Hilfsdienstgesetz*.[43] They disagreed with the government over war aims, over policy towards Belgium and Poland, on the issue of unrestricted submarine warfare, and they were horrified at the proposal to reform the Prussian franchise. Hindenburg and Ludendorff were now strengthened in their determination that the Chancellor should go. The industrialist Carl Duisberg visited headquarters at Pless and then launched the 'Adlon Action' in which he brought together leading figures of industry and the political right at the Hotel Adlon in Berlin to form a powerful group pushing for the replacement of Bethmann Hollweg by Hindenburg. The army's propaganda machine gave extensive coverage of this group's activities.[44]

The Adlon Action misfired. Duisberg was unable to drum up much popular support, for the prospect of a military dictatorship was not something that most Germans found particularly attractive. Hindenburg and Ludendorff also preferred to remain behind the scenes, using the Chancellor, as Ludendorff put it, as a 'lightening conductor' for unpopular decisions. Information was leaked to the liberal and left-wing press and a skillful campaign was mounted by the opponents of the scheme.[45] Undaunted, Hindenburg asked the Kaiser to dismiss Bethmann, but the Kaiser was appalled at the whole affair. He told the chief of his Military Cabinet that 'The representatives of heavy industry . . . are engaged in activities that can only be described by the word "treason", particularly in time of war' and added that they should all be locked up in Spandau jail. He was particularly concerned about the role of Hindenburg and Ludendorff in the Adlon affair. 'For me the most serious aspect of this affair is the carefully prepared impression that the hounding of the Chancellor has been set in motion with at least the silent approval of the High Command, certainly with their cognizance. ' He described the whole business as a 'revolutionary attack on the power of the crown and of the Supreme Warlord, which is a slap in the face of all the traditions of Prussia'.[46] The Kaiser included the promise of suffrage reform in his Easter message for 1917, prompting Ludendorff to denounce the speech as a 'kowtow to the Russian revolution' and the direct cause of the wave of strikes in April, which were in turn the 'insolent answer of the proletariat to a policy dictated by fear'.[47] But the OHL was reluctant to make too open a denunciation of the proposed suffrage reform for fear of being exposed as meddling directly in politics. They preferred to use a more indirect approach. They invited the Kaiser's childhood friend, von Berg, the President of East Prussia, to headquarters and told him that Bethmann was too weak, was opening the door to revolution and had to go. Berg promptly went to the Kaiser and told him that the Chancellor's dismissal was demanded by 'all patriots'.[48] Wilhelm II was deeply impressed by his friend's arguments and began to distance himself from Bethmann.

On 6 July Erzberger gave a highly ambiguous speech in the Reichstag, stressing the gravity of the military situation and the need to begin peace negotiations. The effect of the speech was dramatic, heightened by the fact that it was widely but incorrectly believed to reflect the thinking of the OHL.[49] Hindenburg and Ludendorff were urged by the War Minister, von Stein, to come to Berlin to discuss the military implications of the speech with the Kaiser and the OHL felt that the moment was ripe to finish off a Chancellor who had allowed the Reichstag to get out of hand. However, Bethmann got to the Kaiser first and was able to convince him that the whole matter had been exaggerated out of all proportion. Hindenburg and Ludendorff were rather startled to be treated to a long diatribe from the Kaiser about the damaging effects of the military meddling in politics and they were ordered back to headquarters immediately.

The OHL continued to treat with Erzberger after his speech and used him to let it be known that they welcomed bringing politicians into the government and were in favor of the greatest possible openness between the OHL and the Reichstag. All this preposterous pretense was designed to win the politicians' support for their campaign against the Chancellor.[50] While the OHL assured the Reichstag members that they supported their efforts to win greater political power, they attacked the Chancellor for caving in to parliament.

Meanwhile, Bethmann was locked in battle with the Prussian Ministry of State, which threatened to resign *en bloc* if Bethmann pressed ahead with his plans for an equal suffrage for Prussia. Bethmann countered by threatening to resign if he did not get his way, and the Kaiser remarked wistfully: 'I am supposed to dismiss that man who stands head and shoulders above all the others'.[51]

The OHL then mustered the support of the Crown Prince who discussed the dismissal of Bethmann with leading members of the Reichstag carefully chosen by the OHL for their opposition to the Chancellor. During these talks Colonel Bauer hid behind a curtain taking notes. Bethmann now had little support in the Reichstag. He was too conciliatory for the right, and on the center and left there was a widespread feeling that he was a major obstacle to peace and to a workable relationship between the politicians and the OHL.[52]

On 12 July Hindenburg told the Kaiser by telephone that he could not accept the sentence in the Reichstag peace resolution which read 'Forcible seizure of territory and political, economic, or financial acts of force are not commensurate with such a peace'. Wilhelm II told Bethmann that he agreed with the OHL.[53] Hindenburg and Ludendorff then informed the Military Cabinet that they were offering their resignations if Bethmann were not dismissed. The Kaiser was furious at such blackmail and requested that they should come to Berlin.[54] At this point Bethmann offered his resignation, leaving the Kaiser in an extremely awkward position. Either he gave way to the OHL, thus abandoning the prerogatives of the Crown, or he allowed Hindenburg and Ludendorff to go, which would cause a public uproar.

He took the easier way out and regretfully accepted Bethmann's resignation.

Bethmann suggested a successor whom the Kaiser approved, but in an extraordinary constitutional innovation the OHL pushed for the appointment of Michaelis, a virtual nonentity of whom the Kaiser had never heard. Once again the Kaiser gave in, establishing the OHL's right to dismiss and appoint the Chancellor.[55] In order to stiffen the new Chancellor, Hindenburg drew up a list of Bethmann's misdeeds which had led to his downfall. His foreign policy had been too feeble. He had refused to consult with the OHL. He had dithered too long over the declaration of unrestricted submarine warfare. His policy towards Poland and Belgium had been similarly pusillanimous. His economic policies had lacked drive and energy. He had failed to mount an effective propaganda effort and as a result there was widespread pessimism, cynicism and worst of all, strikes. Hindenburg even had the gall to suggest that Bethmann had seriously weakened the monarchy. In conclusion he warned that Michaelis would only have the OHL's support if he rectified these mistakes.[56]

The OHL was prepared to live with the Reichstag's peace resolution since it was sufficiently ambiguous and they now had the one and a quarter million paying members of the new *Vaterlandspartei* organized by Admiral Tirpitz and Wolfgang Kapp (who was later to lead the eponymous coup against the Weimar Republic) to make sure that it was interpreted in a manner which suited them. Far more important was the question of industry and labor. General Groener was now dubbed the 'red general' for what was considered his conciliatory attitude towards labor and for listening to his adjutant, Captain Richard Merton, an industrialist in civilian life, who argued that profits in heavy industry were excessive and should be controlled by draconian taxation on excess profits.[57] The OHL drew up a memorandum for the Chancellor demanding that workers should be bound to their place of employment, industry should only produce goods deemed essential to the war effort, individual productivity would have to be drastically increased, labor should be fully controlled and more women should be obliged to work.[58] Prompted by the OHL, the War Minister told the commanding generals to ignore the *Kriegsamt's* conciliatory efforts and put down strikes by force. Ludendorff gave further emphasis to this exhortation by issuing an appeal to the commanding generals to render all agitators 'harmless'.[59]

Supported by vociferous representatives of industry, the OHL now began a campaign either to abolish or drastically change the auxiliary labor law and to get rid of Groener. Although Groener had considerable support in the Reichstag and was respected by many of the labor leaders, the OHL had little difficulty in removing him from office. First the *Kriegsamt* was placed securely under the control of the War Ministry, then Groener was informed that his services were no longer required and he was posted to command the 33rd division.

These differences between the OHL and Groener were questions of degree rather than fundamental disagreement. Groener was convinced that he had been dismissed because he had accepted Merton's arguments in favor of a steep tax on profits. In fact the OHL had no sympathy for greedy capitalists amassing vast wealth in time of war and agreed that profits were excessive. The argument was over whether force or conciliation was the best method to increase industrial productivity, which had slipped badly in the first nine months of the auxiliary labor law. The industrialists wanted to become masters in their own house, free from the red tape and interference of the *Kriegsamt* and the War Ministry, but with the army ready to put down strikes and coerce the labor force when they deemed it necessary.[60] The OHL agreed with this position and told Michaelis that the auxiliary labor law would have to be torn up. Michaelis insisted that this was politically impossible. The OHL continued to grumble but gradually came round to a view that was remarkably close to Groener's position. The labor leaders Legien and Gustave Bauer visited headquarters in October and assured Hindenburg and Ludendorff that they were opposed to any strikes and disturbances in war industries.[61] Ludendorff agreed that labor should be allowed to discuss issues such as wages and profits, called for a harmonious relationship between capital and labor and continued to denounce strikes as treason. His summary of the meeting which he sent to the *Kriegsamt* could very well have been written by Groener.[62]

Michaelis proved incapable of providing decisive leadership and as he drifted from side to side on all the major issues of the day – the peace resolution, the Papal peace initiative, the auxiliary labor law, and franchise reform – he soon came under attack from all sides. The initiative for his dismissal came from the majority parties in the Reichstag, the social democrats, the progressives, the center and the national liberals who wanted a firm commitment to franchise reform, the relaxation of censorship and an unambiguous reply to the Papal note. The OHL had no serious complaints about Michaelis, for he was weak, pliable and unwilling to stand up to the soldiers. He was, as Colonel Bauer said, the 'Chancellor of the OHL'. But they had made the mistake of mobilizing the Reichstag against Bethmann Hollweg and in doing so had strengthened the authority of parliament. They realized that Michaelis had to go, but their preferred replacement, Bülow, was unacceptable to the Kaiser. On 1 November the Kaiser appointed the aged Minister President of Bavaria, Hertling. Hindenburg and Ludendorff were furious. They disliked him because he was a staunch Bavarian and a devout Catholic, and they had squabbled with him over a number of issues, including the future of Poland. Even more annoying to them was the fact that they had not been consulted over his appointment. This drove home the realization that their triumph over Bethmann Hollweg was not a complete victory for the military over the civilians.[63] They swallowed their pride and with rather ill grace promised that they would cooperate with the new Chancellor, even giving a luke-warm promise to curb the inveterate political meddler, Colonel Bauer.[64]

Issues of foreign policy dominated relations between the OHL and Hertling. During the negotiations at Brest Litovsk they concentrated their fire on the leader of the German delegation, the Secretary of State for Foreign Affairs, von Kühlmann, and instructed their representative at the peace talks, General Hoffmann, to press for extensive annexations and a decisive influence over the Russian economy. On Christmas Day, when Kühlmann appeared to give way to the Soviet note calling for a peace without reparations, compensation, or annexations and in accordance with the principle of the self determination of peoples, the OHL were determined to get rid of him, even though General Hoffmann knew perfectly well that Kühlmann's ingenious reply left the door open for extensive annexations and reparations.[65] At the end of December Kühlmann, Hindenburg and Ludendorff met in Berlin to discuss the peace negotiations. Hoffmann found himself stuck between the OHL and Kühlmann. He disliked Kühlmann who was overly suave, apparently indolent and a typical diplomatist; but he also knew that the OHL's designs in the east were preposterous, and he deeply resented Ludendorff blaming him for letting Kühlmann commit the 'treachery of 25 December'.[66]

There followed a long and unseemly battle between the OHL and the civilians, in whose camp they counted General Hoffman. Hindenburg and Ludendorff stormed out of a meeting of the Crown Council, at which the Kaiser was present, slamming the door behind them. They launched a scurrilous press campaign against Hoffmann, suggesting that his wife came from 'Semitic circles' and that she held 'parliamentary tea parties'. Ludendorff offered his resignation, letting it be known that he was being hounded out of office by pusillanimous civilians and hinting that were he to go the war would inevitably be lost.[67] Hindenburg also announced in a letter to the Kaiser on 7 January 1918 that he and Ludendorff would resign unless a 'strong' rather than a 'diplomatic' approach were adopted at Brest Litovsk. This shameless letter ended with the plea that: 'Your Majesty would not order honest men who have loyally served Your Majesty and the Fatherland to have their authority and their name involved in actions that they realize from the bottom of their hearts to be harmful to the Crown and to the Reich'.[68]

The OHL thus insisted that it was their right and their duty to influence and even decide vital political issues, all the while claiming that they were merely offering military advice. They argued that the war had to be fought until victory was won, a victory which would ensure almost unbelievable annexations which would not only secure the Reich against any future attack but which would also reinforce the political and social order which was beginning to fall apart under the strains of a lengthy and almost total war.[69] It was important to them that the Chancellor gave the appearance of exercising political power while they controlled the substance. Theirs' was the harlot's prerogative – the maximum of power with the minimum of responsibility.

In the OHL's eyes the villains of the current piece were Kühlmann, Valentini, General Hoffmann and Admiral Müller, and they were determined to secure the dismissal of at least the first two. Hindenburg had an audience with the Kaiser on 14 January and suggested that unless Valentini was replaced by Wilhelm's old school-friend, the arch-reactionary Berg, in some mysterious way the leftward swing in German domestic politics would continue and the offensive on the Western front would inevitably fail. Once again Hindenburg threatened that he and Ludendorff would resign if Valentini were not dismissed. The Kaiser was furious at such impertinence and stormed out of the room shouting that he had no need for Hindenburg's paternal advice.[70] On reflection the Kaiser began to fear that Hindenburg and Ludendorff might make good their threat and he therefore decided to let Valentini go, wistfully telling Berg that he had been asked to make him a chief of the Civil Cabinet.[71]

The Crown Prince, who had played a vital role in the intrigue which led to Valentini's dismissal, realized that he had played a fateful role in undermining the authority of the Crown which he vainly hoped one day to wear. He petulantly told Hindenburg and Ludendorff: 'You cannot demand of my father that he dismiss a statesman every five minutes just because you don't like him'. Graf Roedern from the Treasury and von Radowitz from the Chancellery tried to stiffen Hertling against the encroachments of the OHL, but the Chancellor was not the man to stand up to the concerted and determined attacks of the military.[72]

The OHL got their way over the terms of the treaty of Brest Litovsk. Convinced that the Bolsheviks were 'tigers' and that the German army should 'round them up and shoot them', the Kaiser proclaimed that the Russians were now prey to the Jews, and that the Bolsheviks were part of a world-wide Jewish conspiracy aided by the Freemasons. He therefore sided with Hindenburg and Ludendorff. Kühlmann, whose differences with the OHL were matters of expediency and temperament rather than of principle, let drop his objections.[73]

Although Kühlmann had achieved everything the OHL wanted at Brest Litovsk and then negotiated a draconian peace treaty with Rumania, Hindenburg and Ludendorff were determined that he should go. They sent spies to Bucharest to try to catch Kühlmann in a compromising position. Hindenburg reported to the Kaiser that Kühlmann spent his time playing 'an American game of chance by the name of poker', and when he was not gambling he was out shooting duck with his Austrian counterpart, Czernin.[74] His chauffeur was in the pay of the OHL and at their prompting fed the *Deutsche Zeitung* with lurid tales of Kühlmann carousing in exclusive Bucharest brothels. Kühlmann sued for libel, but the case never came to court. There were so many libel cases in the heated atmosphere at the end of the war that a general amnesty was proclaimed.

In May 1918 Ludendorff confessed that the war could no longer be won unless he got 200 000 additional men and therefore ordered Colonel Haeften, the OHL's representative at the foreign office, to go ahead with his crackpot peace initiative. Haeften believed that a peace move, supported by demonstrations in Germany in favor of peace, would demoralize the Entente by giving false hopes to the peace movement and thus do as much damage as the missing reserves. Kühlmann gave a speech in the Reichstag on 24 June 1918 based on Haeften's memorandum in which he said that 'a purely military decision without diplomatic negotiations could hardly be expected'. This provoked a series of horrified outbursts from the right, including Stresemann, who announced that there had never been less reason to doubt a military victory. Graf Westarp, on behalf of the conservatives, promptly phoned the OHL and Hindenburg demanded of Hertling whether this was merely Kühlmann's personal view, or whether it was shared by the Chancellor. He complained of the 'shattering effect' the speech had had on the troops and demanded that the peace initiative should be dropped instantly. The following day a spokesman of the OHL told a press conference that Hindenburg and Ludendorff did not share Kühlmann's view that victory was impossible.[75] Hindenburg would not accept Hertling's lame excuse that Kühlmann had given such a poor performance in the Reichstag because he had not had a proper breakfast and told the Chancellor that he refused to continue working with him. Kühlmann was pointedly not invited to an important conference on war aims attended by most military and civilian leaders.

He arrived at Spa shortly after the conference ended, only to be told by the Kaiser that their ways would have to part. This capable diplomat, unable to share the fantasies and illusions of the OHL, earned their undying hatred, and once again they secured the dismissal of an important rival.[76]

Kühlmann's successor was Admiral Hintze, a blasé and highly ambitious trimmer. He was a favorite of the Kaiser and was very much the candidate of the OHL. Ludendorff called him a 'national man' and was delighted that he was closely associated with the Pan-Germans.[77] Dr Fleischer, a virulent anti-semitic activist, told Colonel Bauer that Hintze would 'realise in a determined fashion the political ambitions of the OHL'.[78] Haeften was alone in warning that Hintze was an opportunist with an eye for the main chance. In fact Hintze, although he lacked Kühlmann's experience and cunning, followed closely in his predecessor's footsteps but still managed to keep on good terms with the OHL.

In spite of their second thoughts in May about the possibility of victory, Hindenburg and Ludendorff persisted with their exotic annexation schemes in the Baltic, the Ukraine and the Crimea and secured the dismissal of those who stood in the path of the realization of these totally unrealistic goals. But the German position on the Western front was deteriorating. The French and American breakthrough at Villers-Cotterets in July convinced General Fritz von Lossberg, an outstanding tactician and the leading specialist in mobile defense, that the army should abandon the impressive gains made in the March offensive and retreat to the Siegfried line. Ludendorff argued that such a move, although militarily justified, would have a shattering effect on morale and threatened once again to resign if the army withdrew. This convinced von Lossberg that Ludendorff had completely lost his grip.[79] In the course of the next few weeks a number of other officers at the OHL began to share Lossberg's misgivings about Ludendorff and suggested that if peace negotiations were not set in train Germany might well suffer a crushing defeat. Admiral Hintze also had serious reservations about Ludendorff. Even Colonel Bauer thought that armistice negotiations were necessary and suggested that a guarantee of Belgian independence and a declaration that Germany would not claim any reparations would provide reasonable grounds for starting discussions.[80]

The OHL continued to place the blame for this unfortunate situation on the home front and demanded stringent measures against the workers, their wages to be reduced to the level of soldiers' pay, and rigorous control of industrial profits. As Bauer put it: 'We shall win the war when the home front stops attacking us from behind!'[81] In their frantic attempt to find a scapegoat, the 'stab in the back' legend was already firmly established.

The Entente failed to follow up their successes and the front stabilized, but in August they broke through the German lines on the Somme making effective use of a massive tank attack. On 8 August, the *dies ater* of the Germany army, experienced and well rested troops, lost their nerve and fled in panic. Ludendorff was plunged into a profound depression and issued disastrously ill-considered orders to the army commanders. He now announced that the Central Powers should adopt a defensive stand, as von Lossberg had suggested, which would wear down the enemy and force them to sue for peace.[82] The OHL now lived in a dream world, imagining that a strategic defensive would result in an annexationist peace, and Hintze, even though he was convinced that the war could not be won, proclaimed that 'the political leadership would give way to the ideas of the greatest general that had emerged in the course of the war'.[83]

Ludendorff continued to believe that the war could still be won, but an increasing number of officers, principal among them the recently appointed chief of the operations division, Colonel Heye, realized the absurdity of this view and were determined either to undermine Ludendorff's position or to oust him. With the Entente pressing hard at Cambrai and Ypres, in the Champagne and on the Meuse, even Ludendorff was forced to concede that an armistice was necessary. Yet he still imagined that it would be possible to hang on to the vast annexations in the east and that an armistice would provide a breathing space for Germany to gather its strength and continue the war.[84]

Admiral Hintze had long since come to the conclusion that the war was lost and discounted as absurd Ludendorff's wild claim in July that the war could be won 'finally and decisively'. He relied on information from the 'pessimistic' officers at the OHL and from commanders in the field. He now planned a 'revolution from above' to meet the very real threat of a 'revolution from below'. This would involve the creation of a new government on a broad national basis. Hertling would have to go and be replaced by a Chancellor who would be acceptable to the majority of the Reichstag. Armistice negotiations could then begin on the basis of Wilson's Fourteen Points.[85]

Hintze met Hindenburg and Ludendorff at the poignant venue of the Hotel Britannique in Spa on 29 September to discuss this scheme. To his surprise and alarm Ludendorff told Hintze that an armistice would have to be signed immediately and the OHL approved the 'Hintze action'.[86] On 1 October Ludendorff spoke to the section chiefs of the OHL looking, as one officer confided in his diary, 'like a truly beautiful German hero. I had to think of Siegfried with the mortal wound in his back from Hagen's spear'.[87] The treacherous *Gibichungs* were the Spartacists and social democrats who had destroyed the German army. On them would be placed the odium of defeat and the disgrace of negotiating an armistice. As Ludendorff said:

> I have asked His Majesty to bring those people into the government who are largely responsible that things have turned out as they have. We shall therefore see these gentlemen enter the ministries, and they must now make the peace which has to be made. They must now eat the soup they have ladled out to us!

The new Chancellor, Prince Max of Baden, insisted that Ludendorff's demand for an immediate armistice would have disastrous political consequences, but Hindenburg fully supported the Quartermaster General. The situation was further confused since the OHL at times talked of the imminent collapse of the front, at others of the need merely for a breathing space. They also made it clear that there could be no question of giving up Alsace-Lorraine or the occupied territories in the east. After lengthy discussion a note was sent to President Wilson on 3 October calling for an immediate armistice. The OHL made sure that the document was signed by the Chancellor and was supported by the representatives of the Reichstag majority in the new Cabinet. In this manner the role of the OHL in the request for an armistice was carefully concealed from the public, and it was hoped that a storm of indignation would fall upon the majority parties for delivering the country to the Entente. Democracy would then be discredited and the old élites could climb back into the saddle.[88]

The government and the OHL now came under attack from the extreme right. Walter Rathenau wrote an article in the *Vossische Zeitung*, which was widely admired in such circles, denouncing the government for losing its nerve and calling for a *levée en masse*. The right-wing parties were horrified to hear that the OHL agreed to abandon occupied territory in the west, even though Ludendorff, insisted that Metz had to be retained 'for reasons of military honor'. Colonel Bauer was working closely with his political associates in Berlin to secure the removal of Ludendorff, whom he now saw as squarely in the camp of the 'pessimists'.[89]

Wilson's second note of 16 October was much firmer in tone than his first reply and strengthened the hand of those who were calling for a struggle to the bitter end. Even Ludendorff began to think of moving troops from the Eastern to the Western front and fighting to the last.[90] He no longer called for an immediate armistice but did not go as far as his erstwhile political supporters on the right who were clamoring that the armistice negotiations should be broken off. The crisis deepened when the Germans received Wilson's third note on 23 October which made it clear that there could be no question of an armistice which would grant the Germans a breathing space. Hindenburg and Ludendorff were determined that the war should continue, Prince Max that the negotiations with the Entente should not be broken off. The Chancellor told the Kaiser that unless Lundendorff was dismissed he would resign. In a stormy interview with the Kaiser, Hindenburg and Ludendorff offered their resignations. The Kaiser accepted that of Ludendorff, but ordered Hindenburg to stay at his post. The aged field marshal bowed his head in acquiescence and Ludendorff stormed out of the room.

With the dismissal of Ludendorff the OHL lost much of its authority, but it had successfully shifted the burden of the armistice onto the civilians. Further constitutional reforms reduced the Kaiser's power of command and placed the army under greater political control. The situation at the front deteriorated rapidly. Discipline was breaking down, in some sectors to the point of outright mutiny. Films of the Kaiser and Hindenburg were booed by the troops. On 1 November the Prussian Minister of the Interior, Drews, told the Kaiser that he would have to abdicate. The Kaiser refused, saying that this would lead to anarchy. Hindenburg supported the Kaiser's position. Groener, who had replaced Ludendorff, said: 'The army stands splendidly; the poison comes from home. The present government is responsible that all authority is attacked in the press and at meetings without being stopped or controlled, and this is also shown in discussions about the future of the monarchy. The issue of abdication must be withdrawn from public discussion by government action'.

Within a week it was obvious that the Kaiser would have to abdicate if the armistice negotiations were to succeed, and the suggestion that the Kaiser could lead his troops back from the front to crush the revolution at home was seen to be totally absurd. Hindenburg lacked the courage to tell his Kaiser and his King this painful truth. He left the unpleasant task to Groener, a Württemberger. On the morning of 9 November he told Wilhelm II: 'The army will march home peacefully and in good order under its leaders and commanding generals, but not at the command of Your Majesty; for it no longer stands behind Your Majesty'.[91]

By sacrificing the Supreme Warlord the OHL did much to preserve the unity of the officer corps and the discipline of the returning army. Even in the moment of defeat, threatened revolution and radical democratization, the officer corps was able to preserve its traditions and its unique position in German society. It did not go the way of the monarchy but remained a powerful, independent and harmful force in the new republic.

The history of civil-military relations in Germany during the Great War provides a classic example of the capitulation of the civilian authorities to the exigencies of the military commanders. A satisfactory balance between the demands and needs of the civil and the military is always difficult to find, even in peacetime; in war it becomes critical since 'purely military' considerations have to be weighed against political goals. Soldiers as the technicians and experts of organized violence frequently have quite different priorities from politicians, who have to think in terms of ends rather than means and of the long-term effects of military actions. The frequently ambiguous canonical texts of Clausewitz on the relationship between the political and the military offer little guidance, and the past can be quarried by either side for supporting arguments.[92] In Germany it was a particularly pressing difficulty, in part because of the very structure of the state and also because of the peculiar status of the army within that society.

At first glance the German Reich of 1871 appears as a monolithic state, dominating central Europe, with an awesome industrial might, an unmatched military machine, and a disciplined, hardworking people, fired by a fervent nationalism, determined to affirm Germany's status as truly a world power. But the reality behind this imposing façade was quite different. The Reich was a remarkably loose federation of states, a coalition of princes who exchanged diplomatic representatives and which was held together by an ill-defined constitution. Although it was dominated by the militaristic power of Prussia, the King of Prussia's sovereignty as German Kaiser resided in the rather humdrum fact that he was the hereditary president of the upper chamber, the Bundesrat. The Prussian Minister President was also Chancellor of the Reich and the Prussian Ministry of State, dependent entirely on the King's prerogative, functioned in part as the imperial government. The Reichstag, elected by universal male suffrage, had limited power, ministers were not responsible to it, and it was widely regarded as an undesirable foreign import. The industrialized, bourgeois, liberal West looked to France and to England for its political inspiration. The agrarian, aristocratic, authoritarian East more closely resembled Russia and even, one is tempted to say, the Ottoman Empire with its Sultan/Kaiser, Grand Vizier/ Chancellor.

Wilhelm I, a modest and conscientious monarch, was first and foremost King of Prussia and was only Kaiser in a purely symbolic sense. He left the governance of the new state to its architect, and there was much complaining of Bismarck's dictatorship. It is quite appropriate that Wilhelm II should still be known as 'The Kaiser', for in the early years of his reign he tried desperately to be a truly German emperor, a people's Kaiser, the focal point of this disparate state. He had considerable power at his disposal. He was 'Supreme Warlord' commanding an army which stood largely outside the constitution, he appointed not only the Chancellor and the ministers but also every member of the civilian administration, even university professors. That his enterprise failed was due to his glaring personal shortcomings, but also to economic, social and political tensions within a state structure which lacked the flexibility to accommodate change and absorb conflict.

The decision to go to war in 1914 was dictated in part by a desire to overcome these divisions and tensions and in this leap into the unknown to recreate the heady days of 1871 when the nation seemed united in the pride of victory and the promise of even greater days to come. In a false macho antinomy, so typical of Wilhelmine Germany, it was widely felt that there was a simple choice between 'world power or extinction'. For the military it was obvious that such a serious business could not be affected by the concerns and hesitancies of mere civilians. Had not the great Moltke said that when Bellona spoke the civilians should remain silent? Without the backing of the Kaiser the civilian government was virtually powerless to resist this fateful denial of their duties and obligations.

There were those, led by Colonel Bauer and supported by an influential group of politicians and industrialists in the 'Adlon Group', who felt that the logic of the situation demanded a military dictatorship. Hindenburg and Ludendorff, however, felt that this was too radical a break with the tradition of a highly professional, specialist and 'unpolitical' officer corps, and also saw the enormous advantages to be gained from hiding behind an unpopular government who would bear responsibility for any failures and thus act as a 'lightening conductor' for the OHL.

The unpolitical nature of the army had always been a myth, but it was one which was increasingly difficult to sustain. The political intrigues, the propaganda and the mobilization of the masses which had led to the dismissal of Falkenhayn and the appointment of Hindenburg and Ludendorff to the OHL introduced a semi-plebiscitary element so that the army leaders could claim that they incorporated the will of the people. The army had always seen itself as standing outside the provisions of the constitution, owing its allegiance to the King, and in time of war to the Kaiser. Now, in their wilder moments, they saw themselves as standing above the Kaiser and above the constitution. They were not only the experts with a war to fight and to win, they were also the embodiment of the state. Thus the soldiers who swore their solemn oaths of allegiance to the King and the fatherland, in the end destroyed the monarchy and brought about the ruin of the existing state.

Or so it seemed in the troubled revolutionary months after the armistice. But Admiral Hintze and the OHL had skillfully used the defeat of the German army to discredit the democratic forces and their ingenious fabrication of the 'stab in the back' legend was to provide the forces of the extreme right with their most powerful ideological weapon with which they were to destroy the Weimar Republic. Hindenburg, who had managed to usurp much of the Kaiser's power, was to survive as an ersatz Kaiser in the republic – a symbol of continuity with the past and a foreshadowing of infinitely worse to come. Even with a consitutionally responsible War Minister the army still retained a large measure of independence from civilian control.[93]

Finally, in Adolf Hitler the army found an ally and a master who was to take it from the pinnacle of glory to the ignominy of total defeat. This time the attempt to blame their failure on a mad dictator mercifully met with little success.

If the lesson of the German experience in the First World War is that the military must be firmly under political control, the lesson of the Second is that the political ends which are served must also be rationally and morally justifiable. It is an unfortunate and perplexing problem that the more democratic and humane society, the greater the discrepancy between civil and military values. Soldiers necessarily accept an authoritarian, hierarchical social organization which, when necessary, must devote all its energies to killing fellow human beings. The moral value of soldierly virtues – courage, self-sacrifice, and obedience are determined by the purposes to which they are directed. The soldier's mission to defend the state against attack can all too easily result in a blind and uncritical acceptance of the status quo, or the dedication to perceived notions of the true interest of the state which may well be quite different from that of the majority of the people or their democratically elected representatives. There are no easy solutions to these problems, and they are certainly not overcome by facile talk of the 'citizen in uniform' or bland denials that within a democratic society no such problem exists. Perhaps we do not learn very much from the lessons of the past, but at least the historical record can remind us that a problem exists. Nowhere is this more apparent than in the history of Germany, and the story of civil-military relations during the First World War provides a particularly vivid example of these important issues.

NOTES

1. Conrad, *Aus meiner Dienstzeit 1906–1918*, Vol. IV, Vienna 1921, p. 152. The telegram was received in Vienna on 31 July.
2. Hans-Ulrich Wehler, *Des Deutsche Kaiserreich 1871–1918* (Göttingen: 1973), pp. 60–9 for a useful account of the consitutional position of the Kaiser.
3. For an admirable discussion of the personality and role of Wilhelm II see: John C. G. Röhl and Nicolaus Sombart (eds), *Kaiser Wilhelm II – New Interpretations* (Cambridge: 1982). Also helpful is Isabel V. Hull, *The Entourage of Kaiser Wilhelm II 1888–1918* (Cambridge: 1982).

4. Varnbuler, quoted in Immanuel Geiss, *Juli Krise and Kriegsausbruch 1914*, 2 Vols. (Hannover: 1963). This is still the most useful work on the outbreak of the war.
5. Alfred von Tirpitz, *Politische Dokumente* (Berlin: 1924), p. 20.
6. Isabel V. Hull, op. cit., p. 267.
7. Siegfried Schöne, *Von der Reichskanzlei zum Bundeskanzleramt* (Berlin: 1968), p. 71. For the organization of the OHL see also: Walter Hubatsch, 'Grosses Hauptquartier 1914–18', *Ostdeutsche Wissenschaft*, Vol. 5, 1959; Josef Stürgh, *Im Grossen Hauptquartier* (Leipzig: 1921); Otto von Moser, *Die Obersten Gewalten im Weltkrieg* (Stuttgart: 1931); Hermann Cron, *Die Organization des deutschen Heeres im Weltkriege* (Berlin: 1923).
8. W. Gölitz, *Regierte der Kaiser? Kriegstagebucher. Aufzeichnungen und Briefe des Chefs des Marine-Kabinetts Admiral George Alexander von Muller 1914–1918* (Göttingen: 1959), p. 50.
9. Politisches Archiv des Auswärtigen Amts, Bonn, Akten der Politischen Abteilung (PA), AA Gr. HQ 28 Presse, Band 1, Lersner to Foreign Office 29-4-1917. Ludendorff was insistent that these letters should remain secret.
10. The best critique of the Schlieffen plan and its defenders and the most reasoned analysis of von Moltke's modification and application of the plan is to be found in Jehuda L. Wallach, *Das Dogma der Vernichtungsschlacht* (Munich: 1970), especially on pp. 55–6, 153 and 157–8.
11. Isabel V. Hull, *op. cit.*, p. 242.
12. Wilhelm Deist, *Militär und Innenpolitik im Weltkrieg 1914–1918*, 2 vols, (Dusseldorf: 1970) is a brilliant study of the domestic policy of the army during the war and gives a trenchant analysis of the law on the state of seige pp. xxxi–li.
13. Johanna Schellenberg, 'Die Herausbildung der Militärdiktatur in den ersten Jahren des Krieges', *in Politik und Krieg 1914–1918* (Berlin: 1964), p. 33.
14. Deutsches Zentralarchiv Abteilung 1, Potsdam (DZA), Reichskanzlei: Presse 2438 Hindenburg to Chancellor 16-1-1917.
15. Walter Nicolai, *Nachrichtendienst Presse und Volksstimmung im Weltkrieg* (Berlin: 1920).
16. DZA Potsdam, Vetr. des RK bei der OHL 31, 'Denkschrift der OHL uber die deutsche Volks- und Wehrkraft'. The memo is almost certainly the work of Colonel Bauer.
17. K. Koszyk, *Deutsche Pressepolitik im Ersten Weltkrieg* (Dusseldorf: 1968), p. 80.
18. Fritz von Unruh, *Opfergang* (Frankfurt: 1966), with a foreword by Kasimir Edschmid.
19. Heeresarchiv Stuttgart, Richtlinien fur den vaterländischen Unterricht, Stellv. Generalkommando IXI (2Ks) Armeekorps (Dresden: 15-12-1917).
20. The best study of Falkenhayn is still Karl-Heinz Janssen, *Der Kanzler und der General. Die Führungskrise um Bethmann Hollweg und Falkenhayn* (Göttingen: 1966).
21. Alistair Horn, *The Price of Glory, Verdun 1916* (London: 1962);

Hermann Wendt, *Verdun 1916. Die Angriffe Falkenhayns im Maasgebiet mit Richtung auf Verdun als strategisches Problem* (Berlin: 1931); J. Pericard, *Verdun* (Paris: 1933).

22. For Zabern see Martin Kitchen, *The German Officer Corps 1890–1914* (Oxford: 1968).
23. Bundesarchiv Militärarchiv Freiburg, Nachlass Adolf Wild von Hohenborn, N44/2 diary entry 2-5-1916. Also Josef Graf Sturgkh, *Im Grossen Hauptquartier* (Leipzig: 1921), p. 81.
24. BA Freiburg, Nachlass Wild, diary entry 9-3-1916; Karl-Heinz Janssen, 'Der Wechsel in der Obersten Heeresleitung', *Vierteljahreshefte fur Zeitgeschichte*, Heft 7, 1959, p. 339.
25. Gerhard Ritter, *Staatskunst und Kriegshandwerk*, vol. 3 (Munich: 1964), p. 248.
26. BA Frieburg, Nachlass Wild N44/2, diary entry 25-6-1916.
27. Muller diary 3-7-1916; PA Bonn AA Weltkrieg Geheim, Band 30.
28. A. Scherer and J. Grunewald, *L'allmagne et les problèmes de la paix pendant la première guerre mondiale*, vol. 1 (Paris: 1962), p. 306.
29. Muller diary 27-8-1916.
30. Karl Heinz Janssen, *Der Kanzler und der General* (Berlin: 1967), p. 251.
31. Erich Ludendorff, *Urkunden der Obersten Heeresleitung über ihrer Tätigkeit 1916–1918* (Berlin: 1920), p. 63. It is almost certain that the memorandum was drafted by Bauer for Falkenhayn and was then presented to Hindenburg for signature.
32. *Ibid.*, p. 65. The original draft of the memorandum in BA Koblenz, Nachlass Bauer, Band 2.
33. BA Koblenz, Nachlass Bauer, Band 2.
34. Helfferich summed up the situation when he said 'One can command an army, but not an economy'. Ritter, *Staatskunst und Kriegshandwerk*, vol. 3, p. 423.
35. G. D. Feldman, *Army, Industry and Labor in Germany, 1914–1918* (Princeton: 1966) is the best book on the subject.
36. BA Freiburg Nachlass Wild, N44/2, diary entry 29-10-1916.
37. Ludendorff, *Ur kunden der OHL*, p. 81.
38. For conflicting views of the law see: Feldman, *Army, Industry and Labor*, pp. 204–5 and H. Weber, *Ludendorff und die Monopole* (Berlin: 1966), p. 54.
39. Feldman, *op. cit.*, p. 209.
40. B. A. Koblenz, Nachlass Bauer, Band 16.
41. Memorandum by Helfferich to Bethmann, 7-3-1917 in DZA Potsdam, Reichskanziei, Notständen 2430.
42. DZA Potsdam, Reichskanziei, Allgemeines, 2398/10.
43. BA Koblenz, Nachlass Bauer, Band 2.
44. DZA Potsdam, Reichsamt des Innern, 19683.
45. Conrad Haussmann, *Schlaglichter, Reichstagsbriefe und Aufzeichnungen*, (Frankfurt: 1924). Haussmann played an important role in discrediting the Adlon Action.
46. BA Koblenz, Nachlass Schwertfeger Band 212.
47. BA Koblenz, Nachlass Bauer, Band 17.
48. Rudolf von Valentini, *Kaiser und Kabinettschef* (Oldenburg: 1931), p. 154.

49. Klaus Epstein, *Matthias Erzberger and the Dilemma of German Democracy* (Princeton: 1959), p. 182.
50. PA Bonn, Weltkrieg AA Gr, HQ 29, Band 1, Wahnschaffe to Ludendorff 8-7-1917; Ritter, *Staatskunst und Kriegshandwerk*, Vol. 3, p. 567.
51. Valentini, *Kaiser und Kabinettschef*, p. 162.
52. Karl Helfferich, Der Weltkrieg (Karlsruhe: 1919), p. 451.
53. DZA Potsdam, Reichskanzlei und Grosses Hauptquartier 2403/5.
54. Ludendorff, *Urkunden der OHL*, pp. 406 and 408.
55. Valentini, *Kaiser und Kabinettschef*, p. 167.
56. Fritz Fischer, *Griff nach der Weltmach*, (Dusseldorf: 1961), p. 525. Although the memorandum is signed by Hindenburg it has all the marks of having been written by Colonel Bauer.
57. Richard Merton, *Erinnernswertes aus meinem Leben* (Frankfurt: 1955), p. 367; Wilhelm Groener, *Lebenserinnerungen. Jugend, Generalstab, Weltkrieg*, ed. Friedrich Freiherr von Gaertringen (Göttingen: 1957) p. 520.
58. DZA Potsdam, Stellvertreter des Reichskanzlers 53: 'Notizen für die Besprechungen mit dem Herrn Reichskanzler', 1-7-17.
59. Ludendorff, *Urkunden der OHL*, p. 186.
60. See the arguments put forward to this effect at a meeting of the Dusseldorf Industry Club on 19 August 1917. BA Freiburg, Nachlass Groener, N46/113. Also DZA Potsdam, Reichsamt des Innern, Die Stimmung im Lande 12476.
61. *Deutschland im Ersten Weltkrieg*, Vol. II (Berlin: 1968), p. 779.
62. Ludendorff, *Urkunden der OHL*, p. 94; DZA Potsdam, Reichsamt des Innern, Die Stimmung im Lande, 12476.
63. Bayerisches Hauptstaatsarchiv, Abteilung IV Kriegsarchiv, M. Kr. 1831.
64. Ibid., 8-10-1917. Bauer received an empty reprimand but henceforth made every effort to be pleasant to Hertling.
65. Max Hoffmann, *Die Aufzeichnungen des Generalmajors Max Hoffmann*, Karl Friedrich Nowak (ed.), Vol. 2 (Berlin: 1929), p. 197.
66. Ibid., p. 203.
67. Valentini, *Kaiser und Kabinettschef*, p. 190; Bayerisches Hauptstaatsarchiv, Abteilung IV Kriegsarchiv, M. Kr. 1832, Bevollmächtigte in Gr. HQ 1918, 6-1-1918.
68. DZA Potsdam, Verkehr des Reichskanzlers mit den Gr. HQ 2403/6.
69. For exhaustive details of various war aims see Fritz Fischer's magisterial *Griff Nach der Weltmacht* (Dusseldorf: 1961).
70. DZA Hist. Ab. Merseburg Preussisches Staatsministerium Rep 90a Abteilung B, III, 2b, Nr. 6, Band 167.
71. BA Koblenz, Nachlass Berg, Band 1.
72. BA Koblenz, Nachlass Bauer, Band 18 and Nachlass Schwertfeger. Band 206.
73. For the critical Crown Council at Homburg at which agreement was reached between the civilians and the OHL see: BA Koblenz, Nachlass Schwertfeger, Band 119; *Deutsch-Sowjeysche Beziehungen von der Verhandlungen in Brest-Litovsk bis zum Abschluss des Rapallo-*

vertrages, Band I (Berlin: 1967), p. 403; W. Baumgart and K. Repgen, *Brest-Litovsk* (Göttingen: 1969), p. 57.

74. DZA Potsdam, Reichskanzlei, Beschwerden uber der Friedensverhandlungen in Bucharest 2458/4. Also Kühlmann, *Erinnerungen* (Heidelberg: 1948), p. 563.
75. DZA Potsdam Reichskanzlei Allgemeines 2398/11; DZA Merseburg, Rep 89 H XXXVI Militaria II: BA Koblenz, Nachlass Hertling, Band 41.
76. BA Koblenz, Nachlass Berg, Aufzeichnungen.
77. BA Freiburg, Nachlass Haeften N35/4.
78. BA Koblenz, Nachlass Bauer, Band 13.
79. F. von Lossberg, *Meine Tätigkeit im Weltkrieg 1914–1918* (Berlin: 1939).
80. BA Koblenz, Nachlass Bauer, Band 2.
81. Ibid.
82. BA Freiburg, Nachlass Haeften N35/5, *Errinerungen; Amtliche Urkunden Zur Vorgeschichte des Waffenstillstandes 1918, 2* Auflage (Berlin: 1924), p. 7.
83. *Amtliche Urkunden*, p. 3.
84. BA Freiburg, Nachlass Haeften N35/4, diary entry for 28-9-1918.
85. PA Bonn Weltkrieg 23 Geheim, Band 32.
86. *Untersuchungsausschuss*, IV Reihe, Band 2, pp. 260, 386.
87. Albrecht von Thaer, *Generalstabsdeinst an der Front und in der OHL. Aus Briefen und Tagebuchaufzeichnungen 1915–1919*, Siegfried von Kaehler (ed.) (Göttingen: 1958).
88. That this was the view of the majority of officers at the OHL is clearly seen in a report from the Bavarian military plenipotentiary dated 7-10-1918. Bayerisches Hauptstaatsarchiv, Abteilung IV Kriegsarchiv, M. Kr. 1832.
89. BA Freiburg, Nachlass Haeften N35/3, diary entry 8-10-1918.
90. DZA Potsdam, Reichskanzlei, Beschlüsse des Kriegsrats 2462/1.
91. Kuno Graf Westarp, *Das Ende der Monarchie am 9. November 1918*, Werner Conze (ed.) (Stollhamm: 1952), p. 46.
92. Martin Kitchen, 'The Political History of Clausewitz', *Journal of Strategic Studies*, 1, 1988.
93. F. L. Carsten, *Reichswehr und Politik* (Cologne: 1964).

4 Comment
Thomas C. Kennedy

In the Spring of 1909 Field Marshal Earl Roberts inquired of General Sir William Nicholson, Chief of the Imperial General Staff, about the state of British military aviation. Nicholson's response is quite revealing, especially in light of Alfred Gollin's chapter. 'As regards aeroplanes', Nicholson said, 'we maintain an open mind and hope not to be behindhand, but so far I am not quite convinced about their military value'. Since aeroplanes had to travel at least 30 to 40 miles per hour, Nicholson seriously doubted their value as a reconnaissance arm and 'as regards dropping explosives with any attempt at accuracy', there was, he said, 'Nothing to guide us in forming an opinion'.[1]

Lord Roberts' interest in aircraft had been sparked by his reading, at age 76, R. P. Hearne's pioneering work on *Aerial Warfare*, which had convinced him that 'aerial machines are likely to take a great part in the wars of the future, and that we cannot, therefore, let other nations get ahead of us in the . . . training and practice . . . of aviation'.[2] On the other hand, the tone of Nicholson's remarks would seem to indicate that his views on aviation were similar to those of the American military writer Homer Lea who, at about this time, published a series of articles for *Harpers Weekly* on 'The Aeroplane in War'.[3] In these essays 'General' Lea cast scorn upon the 'delusions' of writers like Hearne who predicted that future wars would be fought 'in the upper heavens by Hertzian waves' while earthbound humanity stood helplessly watching. Lea was certain that wars of the future like wars of the past would be won by fighting men with the proper offensive spirit, wielding the bayonet with deadly skill as the weight of their numbers carried them through the shattered ranks of their bewildered, demoralized foe. Because he believed that moral and psychological factors were more decisive than new-fangled machines, Lea assured his readers that the principles of modern warfare had remained constant through the centuries and could not be altered by mere technology.

> True preparation for war concerns itself alone with the preparation of . . . soldiers for combat, and has nothing to do with the illusions of hope, nor those vain speculations by which men pad their valor and fudge upon the unoffending machines they trundle to and from the field of battle.[4]

I mention Homer Lea's remarks not because I believe that the Chief of the Imperial General Staff actually read such nonsense but because Lea's belief that the destructiveness of machines would always remain subordinate to the militancy of human combatants was, as has been demonstrated in the work of scholars such as T. H. E. Travers,[5] exactly the doctrine of the British War Office prior to 1914. In January 1910, for example, Brigadier General Sir Launcelot Kiggell, one of the 'brains' among British staff planners, told a Staff College Conference that modern wars were won not by firepower but 'by the bayonet, or by the fear of it'. General Sir William Nicholson, who was in attendance, confirmed Kiggell's opinion, presumably classing the aeroplane with the machine gun as a weapon of limited offensive potential.[6]

The point here is that Professor Gollin's discovery of a 'flawed strategy' for early British air defense is entirely of a piece with the general tenor of military planning in the Edwardian period. The men who dominated British military thinking (chiefly cavalry officers, although Nicholson had served with the Royal Engineers) had long since adopted a continental strategy, and it is not surprising that they made a second 'continental commitment' by assigning the entire Royal Flying Corps to support the British Expeditionary Force. Of course, the aeroplane like the machine gun was to have merely an ancillary role since it did not fit conveniently into their plan as to how the next war would be fought. Furthermore, short-sightedness regarding the use of military aviation was not mitigated by a lack of information. There was, as Professor Gollin has noted in *No Longer An Island*, an active Parliamentary Committee on Aerial Defence.[7] And the redoubtable Lord Roberts, even in his eightieth year, was warning all who would listen to him that 'the question of aerial defence is a vital one' which must needs be pursued by 'methodical scientific research and experiment with a view to originating improvement in every direction'.[8]

Gollin has noted that such warnings about aerial defense were not lost upon Winston Churchill at the Admirality; and he was not the only influential politician with some inkling of the significance of military aviation. Indeed, Churchill regularly corresponded with former Prime Minister and Unionist leader Arthur Balfour on military and naval questions and strongly supported Balfour's view, as expressed to Andrew Bonar Law, that: 'Submarines and airships seem . . . to be much more to the purpose of Home Defense than universal conscription and certainly are much cheaper and easier to obtain'.[9] When one contrasts the views of Churchill and Balfour with those of contemporary generals, to whom Admiral 'Jackie' Fisher referred as 'these silly asses who want to have an Army in Flanders',[10] one is again struck by the utter lack of imaginative grasp of so many of the soldiers who were planning the way in which Britain's next war would be fought.

In early 1910, for example, two of those generals, Henry S. Rawlinson and Sir John French, became 'much exercised' at Lord Roberts for writing a preface to Erskine Childers' *War and the Arme Blanche*, a book that questioned the efficacy of Britain's supposed chief offensive thrust, the massed cavalry charge. As Roberts told Spencer Wilkinson:

> It is a mystery to me why Cavalry should have failed to realize that change that has been brought about in Modern Warfare . . . My hope is that Childers' book will cause the people to see the folly of Cavalry trusting mainly to sword and lance and thus bring pressure to bear on Cavalry soldiers.[11]

Of course, this proved to be a vain hope for, as Gollin notes, these generals were willful men not easily deterred from any course they had chosen. Given their insistence, despite all logical arguments to the contrary, on maintaining as the primary cavalry weapon a device chiefly useful for sticking wild pigs, Gollin's revelation of War Office resistance to surrendering a responsibility for air defense that it had neither the means nor the intention of fulfilling comes as no great surprise. Somewhat more surprising, at least at first glance, is Gollin's conclusion that much of the blame for the insufficiency of Britain's early air defense must fall on Prime Minister H. H. Asquith for his failure to take steps to fill this 'bizarre gap' in Britain's strategic defense. Upon further consideration, however, Gollin's point is simply one more illustration of the view expressed some 17 years ago in the definitive history of defense policy in pre-war Britain, viz., that once Asquith had dealt with immediate political issues and 'safeguarded his own position . . . he pushed the profound issues of policy . . . to the back of his mind . . . '.[12] One would be interested to know if Asquith ever really considered air policy long enough to require putting it out of his mind, but whether he did or did not, air defense is one more example of his abdication of leadership responsibility for the sake of political expediency.

But however careless or neglectful British politicians might be regarding military policy, their behavior seems both vigorous and virtuous in light of Martin Kitchen's detailed and fascinating account of the ominous growth of military authority and military duplicity in

Imperial Germany during the First World War. In attempting to come to grips with this formidable study of German civil-military relations, I was struck by the fundamental ruthlessness and even brutality of the internal siege imposed upon German society, and particularly the working-classes, by the Army High Command (OHL). The draconic nature of the 'Hindenburg Program' to seize absolute control of civilian labor and war production stands in stark contrast to fumbling British manpower policies such as the 'combing out' of the industrial workforce to obtain a few thousand more men for the Western Front[13] or with Lloyd George's efforts at subtle diplomacy to resolve labor problems and stoppages.[14] No wonder there was no conscientious objector movement in Germany. How long would German military leaders have put up with the legal niceties evoked by the No-Conscription Fellowship or listened unprovoked to the slashing sarcasm of Bertrand Russell?[15] On the other hand, one can only speculate as to the fate of C.O.s such as Clifford Allen or Fenner Brockway or of troublesome agitators like Russell if some determined British military man, say, General Sir Henry Wilson,[16] had been free to exercise the sort of control that the OHL exerted upon Germany's civilian population.

Another point that struck me forcibly was Kitchen's implication that it took the second battle of Ypres and the catastrophic attack on Langemarck to convince the German military leadership of what Jean de Bloch could have told them, and did, in 1900: that frontal assaults on entrenched positions were nonsense in modern warfare.[17] Of course, they seem to have learned even this graphic lesson badly since at Verdun, as Kitchen notes, they immediately reverted to form at the cost of tens of thousands. Still, they were in advance of their Anglo-Saxon foes in this regard since most British brass hats who had, besides Bloch, G. F. R. Henderson, Robert Baden-Powell and Charles Calwell to warn them, maintained their faith in the dogma of the offensive until the last months of the Great War when they finally realized, as a recent scholar of the war has noted, 'that the path of frontal assault and the vocabulary of attrition was no longer countenanced by the War Cabinet . . . '.[18]

The German generals' failure to learn basic doctrinal lessons seems all the more amazing given their uncanny ability to play every card to their advantage in political battles with the Kaiser and his civilian officials. Their capacity for having it both ways or all possible ways is, by Kitchen's account, truly remarkable. The OHL's success at disguising political decisions as military advice and thus combining a maximum of power with a minimum of responsibility is well-illustrated by Kitchen's example of the High Command using its negotiations with Count Erzberger to win support for a campaign against Bethmann Hollweg while simultaneously attacking the Chancellor for having caved in to the very Reichstag members whom they were wooing. It seems a model of ingenious duplicity. Even more impressive is the 'Hintze action' of October 1918, maneuvering the left-wing opposition into office in order to lay upon them the blame for losing the war. And all of this in an atmosphere that enhanced the stab-in-the-back (*Dolchstoss*) legend the OHL had created and sustained through their control of the press.

Professor Kitchen believes that the story of civil-military relations in Germany during the Great War 'provides a classic example of the capitulation of the civilian authorities to the exigencies of the military commanders'. I think he has made a good case for this assertion. One may indeed account for the OHL's remarkable success at political subterfuge in contrast to its failure of strategic imagination or even military common sense by noting that however unsatisfactory Allied political leaders were, they never permitted their commanders to walk over them with the ease with which the OHL was permitted to trample on German civilian authority.

There is one final question arising from Kitchen's account that I should like to address. Were the OHL's expectations for Brest-Litovsk really 'preposterous', as Professor Kitchen notes, or were they, as A. J. P. Taylor has said in a different context, simply the dreams of the German man in the street or, more correctly, the man in the gutter, to whom Hitler would so successfully appeal?[19] Indeed, OHL dreams of an annexationist peace amidst the eroding situation of September-October 1918 are reminiscent of Hitler's shadow divisions and 'miracle' weapons in the spring of 1945.[20]

Kitchen's characterization of Hindenberg as both 'ersatz Kaiser' and 'proto-Führer' does seem to point to continuity in German military attitudes and aims between 1914 and 1945, and perhaps even of German civilian willingness to be used in pursuit of those aims.

In any case, Kitchen's chapter simply and surely illustrates the soundness of Stanley Hoffmann's ominous evaluation of the impact of the wars of our century upon military and civilian alike:

> What is total war, if not the self-destruction of the rules and institutions of the [traditional] game, a technological Frankenstein that subordinates political calculations to military necessities, a

vampire that injects public passions into the body politic until political calculations disappear altogether, a minotaur that obliges leaders to make choices that exceed the possibilities of ethical calculations.[21]

NOTES

1. Nicholson to Roberts, 13 April 1909, Roberts Papers (RP), 7101–23, 52/132, National Army Museum, London. Nicholson did believe that 'dirigible airships . . . may perhaps be more formidable than aeroplanes'. Also see Alfred Gollin, *No Longer An Island* (London: 1984), pp. 300–2 for a discussion of Nicholson's resolute opposition to military aviation.
2. Roberts to Lord Montagu of Beaulieu, 28 January 1909, RP, 122/7 and to M. A. Duhamel, 27 February 1909, ibid., 122/11.
3. *Harper's Weekley* 54 (20 August 1910): 8–9, and (27 August 1910): 11,26. For Lea, see Eugene Anschel, *Homer Lea, Sun Yat-Sen and The Chinese Revolution* (New York: 1985) and Thomas C. Kennedy, 'Homer Lea and the Peacemakers', *The Historian* 45/4 (August 1983); 473–96.
4. Lea, 'Aeroplane', *Harper's Weekley* 54 (27 August 1910): 26 and *passim*.
5. See Travers' articles 'Technology, Tactics and Morale: Jean de Bloch, The Boer War, and British Military Theory, 1900–1914', *Journal of Modern History*, 51/2 (June 1979); 264–86 and 'The Offensive and the Problem in Innovation in British Military Thought, 1870–1915', *Journal of Contemporary History*, 13/3 (July 1978); 531–53
6. Ibid., 531–2 and *passim*.
7. Gollin, *No Longer An Island*, pp. 463–4.
8. Roberts to Mr Mannon of the Aerial Defence Committee, 20 April 1913, RP, 125/2. One of the chief architects of the continental strategy, Colonel Sir Henry Wilson, did express some misgivings about British lack of progress in aviation when he noted: 'Capper gave us his second lecture on the Aeroplane. Awful the way . . . we are doing nothing', Wilson, *Diaries*, 10 February 1910, Imperial War Museum, London.
9. Balfour to Bonar Law, 22 November 1912, Bonar Law Papers, 27/4/9, House of Lords Records Office, London.
10. Fisher to Balfour, 6 April 1913, Arthur Balfour Papers, Ad. Mss. 49712, British Library, London. Also see Fisher to Balfour, 22 November 1912, ibid.
11. Henry Wilson, *Diaries*, 31 January 2, 4 and 5 February 1910, Imperial War Museum and Roberts to Spencer Wilkinson, 24 March 1910, Spencer Wilkinson Papers, 13/14/107 Army Museum Ogilvy Trust, Whitehall, London. Roberts had clashed with French six years earlier

on the same question, see Hugh O. Arnold-Forster, *Diary*, vol. II, 1904, 29 February and 6 March 1906, Arnold-Forster Papers, Ad. Mss. 50336, British Library, London.

12. See Nicholas d'Ombrain, *War Machinery and High Policy* (London: 1973), p. 260.
13. For a discussion of industrial 'combing out' in Britain see R. J. Q. Adams and Philip P. Poirer, *The Conscription Controversy in Great Britain 1900–18* (Columbus: 1987), pp. 201–2, 225–6. In his recent book on *The Politics of Manpower, 1914–1918* (New York: 1988), pp. 81–2, Keith Grieves notes the similarity between the German Auxiliary Service Law and an idealized scheme of National Service envisioned by Lloyd George and his Unionist allies in late 1916 and early 1917. The differences were, of course, that Britain not only never imposed compulsory industrial service but that is military conscription laws were far milder than their German counterparts. For a detailed consideration of British and German radical responses to domestic military policies, See F. L. Carsten, *War Against War* (Berkeley: 1982).
14. See C. J. Wrigley, *David Lloyd George and the British Labor Movement* (Hassocks: 1976).
15. For the C. O. movement in Britain, see John Rae, *Politics and Conscience* (London: 1970) and Thomas C. Kennedy, *The Hound of Conscience: A History of the No-Conscription Fellowship, 1914–1919* (Fayetteville: 1981). In Germany as in other continental countries, conscientious objectors had no legal status and were treated as deserters; see Carsten, *War Against War*, p. 73.
16. A fellow officer, General F. P. Crozier, called Henry Wilson 'the greatest political soldier of our day . . . the greatest mischief maker and political claptrapper the British army has ever possessed'.
17. For Bloch see Peter van den Dugen, 'The Making of Peace: Jean de Bloch and the First Hague Peace Conference', Occasional Paper Series, No. 12, Center for the Study of Armament and Disarmament, Los Angeles, and Travers, 'Technology, Tactics and Moralé', 265–70. A recent and fascinating discussion of how the OHL and later the Nazis transformed the disaster of Langemarck into the myth of a great moral victory by inspired German youth is Bernd Hüppauf, 'Langermarck, Verdun and the Myth of a New Man in Germany after the First World War', *War and Society*, 612 (September 1988); pp. 70–103.
18. Ibid., 270, 272–5 and Grieves, *Politics of Manpower*.
19. A. J. P. Taylor, *The Origins of the Second World War* (London: 1961), pp. 69–73.
20. See Albert Seaton, *The Fall of Fortress Europe, 1943–1945* (New York: 1981), pp. 179–97.
21. Stanley Hoffmann, *The State of War: Essays on the Theory and Practice of International Politics* (New York 1965), p. 267.

Part III

General Arthur Currie (left) and General John J. Pershing. Reproduced courtesy of the National Archives of the United States of America.

5 The Canadian Military Experience in the First World War, 1914–18

Desmond Morton

Canadians, like other citizens of other smaller nations, resent being overlooked in the great events of history. The price of fame can, of course, be inordinately high, as the Lebanese have found in our time or the Belgians did in 1914. It is, perhaps, nobody's business but Canadians' that the First World War was the major transforming event in their history, akin to the Civil War for Americans or the Napoleonic wars for the British. Four years of war left nothing in Canada untouched, from skirt lengths to taxation to romantic innocence about the world and war. The war divided Canadians and left fault lines which are still visible today. To a degree barely glimpsed by contemporaries, 1914–18 turned out to be Canada's war for independence from the Empire, though Britain was and remained a cherished ally; correspondingly, the war marked Canada's ineluctable transfer to the orbit of the United States.

Futures are visible only in retrospect. When news reached Canada on the afternoon of 4 August that the British Empire had declared war on Germany, revelling crowds extended the hot holiday week-end. American delegates to a convention at Winnipeg got a special dose of cheering so that they could take home word that British patriotism was at fever pitch on the Canadian prairie. In French-speaking Montreal and Quebec, crowds exceeded those in solidly-British Toronto.[1] In Ottawa, where the Minister of Militia had threatened to haul down the Union Jack if Britain 'skunked it', mobilization began with orders to scrap the pre-war mobilization plan. The Minister, Colonel Sam Hughes, would summon volunteers his way.[2] Within days, Parliament had met to promise Britain a division of troops, entirely at Canada's expense. Since the war would be won by Christmas, would they arrive in time? In an attempt to guarantee Canada a place in the victory parade, a special battalion, Princess Patricia's Canadian Light Infantry, was formed by private subscription from British army reservists in Canada.[3]

Fifteen years earlier, Canadians had had their only experience of modern war when popular demand overruled Sir Wilfrid Laurier's Liberal government, and Canadian contingents were sent to the Boer War. They returned with few losses and a high sense of their achievements as both infantry and mounted rifles. It was a war designed for colonial irregulars, and it inspired much the same military self-confidence as the Spanish-American War created in the United States.[4] It also gave the Canadian Militia a role more challenging and realistic than waiting for a renewal of the War of 1812. Military reform became mildly popular. Arms, equipment and training improved. Departmental corps, necessary for a field army, took shape. Since Canadian-born officers had won renown in South Africa, Canadians wondered whether they still needed the tutelage of British generals and staff officers.[5]

No one embodied Canada's prewar militarism better than Colonel Hughes. A rural editor, Conservative politician, promoter of railways, passionate Imperialist, Hughes defied the Canadian self-image of drab moderation. He combined imperialism with a contempt for most Englishmen and his military enthusiasm with outspoken disdain for any senior officer who crossed his will. Hughes was charming, affectionate and vindictive. Though he was a Conservative, it was a Liberal minister of militia, Sir Fred Borden, who allowed him to serve in South Africa, and who won Hughes's undying support for the Canadian-made Ross rifle. When the Liberals lost in 1911, it was Sir Fred who argued for Hughes to be part of the new Conservative government formed by his cousin, Robert L. Borden. As minister, Hughes doubled defense spending, expanded the militia to 60 000, built armories, laid out camps and revelled in the new cadet corps with their compulsory training for high school boys. A feminist, Hughes wanted the same training for girls. In 1913, Canada slid into economic depression, militarism went out of style and suddenly 'Drill Hall Sam' had become an acute political liability. The outbreak of war in 1914 saved him.[6]

Hughes was instantly in his element. Thirty-three thousand volunteers poured into the camp at Valcartier. In uniform and on horseback, the Minister galloped about giving orders, promoting, demoting and cursing anyone who offended his sense of fitness. Workmen hurried to build the biggest rifle range in the world. It was the only training facility Hughes thought necessary in modern war: 'his boys', he insisted, must be able to 'pink the enemy every time'. Vast quantities of equipment poured into the camp, including a shield-shovel Hughes had patented in the name of his secretary, Ena MacAdam. Canadians would advance behind its protection, score bullseyes through its loophole and dig in on the objective.[7] Once embarked, the Canadian troops had their last gift from the Minister, a bombastic order of the day that claimed: 'Soldiers, the world regards you as a marvel . . .'.[8] When they reached Plymouth on 15 October, a good many of the young men spoiled their welcome by getting drunk on the potent British beer.[9] For days, unit search parties hunted for their equipment in vast piles strewn along the road to Salisbury Plain. There, under the worst rains in memory, an elderly British soldier, Lieutenant General Sir Edwin Alderson, helped turn raw Canadians into an infantry division. Part of the job was replacing much of Hughes' cherished equipment with British patterns of boots, wagons and equipment. Hughes and his cronies were outraged; soldiers were more grateful. Nationalism was a poor trade-off for flimsy farm carts and boots that dissolved in the mud. Hughes became 'General Sham Shoes'.[10]

To Canadians, however, Valcartier was a triumph. It seemed amazing that so many men could be collected, trained and dispatched in a few weeks. A Second Contingent was announced in October and 12 regiments of mounted rifles in December. Soon, scores of battalions were recruiting for the Canadian Expeditionary Force, each of them certain to be in the vanguard to Berlin. Colonels appealed to Scots with bagpipes, to the Irish with the promise of kilts, and to 'Pals' with the pledge that they would never be separated.[11] An 'American Legion' drew 1500 men across the frontier, half of whom soon deserted. Hughes travelled ceaselessly, roving across Canada in his private railway car, crossing the Atlantic to see 'his boys' and chastise their officers, always eager to meet reporters for 'seances', to exchange gossip, pass on secrets and deliver threats that he would 'rawhide' his latest critic or troublemaker.[12] If it was absurd and undignified, what else was a peacable democracy in the throes of its first real war? Critics complained to the Prime Minister, particularly when Hughes raged against British mismanagement of the war. Sir Robert Borden could only plead with Hughes to be more discreet: 'You do not represent yourself alone as Minister of Militia, but the government of which you are a part'.[13] His tempestuous minister wondered aloud what his prime minister privately feared: were Canadians dying in vain because of the stupidity of British generals?[14]

Overseas, the perspective was different. In February 1915 Alderson's division went to France. On 22 April, the Canadians found themselves guarding the hills east of Ypres when the Germans attacked behind a cloud of chlorine gas. In a week of savage fighting, the Canadians lost ground and suffered 6000 casualties. Somehow the line held. At Ypres, the romance of war was dispelled faster than the gas. There had been no victory by Christmas in 1914; there would be none in 1915 or 1916 either. In September, a second Canadian Division arrived in France; early in 1916 a third Division was formed and a fourth Division joined the Canadian Corps during the autumn battle on the Somme. Each had its grim baptism. At St Eloi in March 1916, thousands of men of the second Division were lost in a struggle for mine craters, because their generals could not locate them in the mist and confusion, and misdirected artillery support. At Mont Sorrel in June, a sudden savage German assault killed the 3rd division's commander and annihilated one of his brigades. The 1st Division, battle-hardened and experienced, waited two weeks and took the ground back. The 4th Division learned its lesson late in the Battle of the Somme, failing miserably in its first assault, succeeding in its second.[15]

For the Canadian Corps, 1916 was a learning year. Despite a persistent myth, the British had no plan to divide up the Canadians as later they would hope to share out the AEF. The British believed that men fought better among friends and free of political meddling. Though the Canadians technically became part of the British Expeditionary Force – 'Imperials' under the Army Act – Ottawa had insisted on paying the bills (unlike its South African contingents) and therefore Canada retained a voice.[16] It was exercised on Hughes' behalf by that consummate Canadian-born intriguer, Sir Max Aitken, who warned Hughes that Alderson was criticizing the cherished Ross rifle and who claimed, less accurately, that he was promoting British staff officers at Canadian expense. It was Aitken who insisted that Canada would not sacrifice the two incompetent Canadian generals partly to blame for the St Eloi fiasco but that Alderson, as a British officer, could be the scapegoat.[17]

Sir Douglas Haig agreed, in return for a second British commander for the Canadians, Sir Julian Byng. Without genius or pomposity, Byng soon won the hearts and the confidence of his Canadians.[18] He was helped by an undeserved Canadian pride in their first tactical invention, the trench raid.[19] A short-run success and a long-term curse which would cost thousands of lives in return for a few scraggly prisoners, trench raids delighted General Headquarters and gave Byng enough credit as a 'thruster' that he could be forgiven the time he took to prepare his men for real battle. Byng's apotheosis came on 9 April, Easter Sunday, 1917, when his four Canadian divisions rose in line and walked forward through driving snow to capture Vimy Ridge. Three months of weary preparation and the biggest British artillery barrage of the war won a long hill that had defied French courage and ingenuity in 1915 at a cost that seemed reasonable in 1917 – ten thousand dead and wounded. The Canadian Corps that day became a national institution. It had served its apprenticeship.[20]

Nations, said Ernest Renan, were made by doing great things together in the past. To contemporaries, taking Vimy Ridge seemed a great thing, but Canadians had not done it together. The French-speaking 22nd Battalion did not represent Henri Bourassa, the *nationalistes* and others who spoke for French Canada in *Le Devoir, Le Droit* and *La Presse*.[21] There were English-speaking Canadians – pacifists, socialists, people with German roots, or simple isolationists who also opposed the war, but their voices were generally silent. Internment camps confined 6000 enemy aliens, most of them guilty of unemployment.[22]

Canada's Prime Minister, Sir Robert Borden, has been regarded as a colorless politician, a progressive with a passion for the honest, efficient government most of his colleagues managed to thwart. The war revealed Borden to be a fighter, profoundly moved by the wounded soldiers he visited at every chance, convinced that he must win the victory their suffering had earned.[23] It was not a universal conviction. Colleagues worried about party prospects; businessmen fretted about profits. Visiting Britain in 1915, Borden was dismayed by the indolent defeatism of the Asquith government. Borden committed Canada to send a quarter-million men; at New Years, 1916, hoping to infect the British with his earnestness, he doubled the total to 500 000 from a population of eight million souls.[24]

Was it too many? Major General Willoughby Gwatkin, a British officer, forced against his will to serve as Hughes' Chief of the General Staff, had warned that two divisions might be all Canada could keep in the field with volunteers. Borden had pledged in 1914 that there would be no conscription. So had Hughes: he could, he boasted, raise eight, ten – any number of divisions – by his own personal appeal.[25] Perhaps he could. By the end of 1915 218 000 men had enlisted; in the first four months of 1916, redoubled pressure from recruiting leagues and dozens of new CEF battalions brought in 108 983 more. Yet few could perceive, thanks to Hughes's organizational muddle, that more and more recruits were unfit and that after April 1916 totals would fall dramatically.[26] Farmers kept sons home to raise crops at wartime prices. The munitions industry, torn from Hughes' control, clamored for labor. Young men endured the slur of 'slacker' for the sake of work, wages and survival. Patriots cried for conscription. Bourassa, who had split with Laurier in 1900 by opposing the South African contingent, led an answering chorus. Canada's frontier was at Halifax, not Flanders, he insisted; its young men should stay home to grow food, or make munitions.[27] French Canada overwhelmingly agreed.

Borden avoided the debate. Throughout 1916 he focused on improving Canada's war effort, usually by separating Hughes from responsibilities and handing them to commissions of businessmen.[28] A major problem was Canadian military administration in Britain. To preserve his own power over even minute decisions, Hughes had left three senior officers with the impression that each had full control. Every quarrel was referred to the Minister. In the summer of 1916, Borden sent Hughes to England to solve the humiliating and costly problem. When Hughes merely created a committee of cronies, with his son-in-law to monitor decisions, an exasperated Borden finally acted. Sir George Perley, Canadian High Commissioner in London, was named Minister of Overseas Military Forces. A quiet by-product was the first official Canadian assertion of authority over its overseas troops; hitherto, they had been assumed to be British. After an acrimonious correspondence, Hughes was fired in November. 'I do not like to kick a man when he is down', wrote Colonel J. J. Creelman of the Corps artillery, 'but I am willing to break nine toes in kicking Sam'.[29]

Having a Canadian minister in London made less difference than the removal of Hughes. Officers whose competence had been proved in France were brought back to England to take charge of the Canadian administrative and reinforcement system. While the traditional hostility between the front and the base soon resumed, it was far less justified. As the Canadians belatedly got their affairs in order, they could reach out for growing authority over their troops in France. Hughes' emotional nationalism, which had protected incompetent commanders and the execrable Ross rifle, was replaced by an overdue determination to manage Canadian military affairs with the same efficiency the Canadian Corps had achieved.[30]

During 1916, Canada painfully organized itself for the war its more powerful allies seemed to be losing. France was bled white at Verdun. Maps and casualty lists mocked British claims of victory on the Somme. On the Russian front, Rumania was overrun and the Brusilov offensive, begun in triumph, ended in disaster. In the west, only Britain and its dominions could still dream of victory. For that they needed a leader. Change came in December, when Sir Max Aitken, freed by Hughes' stormy dismissal, lent his conspiratorial talents to David Lloyd George.[31] Britain got a new Prime Minister and Aitken got a peerage as the new Lord Beaverbrook. Borden was delighted. Whatever Lloyd George's dubious political past as a Liberal and pro-Boer, he had struck the Canadian Prime Minister in 1915 as the only British leader with a will to win. In turn, Lloyd George needed the Dominion prime ministers. 'We can hardly ask them to make another great recruiting effort unless we ask them to come over and discuss the situation with us.'[32]

Borden was eager to come. A year earlier, he had written to warn the British that Canada would not provide half a million men 'and willingly accept the position of having no more voice and receiving no more consideration than if we were toy automata'.[33] Borden had long believed that Canada's destiny lay within a form of British imperial federation. Now, through Lloyd George's Imperial War Cabinet, it could be realized. So could unified direction of the war.

Lloyd George had no intention of conceding either consultation or federation. Instead, by revealing enough of the grim Allied situation to make the Dominion premiers' flesh creep, he sent them home for more men.[34] For Borden, that meant a crisis. Getting rid of Hughes had clarified the facts about recruiting. With the volunteers available, Canada could sustain only three of its four divisions in France and certainly not the 5th Division Hughes had organized in England as a command for his son, Garnet. Yet, even with the Americans about to enter the war, the Allied cause was too desperate for a slackening of effort. Visits to wounded Canadians steeled Borden's heart: unless more men were sent, these were soldiers who would be forced to return again and again to the trenches until they were dead or human wreckage. To underline the point came news of the triumph and the losses at Vimy Ridge. Borden went grimly home to his divided country: on 18 May 1917 he told Parliament that his government would conscript men for overseas service.[35]

Later, the Liberals would claim that Borden dreamed up conscription to save his political skin. Conservative scandals and railway bankruptcies would be buried in patriotic grace. This was absurd. Borden was a cautious, even a timid politician, and he knew the depth of opposition to conscription. Australia, more British by far than Canada, had already rejected conscription in a plebiscite, and it would do so again. Having chosen his goal, Borden was patient and flexible on the means. He offered the aged Sir Wilfrid Laurier a coalition.

Laurier refused. When the Military Service Bill appeared, modelled on the US draft, it was so full of exemptions and appeals as ultimately to prove almost unworkable. It was and still is labelled an engine of oppression.[36] In August, the government enfranchised soldiers, their wives, sisters and mothers, while robbing citizens born in enemy countries before 1902 of their right to vote.[37] The Wartime Election Act, shocking at the time and since, had the effect of convincing prominent pro-conscription Liberals that it was time to desert their party and join Borden in that promised coalition. It was as head of a Union government that Sir Robert campaigned through the fall of 1917, pledging votes for women, railway nationalization and prohibition of liquor as well as earnestness in the war effort and exemptions for farmers' sons.[38]

It was a dirty, bitter campaign. In French Canada Laurier was unchallenged. Even Henri Bourassa, an enemy since 1900, was briefly reconciled to him. Outside Quebec, Borden by no means had his own way. At Kitchener, a German-speaking Ontario city compelled to change its name from Berlin, an angry crowd shouted Borden off the platform. Only exemptions for their sons steadied the farm vote – and the implied promise that the Military Service Act would fall chiefly on the Catholic, French-speaking slackers in Quebec. On election day Borden won 153 seats to Laurier's 82. Without the soldier vote, Borden's margin in votes was a bare hundred thousand. In Quebec the Unionists won a mere three seats.[39]

An election may not seem a substantial wartime experience. To a people separated by the Atlantic from the sounds and sights of combat, the 1917 contest, with its savage emotions and the rending of party and social unity, brought the war home. Winners and losers could never forget the conscription issue, all the more because the next election in 1921 would so completely reverse the 1917 result. Canada's history would be written, in great part, by the Liberal losers of 1917; they would shape the inherited experience of the First World War as the national government in 1939–45.[40]

There remained a war to fight, a long and idealistic political program to implement and conscription to impose. The last proved difficult. To get a hundred thousand men, the government called 404 395 men; 380 510 promptly appealed. Local tribunals, formed jointly by Liberal and Conservative nominees, granted blanket exemptions to young *Québécois* though, the central appeal judge, Mr Justice Lyman Duff, later claimed, they 'applied conscription against the English-speaking minority in Quebec with a rigor unparalleled'.[41] None of this would help the Corps in France.

As the overseas Ministry and other reforms helped Canada gain more control of its troops, the men themselves looked and sounded more Canadian. In 1914 60 per cent of the 'Old Originals' had been British-born and the survivors formed a non-commissioned backbone for later contingents. By 1917, however, time and war's toll left the Corps to the Canadian-born and their flat North American accents.[42] In June, when Byng was promoted to command the British Third Army, one of the Canadian-born took his place.

Arthur Currie was as important in Canada's war effort as Hughes. An insurance agent and land dealer from Victoria on Vancouver Island, Currie's pear-shaped bulk and solemn demeanor hid the young athlete he had once been when he joined the militia artillery in 1897. Currie had risen fast, excited by the technicalities of his branch and eager for social recognition.[43] Perhaps he had spent too much time in soldiering; in 1914 the depression left him in hopeless debt. A government check for $10 000, illegally converted, saved him from bankruptcy; the war saved him from the consequences.[44]

In 1914 Hughes had accepted Currie, a Western Liberal, at the urging of his son, Garnet. At Ypres, Currie more than earned his rank by reorganizing his shattered brigade, though a British general condemned his action in going back for help. A year later, Currie masterminded the 1st Division's recapture of Mont Sorrel.[45] Before Vimy, Currie refused to waste his division in futile trench raids. Byng, he later recalled, 'walked around me like a cooper round a barrel until I suggested that he needed some leave'.[46] The quarrel was forgotten, other divisions were left to sacrifice their keenest officers and men in futile raids and the 1st Division was the first to consolidate its Vimy objective. Currie was Byng's only choice to command the Corps.

Promotion came with a knighthood and a crisis. The $10 000 fraud had finally been traced. The Hughes faction threatened to reveal all if Garnet, found useless in command, was not given Currie's old division. Sir Arthur kept cool, persuaded two wealthy subordinates to lend him the necessary money, defied blackmail and left the government to cover up.[47]

Currie inherited a Corps that had developed a very largely Canadian staff. Its units had been tested in battle, improved by experience rather than systematic training. That made possible acceptance of ideas professional soldiers would have regarded as unconventional, although it contributed to a certain inflexibility in practice – a combination familiar to those who worked with the self-educated. The new Corps commander brought, from his militia days, a special enthusiasm for artillery and a belief in overwhelming firepower, whatever the cost, which went far beyond the more frugal British expectations. To Currie, shells were cheaper than lives. In his division he had also tried to overcome the paralysis that overtook infantry at or near the objective by imbuing an equally unfashionable enthusiasm for small-unit maneuvering at the platoon and section (US squad) level. 'Maps to section leaders' was a 1st Division slogan. Corporals sometimes even got the scarce new air photos. Canadians, less preoccupied by rank and uncertain in any case of the knowledge and authority of commissioned officers, may have been more willing than their British counterparts to get the job done by whoever was willing to do it – captain, corporal or private.[48]

That summer the Canadian Corps' first major assignment came in August. To pull Germans away from the disastrous British offensive at Passchendaele, Currie was ordered to capture the mining town of Lens. He took one look and refused. Nestled between two hills, Lens would be a deathtrap. Why not capture one of the hills, pour in machine gun and artillery cover and let the Germans bleed themselves white in the inevitable counter-attacks. On 15 August the Canadians took Hill 70, rushed up protective firepower and withstood 21 German assaults in two weeks. They lost 9612 casualties, half the German toll. It was, Currie later claimed, his best battle.[49]

In October it was the Canadian turn to share in Haig's drive on Passchendaele. Currie protested. Haig insisted; there were reasons he could explain only after the war. In that case, Currie insisted, he would fight the battle in his own methodical way. As pelting rain flooded the vast, glutinous morass, engineers built and repaired roads, paths and light railways. Gunners hauled artillery onto wooden rafts and waited while scores of missing guns were replaced. On 26 October two divisions pushed forward a few hundred yards at the cost of 2600 dead or wounded. Four days later they tried again, losing 2321 in the struggle for German pillboxes. Then Currie switched divisions. A week later, with all as ready as it could be, fresh troops inched further up the slope to dryer land. Again there was delay until, on 10 November the last assault reached the useless but symbolic Passchendaele – now a smear of brick dust in the mud. Currie had warned Haig that Passchendaele would cost him 16 000 casualties; the actual price was 15 654 dead and wounded, 3000 of them among the engineer and pioneer units who had borne the brunt of Currie's insistence on painstaking preparation.[50]

That insistence became the style of the Canadian Corps. These were not, like the ANZACS, wild colonial boys. There was not a trace of charisma in their plump commander. Most of his men seem to have disliked him as they detested most of their generals and staff officers.[51] The few exceptions, Major-General 'Batty Mac' Macdonell, Currie's successor in the 1st Division, L. J. Lipsett, the British exchange officer who had risen from the 8th Winnipeg Rifles to command the 3rd Division, were admired for their frequent appearance in front-line trenches.[52] Currie was there too, at times: few generals in that war were more committed to seeing ground for themselves, as he had at Lens, Vimy and Passchendaele. Few, even among Canadians, were more willing to learn from others in an army of part-timers, full of strange expertise. There was Andy McNaughton, a chemistry professor from McGill, a brilliant gunner who applied sound-ranging and flash spotting to counter-battery operations.[53] There was Charlie Mitchell, a railwayman who became Director of Light Railways for the BEF or Major General Bill Lindsay, Currie's Chief Engineer. 'Foghorn' Macdonald, a miner and a corporal sat seething one day as Currie issued orders to his officers and then broke in: 'Look here, old man Currie, you don't know the first thing about mines. I have forgotten more about them than you'll ever know. You may say what you like about the rest, but don't try coming over me about the mine just because you're stud duck in this puddle'. Currie laughed, sat down and learned from the expert.[54]

Few soldiers saw that. Nor could they know, in their sacrificial role, of Currie's growing insistence that shells, barbed wire, picks and shovels and every form of *matériel* that could save lives would be supplied to the Canadians and used. Before Vimy, Byng had laid out replicas of the objective and forced every unit to rehearse. Currie continued and improved on Byng's methods. Units instinctively evolved the battle drills that would be taught in a later war. They compensated for inexperienced junior officers. A systematic, methodical style fitted the needs of hastily-promoted Canadian commanders and staffs – though a few key positions at Corps and division level were held by some outstanding British officers almost to the end of the war. Keeping the Corps together forged a confidence and cohesion missing in British divisions which were shifted from corps to corps.[55]

That was a factor when, in early 1918, manpower shortages forced the British to cut their divisions from 12 to nine battalions of infantry – in theory so that Americans could fill the gaps. With conscription, the Canadians could have followed suit and add a 5th and a 6th Division, allowing for two corps and a small Army. National pride and hosts of surplus senior officers in England would have been satisified.[56] The Allies could boast of added strength.

Currie refused. More divisions meant more untrained and incompetent officers and an end to the marvellous cohesion of his Corps. Reluctantly, since it meant frustrating ambitions and dissolving the 5th Division in England, Ottawa agreed.[57] By now, the British had learned not to interfere. When Haig had grumbled earlier about Canadian assertiveness, the Secretary of State for War, the Earl of Derby, warned: '. . . we must look upon them in the light in which they wish to be looked upon rather than the light in which we would wish to do so'.[58]

It was a warning made more painful when the German offensives in March shattered the British Fifth Army and brought the Allies to the brink of defeat. Currie's Corps, back in front of Vimy, missed each of the German thrusts, but, when Haig insisted on using Canadian divisions to plug his gaps, their Corps commander used his new channels to protest. A furious Haig was compelled by Whitehall to restore most of Currie's divisions. Without formality or signatures, Canada had become a junior but sovereign ally whose army, seemingly British in all but its badges and its new sense of nationality, now had its own chain of command and a measure of autonomy.[59]

The German offensives had their impact in Canada too. In Ottawa, the censors' attempt to conceal the awful setbacks only made the truth seem worse. Clearly men would be needed. Warnings came from the Overseas Military. The force of the Military Service Act would be ended. By Cabinet order, the exemptions from conscription were cancelled. Farmers lost their sons, just as seeding time began. In Quebec City there were riots, ended when soldiers from Toronto shot five civilians and the Catholic archbishop commanded obedience to civil authority.[60] Neither farmers nor *Québécois* would forget their added sense of betrayal but almost a hundred thousand conscripts – MSA men was the usual term – were available and on their way.

Ironically, they were not needed. The German offensives failed. The Canadian Corps, stretched thin behind its masses of barbed wire, was not attacked. Well-trained men from the 5th Division swelled each fighting battalion far beyond its regulation strength. Only the AEF had more abundant manpower by war-weary 1918. Indeed, Canadians had spread far beyond the Corps, operating railways, cutting forests and piloting barges. Above all, they were in the air, where close to a quarter of the pilots in the Royal Air Force and two of its top five aces were Canadians, many of them trained at new flying schools in Canada and Texas.[61]

In the spring of 1918, Borden came again to England. This time Lloyd George was serious about consultation. When Borden, briefed by Currie, delivered a memorable denunciation of the Passchendaele fiasco, the British Prime Minister summoned the generals and forced them to listen. 'Let the past bury its dead', stormed the usually taciturn Canadian, 'but for God's sake let us get down to earnest endeavor'. If there were more Passchendaeles, he warned, not a single Canadian would sail for Europe.[62] Instead, Borden got a share in planning. His committee insisted that Russia must be restored to the Allies and, to back his word, thousand of Canadians set sail for Archangel and Vladivostok in the summer of 1918.[63]

Victory, Borden and his fellow prime ministers agreed, could not come before 1919 or even 1920. The offensive planned for Amiens on 8 August would do no more than put distance between the Germans and a vital rail link. Elaborate security concealed the Canadian arrival. On a misty dawn, they and the Australians rolled forward behind a short, intense barrage. For once, tanks were welcome; so was the innovation of close support from aircraft. Platoons, drilled in fire and movement, imitated the German tactics of March 1918. Wholly unexpectedly, the German line crumpled. The Canadians advanced eight miles, the Australians seven. As resistance finally hardened, Currie pleaded for a chance to switch fronts, to launch an attack the Canadians had already rehearsed. Haig agreed.[64]

On 26 August, led by barrage lines and fighter-bombers with fragmentation bombs, two Canadian divisions began systematically forcing their way through the Drocourt-Quéant line. By 3 September, at a cost of 11 000 casualties, the Corps had broken both the old British and the old German lines. Beyond lay the Canal du Nord and Cambrai. With unexpected boldness, Currie proposed to force a narrow crossing and push 50 000 men through the funnel. While British superiors and Currie himself waited nervously, on 26 September the Canadians carried it off. Then, four bitter days of fighting followed as the Germans struggled to save Cambrai. For once, the Canadians were stopped. But, when the attack resumed on the night of 8–9 October, resistance wilted. Thereafter, the Canadians turned east through Valenciennes to Mons where the war had begun for the British and where it ended for the Canadians on 11 November.[65]

Americans, too, had forged a victorious tradition that autumn in France, and the French and British armies could claim their share of triumphs. In the nature of nations, each had eyes for its own accomplishments. Long after the war, Canadians would remember Ypres or Vimy more clearly than they recalled what contemporaries called 'the Hundred Days'. Nor would Canadians remember that their heaviest casualties by far occurred in those days. Perhaps half the fighting strength of the Corps, 30 802 men, fell between Amiens and Cambrai.[66] The Australians, who suffered comparable losses, had no replacements. By October, some AIF units mutinied rather than face fresh slaughter. The Canadian battalions could be filled with 'MSA men', unwelcome and disparaged conscripts but willing to follow the example of hard-bitten comrades in arms. Canadians have been told that conscription was unnecessary and a failure. Both claims are wrong.[67]

Experience, of course, is not necessarily based on truth. For most Canadians, the First World War remains, as it does for most who remember it, a tragedy for Western civilization and the firmest *quietus* to the illusion that war can be a glorious adventure. Sixty thousand of the Canadians who went to war did not return; at least another 60 000 came home so maimed in mind or body that their lives were lived in agony.[68] The crass could note that the war tripled the national debt. The National War Income Tax, a temporary, emergency device, is with Canadians still. During the war Canadian women gained the vote and all Canadians lost the right to drink, though most of them had gained it back in 1925. In the wake of the war, Quebeckers voted Liberal, farmers created their own Progressive Party, the Conservatives came a poor third in the 1921 election and never again would Canadians know the simplicity of a two-party system.[69]

Among the casualties of war was the dream of an Imperial Federation through which, in Sam Hughes' fanciful vision, Canadians would emerge as the supermen of the Empire and the fittest rulers of its domain. Borden, innocent of such fantasies, had merely expected competence and consultation in Whitehall. In searching for it, he imperilled his constituency at home and won little for Canada abroad; a signature, slightly indented below Britain's at American insistence, on the Treaty of Versailles and another on the Charter of the League of Nations. That was Canada's reward for the war and most Canadians, not surprisingly, thought it insufficient.[70] Article X of the Covenant, with its pledge of collective security, became anathema to Canadians as well as Americans, even to Borden and his colleagues. Canadians, in the words of their chief delegate to the League in 1924, 'live in a fireproof house, far from the sources of conflagration'.[71] In their own eyes, many Canadians live there still.

Canadian soldiers, of course, had their own special memories of the war. Because there was no separate Canadian air force until the very end of the war and because the Royal Canadian Navy was allowed to do little, only the army brought home a tradition from the war. It was explicit in the two extra permanent force regiments permitted after the war, the Princess Patricia's Canadian Light Infantry in the West and the Royal 22e Regiment in memory of the heroic but lonely French Canadian battalion in the Corps. While at least the more thoughtful British officers learned much from the war, Canadians had the smugness of those who had seemingly surpassed their mentors. Wartime experience confirmed the dominance of artillery and infantry. Canadians, as it happened, had none of the connection with tanks that they had gained with air forces, and gave armor no thought in the two post-war decades. The methodical stolidity which characterized the Canadian Corps and its commanders became, sadly but unquestionably, the style of the Canadian Army in the Second World War.[72] There are worse sins in a general than spending time, money and ammunition to save lives. Victory is absolution for any sin. It is also a preservative of complacency.

NOTES

1. Manitoba *Free Press*, 5 August 1914. On the mood at the outbreak, see Wilson, *Ontario and the First World War, 1914–1918* (Toronto: 1977), pp. xvii–xix.
2. On the outbreak: C. F. Winter, *Lieutenant-General Sir Sam Hughes: Canada's War Minister* (Toronto: 1930), pp. 132–6; G. W. L. Nicolson, *Canadian Expeditionary Force: The Canadian Army in the First World War, 1914–1919* (Ottawa: 1960), pp. 5–6. On Parliament: R. C. Brown, *Robert Laird Borden: A Biography* (Toronto: 1980), vol. II, pp. 9–12.
3. Jeffrey Williams, *Princess Patricia's Canadian Light Infantry* (London: 1985), pp. 1–6.
4. On the Canadians and South Africa, see Norman Penlington, *Canada and Imperialism, 1896–1899* (Toronto: 1965), pp. 226–63; R. A. Preston, *Canada and 'Imperial Defense': A Study of the Origins of the British Commonwealth's Defense Organization, 1867–1919* (Toronto and Durham: 1967) ch. IX; Desmond Morton, *Canada at Paardeberg* (Ottawa: 1986) Desmond Morton, *The Canadian General: Sir William Otter* (Toronto: 1974), pp. 169–236.

5. Carman Miller, 'Sir Frederick William Borden and Military Reform, 1896–1911', *Canadian Historical Review*, L, 3, 1969; Desmond Morton, 'The Cadet Movement in the Moment of Canadian Militarism, 1909–1914', *Journal of Canadian Studies*, XIII, 2, 1978. On the state of the Militia, see Nicholson *Canadian Expeditionary Forces*, pp. 6–13.
6. On Hughes see Ronald G. Haycock, *Sam Hughes: The Public Career of a Controversial Canadian, 1885–1915* (Waterloo: 1986), pp. 15–134; Alan R. Capon, *His Faults Lie Gently: The Incredible Sam Hughes* (Lindsay: 1969).
7. On events at Valcartier: Nicholson, *Canadian Expeditionary Force*, pp. 20–8; A Fortesque Duguid, *The Official History of the Canadian Forces in the Great War, 1914–1919 – General Series* (Ottawa: 1938), vol. I, pp. 46–93; *Appendices*, pp. 43–121.
8. *Ibid.*, p. 104; Appendix 149, p. 122
9. For a somewhat jaundiced view: J. F. C. Fuller, *Memoirs of an Unconventional Soldier* (London: 1936), pp. 37–43.
10. On Salisbury conditions: Nicholson, *Canadian Expeditionary Force*, pp. 35–7 and on equipment problems, pp. 25–8; Desmond Morton, *Peculiar Kind of Politics: Canada's Overseas Ministry in the First World War* (Toronto: 1982).
11. On recruiting see Haycock, *Hughes*, pp. 198–224; R. C. Brown and Donald Loveridge, 'Unrequited Faith: Recruiting the C. E. F., 1914–1918' in *Revue Internationale d'Histoire Militaire*, no. 51, 1981.
12. On Hughes's 'seances': Winter, *War Minister*, pp. 76–8; Haycock, *Hughes* p. 180.
13. Public Archives of Canada, R. L. Borden Papers, Borden to Hughes, 8 June 1915, f. 12693.
14. On Borden's views, see Brown, *Borden*, II, pp. 27–8, 32.
15. Nicholson, *Canadian Expeditionary Force*, ch. V; J. A. Swettenham, *To Seize the Victory: The Canadian Corps in World War* (Toronto: 1965), pp. 79–90, 101, 113. D. J. Goodspeed, 'Prelude to the Somme: Mont Sorrel, June, 1916' in Michael Cross and Robert Bothwell (eds), *Policy By Other Means: Essays in Honor of C. P. Stacey* (Toronto: 1972).
16. Morton, *Peculiar Politics*, p. 25; Canada, House of Commons, *Debates*, 21 August 1914.
17. On Aitken's role see Preston, *Canada and 'Imperial Defense'*, pp. 470–80; Morton, *Peculiar Politics*, pp. 72–5.
18. On Byng: Jeffrey Williams, *Byng of Vimy: General and Governor General* (London: 1983), pp. 127–9 and *passim*.
19. On Canadians and trench raids: Dennis Winter, *Death's Men: Soldiers of the Great War* (London: 1979), p. 92; John Ellis, *Eye-Deep in Hell: The Western Front, 1914–1918* (London: 1976), p. 76. Maurice Pope, *Soldiers and Politicians* (Toronto: 1962), p. 34.
20. A long list of books deal with Canadians at Vimy. Among others are Pierre Berton, *Vimy* (Toronto: 1986); Kenneth Mackesy, *The Shadow of Vimy Ridge* (Toronto: 1965); Alexander McKee, *Vimy Ridge* (London: 1966) and H. F. Wood, *Vimy*! (Toronto: 1967). See also, Williams, *Byng*, pp. 146–66; Nicholson, *Canadian Expeditionary Force*, pp. 233–68. E. L. M. Burns, *General Mud: Memoirs of Two World Wars* (Toronto: 1970), pp. 32–50.

21. On French Canadians and the war: Jean-Pierre Gagnon, *Le 22e bataillon (Canadien-Français) 1914–1919: Etude sociale-militaire*, Quebec and Elizabeth Armstrong, *The Crisis of Quebec* (New York: 1937); Desmond Morton, 'The Limits of Loyalty: French Canadian Officers and the First World War', in Edgar Denton III (ed.), *The Limits of Loyalty* (Waterloo: 1980).
22. On internment: Desmond Morton, 'Sir William Otter and Internment Operations in Canada During the First World War', *Canadian Historical Review*, LV, 1, 1974; Lubomyr Lucivk, *A Time for Atonement* (Ottawa: 1988); see also David Smith, 'Emergency Government in Canada', *ibid.*, L, 4, 1969.
23. See R. C. Brown, 'Whither Are We Being Shoved?': Political Leadership in Canada During World War I' in J. L. Granatstein and R. C. Cuff, *War and Society in North America* (Toronto: 1971).
24. On commitments: C. P. Stacey, *Canada in the Age of Conflict* (Toronto: 1977), vol. I, pp. 188–92. See also Brown, *Borden*, vol. II, p. 22.
25. On voluntarism and conscription: J. L. Granatstein and J. M. Hitsman, *Broken Promises: A History of Conscription in Canada* (Toronto: 1977); Haycock, *Hughes*, pp. 203–8; Public Archives of Canada, Gwatkin Papers, Gwatkin to Col. J. Mason, 3 July 1915, file, 2; see Borden Papers, Gwatkin to Loring Christie, 24 May 1915, f. 109601.
26. Brown and Loveridge, 'Unrequited Faith', pp. 57–61.
27. On Bourassa, French Canada and conscription: Armstrong, *Crisis*, pp. 131, 135–9; Joseph Levitt, *Henri Bourassa on Imperialism and Biculturalism* (Toronto: 1970), pp. 160–9; Real Belanger, 'Albert Sévigny et la participation des canadiens français a la grand guerre', *Revue Internationale d'Histoire Militaire*, no. 51, 1982. On the war and prairie agriculture, see John Herd Thompson, *The Harvest of War: The Prairie West, 1914–1918* (Toronto: 1978), esp. pp. 45–72.
28. Among areas transferred were munitions and military hospitals. See J. M. Bliss, *A Canadian Millionaire: The Life and Business Times of Sir Joseph Flavelle, Bart, 1858–1939* (Toronto: 1978), pp. 238–328; David Carnegie, *The History of Munition Supply in Canada, 1914–1918* (New York: 1925), Desmond Morton and Glenn Wright, *Winning the Second Battle: Canadian Veterans and the Return of Civilian Life* (Toronto: 1987).
29. Public Archives of Canada, Creelman Papers, Diary 19 November 1916, p. 77. Morton, *Peculiar Politics*, pp. 76–92 and *passim.*; D. M. A. R. Vince, 'The Acting Overseas Sub Militia Council and the Resignation of Sir Sam Hughes', *Canadian Historical Review*, XXXI, I, 1950; Haycock, *Hughes*, pp. 301–10.
30. Morton, *Peculiar Politics*, pp. 93–105. On the Ross rifle: Duguid, *Official History*, Appendices, no. 111, pp. 75–99; Haycock, *Hughes*, pp. 245–52.
31. Lord Beaverbrook, *Politicians and the War* (London: 1960), pp. 206–7; A. J. P. Taylor, *Beaverbrook*, (London: 1972), pp. 101–27.
32. Stacey, *Age of Conflict*, pp. 210–11; Nicholson, *Canadian Expeditionary Force*, pp. 341–2; (Lloyd George and Walter Long, 12 December 1916) David Lloyd George, *War Memoirs* (London: 1938), vol. I, p. 1026 for citation.

33. Public Archives of Canada, Perley Papers, Borden to Perley, 4 January 1916, vol. 5. f. 127a; Stacey, *Age of Conflict*, pp. 191–2 notes that Borden was weary and suffering from lumbago when he expressed himself with such uncharacteristic heat. The letter was not communicated to the British but it was reprinted in Borden's memoirs. See also R. C. Brown, 'Sir Robert Borden, the Great War and Anglo-Canadian Relations' in J. S. Moir (ed.), *Character and Circumstance: Essays in Honor of Donald Grant Creighton* (Toronto: 1970), pp. 211–4; Brown, *Borden*, vol. II, pp. 34–5.
34. Stacey, *Age of Conflict*, pp. 210–11; Nicholson, *Expeditionary Force*, pp. 341–2; Granatstein and Hitsman, *Broken Promises*, pp. 61–5.
35. Canada, House of Commons, *Debates*, 18 May 1917, pp. 1515 *et seq*. Brown, *Borden*, vol. II, pp. 84–95.
36. Nicholson, *Canadian Expeditionary Force*, pp. 344–5; A. M. Willms, 'Conscription, 1917; A Brief for the Defense', *Canadian Historical Review* XXXVII, 4, 1956.
37. *The Military Voters' Act*, 7–8 Geo. V. c. 34; *The War Time Elections Act*, 7–8 Geo. V. c. 39.
38. For the Unionist platform see Edward Carrigan, *Canadian Party Platforms* (Toronto: 1968), pp. 74–8; John English, *The Decline of Politics: The Conservatives and the Party System, 1901–1920* (Toronto; 1977), pp. 162–72.
39. *Ibid.*, pp. 173ff, R. C. Brown and Ramsay Cook, *Canada, 1896–1921: A Nation Transformed* (Toronto: 1974), ch. XV.
40. For years, the main text cited on conscription outside rare references to (usually unspecified) official documents was O. D. Skelton's adulatory biography of Sir Winfrid Laurier. On a continuing interpretive theme, see Granatstein and Hitsman, *Broken Promises*, ch. III.
41. Queen's University Archives, Grant Dexter Papers, Lyman Duff to Dexter, 22 December 1941.
42. On the composition of the original contingent: Duguid, *Official History, Appendices*, no. 86, p. 58. On the influence of origins, see W. D. B. Kerr, *Arms and the Maple Leaf* (Seaforth: 1943); R. H. Roy (ed.), *The Journal of Private Fraser, 1914–1918, Canadian Expeditionary Force* (Victoria: 1985); Bridget Fialkowski, *John Launcelot Todd* (Senneville: n.d.), p. 334.
43. H. M. Urquhart, *Sir Arthur Currie: The Biography of a Great Canadian* (Toronto:1950), pp. 11–28; Daniel G. Dancocks, *Sir Arthur Currie: A Biography* (Toronto: 1985), pp. 10–28.
44. R. C. Brown and Desmond Morton, 'The Embarrassing Apotheosis of a Great Canadian: Sir Arthur Currie's Personal Crisis in 1917', *Canadian Historical Review*, LX, 1, 1979, pp. 46–53.
45. Currie's record at Ypres was bedevilled by the fact that he had walked back to get reinforcements for his brigade. While justifiable in the circumstances, it was easily misinterpreted by enemies. So was the fact that a namesake, Lt. Col. J. A. Currie, was removed from command of his battalion after the battle and returned to Canada where, as a Conservative MP and friend of Hughes, he was promptly promoted. On Currie at Ypres: Dandocks, *Currie*, pp. 46–55; Swettenham, *To Seize the Victory*, pp. 84–90.

46. *The Legionary*, August 1928 (Charles Vining interview).
47. Brown and Morton, 'Embarrassing Apotheosis', pp. 58–9.
48. On the evolution of Canadian Corps method: Dancocks, *Currie*, pp. 83–91; Berton, *Vimy*, pp. 103–4; Burns, *General Mud*, pp. 35–6 and *passim*.
49. *The Legionary*, August 1928; Nicholson, *Candian Expeditionary Force*, pp. 284–97; Swettenham, *To Seize the Victory*, pp. 173–8.
50. Nicholson, *Canadian Expeditionary Force*, pp. 311–30; Daniel G. Dancocks, *Legacy of Valour: The Canadians at Passchendaele* (Edmonton: 1987).
51. Currie's awkward aloofness in the presence of his men is described by Urquhart, *Currie*, pp. 223 and *passim*. W. D. B. Kerr; later an academic historian, was an eloquent critic from the ranks. See *Arms and the Maple Leaf*, pp. 27–8, 44–8; W. D. B. Kerr, *Shrieks and Crashes; Being Memories of Canada's Corps, 1917* (Toronto: 1929), p. 40. A. M. J. Hyatt, *Sir Arthur Currie: A Military Biography* (Toronto: 1987), pp. 108–10.
52. W. R. Bird, *Ghosts Have Warm Hands* (Toronto: 1968), pp. 21, 197 on Lipsett and p. 56 on Macdonell – rare praise for senior officers. On Canadian generals: H. F. Wood, *Vimy!*, pp. 68–73; A. M. J. Hyatt, 'Canadian Generals in the First World War and the Popular View of Military Leadership', *Histoire Sociale/Social History*, XII, 24, 1979, in response to Charles Y. Harrison *Generals Die in Bed* (London: 1930).
53. McNaughton, who commanded the Canadian Army overseas in the Second World War has alone received extensive biographical treatment: J. A. Swettenham, *McNaughton* (Toronto: 1968), vol. I. Another officer, brilliant but condemned by McNaughton, was Raymond Brutinel. See Larry Worthington, *Amid the Guns Below* (Toronto: 1965).
54. Cited in J. E. B. Seeley (Lord Mottistone) *Adventure* (London: 1930), pp. 234–5.
55. Williams, *Byng*, pp. 146–56; Pope, *Soldiers and Politicians*, pp. 41–2; Burns, *General Mud*, p. 62–8.
56. Morton, *Peculiar Politics*, pp. 151–6; Dancocks, *Currie*, pp. 127–30.
57. Urquhart, *Currie*, pp. 198–202; Public Archives of Canada, Turner Papers Currie to Sir Richard Turner, 7 February 1918, pp. 8–54. Hyatt, *Currie*, pp. 100–1.
58. Derby to Haig, 2 November 1917, cited by Robert Blake (ed.), *The Private Papers of Sir Douglas Haig* (London: 1952), p. 266. See Borden Papers, Sir Edward Kemp to Borden, 24 February 1918; Preston *Canada and 'Imperial Defense'*, pp. 488–92.
59. Blake, *Private Papers*, pp. 303–4; Nicholson, *Canadian Expeditionary Force*, pp. 379–81; Preston, *Canadian and 'Imperial Defense'*, pp. 487–9.
60. Jean Provencher, *Quebec sous la loi des mésures de guerre, 1918* (Trois Rivières, 1971). On cancellation: Nicholson, *Canadian Expeditionary Force*, pp. 347–8; Granatstein and Hitsman, *Broken Promises*, pp. 88–94.
61. On Canadians in the air: S. F. Wise, *Canadian Airmen and the First World War: The Official History of the Royal Canadian Air Force*, vol. I (Toronto: 1980).

62. Brown, *Borden*, II, 137–8; Stacey, *Age of Conflict*, pp. 219–21.
63. Brown, *Borden, II, pp. 137–8; J. A. Swettenham, Allied Intervention in Russia, 1918–1919 and the Part Played by Canada* (Toronto: 1967), pp. 127–9 and ch.5.
64. Nicholson, *Canadian Expeditionary Force*, pp. 386–424; Swettenham, *McNaughton* pp. 133–5; Overseas Military Forces of Canada, *Report of the Ministry*, 1918 (London: n.d.), pp. 126–46.
65. *Ibid.*, pp. 146–85; Nicholson, *Canadian Expeditionary Force*, pp. 425–82.
66. *Ibid.*, pp. 419–60.
67. Willms, 'Conscription, 1917'.
68. On casualties, Nicholson, *Canadian Expeditionary Force*, p. 548; Sir Andrew Macphail, *Official History of the Canadian Forces in the Great War, 1914–19: The Medical Services* (Ottawa: 1925), pp. 246–54; Public Archives of Canada, R. G. 24, vol. 1883a, f. 27 (cited in Morton and Wright, *Winning the Second Battle*, pp. 230–1 and *passim*); Desmond Morton, 'Military Medicine and State Medicine: Historical Notes on the Canadian Army Medical Corps in the First World War, 1914–1919' in Pauline Mazumdar (ed.), *Medicine and the State in Canada* (Toronto: t.b.a.).
69. English, *Decline of Politics*, pp. 204–21; Brown and Cook, *Canada, 1896–1921*, pp. 294–331.
70. Stacey, *Age of Conflict*, I, pp. 228–318.
71. Cited address to the League of Nations Assembly, 2 October 1924 in W. A. Riddell (ed.), *Documents on Canadian Foreign Policy, 1917–1939* (Toronto: 1962), pp. 462–3; Stacey, *Age of Conflict*, II, pp. 60–1.
72. A frank view of the general state of Canadian generalship in the Second World War by the Canadian Army's official historian is C. P. Stacey, 'Canadian Leaders in the Second World War', *Canadian Historical Review*, LXVI, 1, 1985. American and British authors, not always with justice, have accused Canadian generals in the Normandy campaign of being too cautious.

Logistics support for the Allies, near Esnes in the Argonne, late in the war. Reproduced courtesy of the National Archives of the United States of America.

6 'Maconochie's Stew': Logistical Support of American Forces with the BEF, 1917–18

Charles R. Shrader

The relative success of the Allied and Associated Powers of the First World War in overcoming the problems of effectively coordinating their economic and military resources was a major factor in their ultimate victory. France, Great Britain, Belgium, Italy, Russia and the United States each possessed an army with its own particular strengths, weaknesses, organization, weapons, doctrine, leadership, and level of experience. In no respect did these armies differ more significantly than in the logistical systems designed to support them in the field. Nowhere was cooperation more needed or ultimately more effective.

The mechanisms by which effective logistical cooperation among the Allies was achieved at the higher levels are relatively well-understood. How inter-Allied logistical cooperation actually worked at the level of execution is less clear. With the forces in the field all of the differences of the coalition partners were intensified by the pressures of active operations against a competent and well-armed enemy. The story of how those differences were overcome in the case of the American troops who served with the British Expeditionary Forces (BEF) in France, although only a small part of the overall picture, embodies in a restricted scope the entire range of logistical problems faced by the Allies throughout the war.

One third of all the American divisions which saw combat in France in the First World War, as well as a number of other units, spent some time in training or actual operations with the BEF. In all, over 200 000 American soldiers served in the British sector. The British were responsible for almost complete logistical support of the American troops in their sector, and the relative isolation of the Americans from their own sources of supply forced a real test of the feasibility of having one army support another with all the essential means of war-making.

The length of time over which this arrangement existed, although relatively brief, was sufficient to test the concept and to evoke both clear reactions and tentative solutions to the many problems which arose.

THE DECISION TO ATTACH AMERICAN COMBAT TROOPS FOR TRAINING WITH THE BEF

Britain and France viewed America's potential as an ally almost exclusively in terms of the manpower which might be supplied to replace their enormous losses of men since 1914. Both recognized that American manpower had to be brought into play at the earliest possible time if disaster was to be avoided. However, it was obvious that a considerable length of time would be required to mobilize, equip, train, and move to France any appreciable American force. Thus, the most rapid means of applying American manpower to the Allied cause appeared to be the integration of American troops into the existing allied formations. Although firmly committed to the formation of an independent American Army in France, the Commander-in-Chief of the American Expeditionary Forces (AEF), General John J. Pershing, was forced by circumstances to permit the attachment of selected American troops to the Allied armies for limited periods. At first only specialist units were so attached, but events later required the assignment of American combat troops for training and employment under Allied command.

In December 1917 the British began to put forth definite proposals for the training and employment of American combat forces with the BEF. Plans for the training of American troops with the British solidified at the end of January 1918 in the form of the so-called 'Six Division Plan'. On 24–25 January 1918 at a conference held at Compiègne and the Hotel de Crillon in Paris Pershing presented a plan for the British to transport to France six complete US divisions.[1] These divisions, less their artillery, were to train with the British. The artillery would be equipped by the French and trained in American camps in the French zone. At the end of the training period the divisions would be reunited and employed under American command. At Versailles on 29–30 January the British accepted Pershing's scheme, and it was agreed that related questions of supply, arms, and equipment would be arranged later between the American and British Commanders-in-Chief. The details of the training program were subsequently worked out by staff officers at British General Headquarters (GHQ) on 4–5 February 1918.[2]

Although the Allied pressure for amalgamation never entirely receded and the details of the Six Division Plan continued to change over the following six months, the program for training American troops with the BEF was carried out essentially in the form proposed by Pershing in January 1918. The early successes of the long-awaited German offensive which began on 21 March 1918 doomed the plan to modification before the shipment of troops for its fulfillment had ever begun. Urgent discussions with the hard-pressed British and decisions taken in the Allied Supreme War Council limited the British transport of American troops to infantry and machine-gun units. By hard bargaining Pershing was able to reach an agreement with the British in London on 24 April which provided that in May American and British shipping would be devoted to transporting the infantry and machine-gunners, engineers, signal troops, and division and brigade headquarters of the six divisions.[3] Further minor modifications and extension of the shipping program to July resulted from further conferences at Abbeville on 1–2 May and Versailles on 1–2 June.[4] The fruit of all these discussions was the transportation in round numbers of 246 000 men in May, 276 000 men in June and 307 000 men in July. Included in this three-month program were ten American divisions destined for training on the British front.

THE FIRST AMERICAN UNITS WITH THE BEF

Long before the first American combat troops of the Six Division Plan reached France, American soldiers were already serving with the BEF. In late April 1917 British and French commissions arrived in Washington to discuss America's contribution to the war effort. Their first request was for technical troops, particularly medical, engineer, and other support units. At a White House dinner on 23 April 1917, the British Commissioner, Arthur J. Balfour, accosted Dr Franklin H. Martin in the receiving line and requested the immediate despatch of American doctors to France to support the BEF. Acting on his own, Dr Martin agreed to provide 1000–1200 medical officers. He subsequently obtained the support of Secretary of War Newton D. Baker and the decision was made to provide immediately 1000 medical officers and six base hospitals for the British as well as 2500 ambulances and 5000 drivers for the French.[5] Eager to join the fray, the United States quickly formed a number of such units and hastened them to France. Most of the initial contingents were attached to the BEF in Flanders where they saw continuous service until the Armistice. For all practical purposes these units were integrated into the British forces and received most of their logistical support from the British.

As early as September 1915 officers of the newly formed US Army Medical Officer Reserve Corps had begun to organize a small number of military hospital units under American Red Cross auspices at several of the prominent civilian hospitals in major American cities.[6] These infant organizations were called upon to provide the six base hospitals for the BEF. Beginning in late April the six units were recruited to authorized strength, mobilized, organized, equipped, and sailed for France in May.[7] Base Hospital No. 4, formed at the Lakeside Hospital in Cleveland, Ohio, under the medical direction of Dr George W. Crile, was the first American unit to arrive in France. The unit sailed from New York on 8 May 1917 and after a short layover in England disembarked at Rouen on 25 May 1917 and proceeded to relieve BEF General Hospital No. 9.[8] Base Hospital No. 5, formed at Harvard University under the medical direction of Dr Harvey Cushing, arrived at Boulogne the same day and on 31 May took over from BEF General Hospital No. 11 at Dannes-Camiers.[9] The four remaining units followed in June.[10] In addition to the organized hospital units more than 1400 American doctors were sent to the British zone as 'casuals'. These young officers, mostly from the Medical Officer Reserve Corps and without military training, began to arrive in France in June 1917 and were attached individually to front-line British units where they rendered excellent service under the most trying conditions far from any American support.[11]

The medics were quickly followed by three regiments of railway engineers. Organized in May 1917 in response to the urgent Allied request for technical troops, the 11th, 12th and 14th Railway Engineers arrived in France in August 1917.[12] The 11th Engineers sailed from New York on 14 July 1917 and after a short stay in England landed at Boulogne on 7 August. Elements of Company E arrived at 'Plateau' Base near Peronne on the morning of 13 August, thus becoming the first US troops, other than medical personnel, to enter the combat zone in France.[13] From August 1917 to the end of January 1918 they built and maintained railway lines and other British logistical facilities in the general vicinity of Peronne under the direction of the British Third Army's Assistant Director of Light Railways. The 12th and 14th Railway Engineers sailed from New York on 17 July 1917.

After a layover in England, which included the famous parade through London on 15 August, both units crossed to France. The 12th Engineers disembarked at Boulogne on the morning of 18 August and arrived on 21 August at Montigny Farm-Roisel. The 14th Engineers took station at Boisleaux on 21 August 1917. Both units were employed maintaining and operating narrow gauge railways and in other engineer tasks in the advance zone of the British Third and Fifth Armies until their transfer to the AEF in mid-1918.[14]

Concurrent with the arrival of the American medical and engineer units in the British zone suitable command and control elements were also established. A liaison office was established in London on 17 June 1917 to handle the medical personnel loaned to the British.[15] Soon after their arrival the engineer regiments were organized as a Railway Engineer Brigade under the command of Brigadier General John Biddle.[16] On 12 July 1917 an American liaison officer was sent to GHQ BEF, and on 8 January 1918 a full-fledged Military Mission at GHQ BEF was opened.[17] The Mission was headed by Brigadier General William W. Harts who also assumed control of all the US troops in the British zone as Commander, Headquarters, United States Army Troops on duty with the British Expeditionary Forces. The troops under General Harts' control corresponded to Army service troops and as such not only received support from the British logistical system but were in fact an important element of that system themselves, providing as they did important medical services and light railway support to the British forces. On 11 May 1918 they numbered some 11 410 American officers, men, nurses, and civilian support personnel.[18]

The American units attached to the BEF in 1917 were deployed with complete equipment insofar as it was possible to obtain it before they left the United States. Once in France they drew whatever support they could from the growing AEF logistical system, but for the most part they had to rely on the British for all types of supplies and services. The initial contingents seem to have fared well under a rather haphazard system. Indeed, their complaints were few when compared to the storm of protest raised by the American combat troops attached to the British for training in 1918.

PRELIMINARY ARRANGEMENTS FOR LOGISTICAL SUPPORT

In all of the proposals for the service of American troops with the BEF it was assumed that the British would provide, at least in part, the necessary logistical support. The implications of undertaking the support of some 150 000 additional troops with different organization, procedures, and tastes were staggering.[19] The eagerness with which the British actively sought the burden was, first and foremost, a measure of their desperate need for manpower. Then, too, in view of the British losses in France already sustained and anticipated, the problem may have appeared to be one of continuing to provide about the same overall level of logistical support rather than one of increasing requirements. Compatibility of the American forces did not appear to be a major consideration. The British logistical system was already geared to supporting an extremely diverse force, including as it did the Portugese as well as elements from throughout the Empire. Furthermore, a sizeable contingent of American units had already been serving with the BEF for nearly a year, and the support of those troops had proven manageable. Thus, the British were sufficiently confident in their ability to support large numbers of American troops that they did not hesitate to offer full logistical support for the American combat divisions to be sent to the BEF under the Six Division Plan.

Pursuant to the agreement reached at Versailles on 28–29 January 1918, Pershing notified the Chief of the Imperial General Staff on 31 January that the 150 000 Americans would arrive with personal baggage but without organizational transport and requested that the British provide food and other needed supplies.[20] The same day he sent a note to Field Marshal Haig suggesting an early meeting of their staffs to work out the details of the plan.[21] Representatives of GHQ AEF subsequently met with their counterparts at Montreuil on 4-5 February and established the general framework of both the training plans and the logistical support arrangements for the American divisions. It was agreed that the American divisions, less their artillery and ammunition trains, would arrive in France with complete personal equipment and individual weapons but without transport or reserve stores. Transport, replacement clothing, and rations would be supplied by the British.[22]

On 12 February Pershing expressed to Haig his satisfaction with the general arrangements and proposed sending to GHQ BEF as soon as possible a number of staff officers to work out the final details including the use of the British rifle by American forces '. . . if it appears the the use of the American arm would seriously complicate the question of ammunition supply'.[23] To serve as the focal point for all arrangements regarding the training, support, and eventual employment of the American divisions with the BEF, Headquarters, US II Corps was activated on 20 February 1918.[24] Lieutenant Colonel (later Brigadier General) George S. Simonds was named Chief of Staff, US II Corps and was charged with making all arrangements for the reception, training, and maintenance of the American troops. The assignment of a corps commander was postponed and Simonds was instructed to report directly to Major General James G. Harbord, the AEF Chief of Staff.[25]

Simonds was notified of his assignment on 19 February and was provided with a two and one-half page directive which stressed that training was to be under American control and doctrine.[26] Harbord informed him that ' . . . the deal with the British provided that they were to furnish additional shipping, equipment and supplies of all kinds from British sources' but that 'no detailed arrangements had yet been made, that my detail at that time had been made for that purpose and that I had full authority to make such arrangements with British GHQ'.[27] The selection of Simonds for the complex and difficult task of working out the arrangements with the British and overseeing the training and support of American units assigned to the BEF was fortuitous. Intelligent and diplomatic, Simonds faced with aplomb the tremendous task of formulating training programs, solving logistical problems, and adapting American principles of organization and administration to those of the British. He proved equal to the task in every respect and worked 'surely and methodically to the accomplishment of his mission' while gaining the respect of both the British and the Americans in the BEF.[28]

Simond's first action was to make an estimate of the situation and he noted: 'Since our troops were to use British supplies, and were to be trained in British areas, it was clear that the two *main* problems in making prelimary arrangements with the British authorities would be logistics and training'.[29] Wisely deciding to scout the situation before asking for a large staff, Simonds left Chaumont for Montreuil on 23 February with ' . . . office paraphernalia consisting of notebook and dispatch case. . . . '[30] He was accompanied by two officers, both logisticians: Lieutenant Colonel Harold S. Hetrick was to be Assistant Chief of Staff G-4 and Lieutenant Colonel E. S. Walton was to be Quartermaster.[31] At Montreuil the three officers were given a small office and set to work to make the necessary arrangements for the reception and training of the American divisions.

Simonds at once went into conference with the key British staff officers. The British knew only that six divisions without artillery were coming to be trained and supplied. Although reluctant to discuss the details of the actual training, ' . . . with regard to supply and equipment, their attitude was quite different. They expressed a complete willingness to furnish us everything we might need in so far as their resources would permit, and requested us to acquaint them with our organization and requirements'.[32] On his second day at GHQ BEF Simonds presented a plan by which the British would furnish rations, weapons, tranportation, and all items of equipment except distinctive items of American uniform. He then proposed that a set of supply and equipment tables adapting the British issue scales and procedures to American organization be made out with the assistance of British supply officers.[33] He also suggested that the British should furnish storage for the American weapons and other equipment to be turned in by the American troops on arrival.

On 1 March 1918 Simonds reported to Harbord that the preliminary points had been agreed upon.[34] Subsequently, the arrangements worked out by Simonds were confirmed by both the British and American headquarters. American divisions, less their artillery brigades and ammunition trains, were to arrive at full strength with all American individual and unit equipment except for transport, machine-guns, automatic rifles, Stoke mortars, and 37-mm. guns. The 37-mm. guns would be provided by the French. The American Springfield rifle would be exchanged for the British Lee-Enfield and the British would also provide automatic rifles, machine guns, and trench mortars as well as the necessary ammunition. All subsistence, clothing, and transport would be obtained from British sources. The American units were to bring with them any specialized transport such as engineer shop vans and signal vans, and it was hoped that the British Stokes mortars and animal transport would be retained permanently by the US units when they were transferred to the AEF for active service. The logistical administration of the American units would be undertaken by the British corps to which they were attached. Procedures for requisition and issue as well as scales of allowances would be those already in use in the BEF with only minor modifications.

The provision of British logistical support was not to be free. Even as the details of what support would be provided were being worked out, Colonel Walton began making arrangements for US reimbursement of the British.[35] The final arrangements were decided only after extended discussion among representatives of US II Corps, the British Financial

Advisor, the chairman of the AEF Board of Contracts and Adjustments in Paris, the chiefs of the British supply departments, and officers in charge of the major British depots.[36] Neither side sought to take advantage of the other and the negotiations, although complex and extended, were not rancorous. At first it was not known whether repayment would be on a direct (per item received) basis or on a *per capita* basis. In the end a combination system was worked out in which initial issues were to be paid for by direct reimbursement. The costs of other supplies and services, such as transportation, rations, ammunition, shelter, medical supplies and services, clothing, and forage, were worked into a capitation rate on the basis of which the United States would repay Great Britain. The British accounting officers knew 'to the fraction of a farthing' the average cost per man for even the most intricate items and Walton supplied the figures for the number of Americans supported.[37] Final agreement on the capitation rate was not reached until September 1918 and the formal agreement was not signed by both parties until after the Armistice.[38] Walton had left the II Corps by the time the final capitation rate was determined, but he later recalled that it was about £6/6 (or $30.24) per man per day which he considered to be a real bargain.[39]

GENERAL PROBLEMS ASSOCIATED WITH BRITISH SUPPORT OF AMERICAN FORCES

Once the basic decision to support the American divisions almost entirely from British resources was taken certain problems were inevitable. The shortage of certain items, the normal confusion of active combat operations, and the increased and rapidly fluctuating number of troops supported aside, the problems encountered fell into three main areas.[40] There were problems caused by the differing organization of the two armies and by their different procedures for providing support to forces in the field. Perhaps most irritating were the many minor problems arising from differences in taste and national custom. Simple expedients solved most of these problems, and in the end the arrangement proved eminently workable, at least in the short run.

Differences in Organization

While the British and American armies were in many ways very similar, sufficient differences in size, unit organization, and tables of allowances existed to cause some problems. In most cases effective solutions were obtained simply by changing the American organization. Although this required some time and was often tedious, the differences were successfully adjusted and the two organizations meshed satisfactorily.

The American division differed substantially from the British division in the number of men and amount of equipment. The 1918 American division at full strength included 28 059 officers and men. The authorized strength of the British division in 1918 was officially about 15 000 officers and men but British divisions frequently had only 8000–9000 or even as few as 5000 men present for duty.[41] American subordinate units were proportionately larger and it took some time for the British to adjust. The amount of arms and other equipment required by the American division was greater not only because the American division was larger but also because American tables of equipment allowances were more liberal. The American and British staff officers set to work out the modified allowance tables suggested by Colonel Simonds had a good deal of difficulty in reconciling the British equipment scales and the American organization and many adjustments were necessary. The British were frequently appalled at the totals arrived at, but, generally speaking, they accepted them and assured the Americans of their best efforts to meet the requirements.[42]

Certain changes in American organization at every level were necessitated by attachment to the BEF. Normally, the US army corps in the First World War was a tactical headquarters and performed very little in the way of administration. However, since the US II Corps operated virtually as an independent Army, an Assistant Chief of Staff G-4 was provided to handle matters of supply normally handled by the Army G-4. The Americans also had to accommodate themselves to the British division of staff responsibilities and in some cases Quartermaster and Ordnance functions at division level were combined.[43] The retention of the US II Corps and the 27th and 30th Divisions for active operations in the British zone raised another difficulty. Lacking a full complement of corps troops, the US II Corps had to be augmented by over 30 000 men from British combat and logistical units, and at one point Headquarters, US II Corps had more British than American troops under its command.[44] These supporting forces represented a significant dedication of specialist manpower to facilitate the use of American combat troops in the BEF.

Similar adjustments were made at lower levels. The regimental headquarters and headquarters company found in the American forces did not exist in the British Army and the British found it difficult to provide for its supply. For them the regimental headquarters and its appendages were so much excess baggage since the British battalion performed the important administrative functions which were handled in the American service at the regimental level, the American battalion being entirely a tactical organization. Adjustments were made to conform to the British scheme by making the American battalion more of an administrative unit than it normally was. Most US divisions left the BEF before it was necessary to adopt more than *ad hoc* arrangements, but in the 27th and 30th Divisions the battalions were reorganized to play a greater administrative role.[45]

Differences in Procedures

The most obvious differences between the British and American logistical systems were procedural. Although seemingly complex, the British supply procedures were, if anything, even simpler than the American ones. The British required few reports and unit paperwork was minimal.[46] Items of daily consumption, such as rations and forage, were supplied automatically, based on predetermined scales and the strength figures submitted by the receiving unit. Other items were obtained by means of the 'indent' (or 'requisition' in American parlance). Battalion supply officers made out indents daily or on pre-arranged schedules and forwarded them to division headquarters. The indents were consolidated at division on one form for transmittal to the Deputy Assistant Director of Ordnance or the Deputy Assistant Director of Supply at Army headquarters, depending upon the type of item required. That official in turn passed the requirement to the appropriate base depot for shipment.

The British Expeditionary Forces in France were supplied from Britain by cross-Channel transportation to one of four main bases: Boulogne, Calais, Le Havre or Rouen, with Dunkirk and Dieppe as subsidiary ports. Two main lines of communication ran to the front: the Northern LOC from Boulogne and Calais and the Southern LOC from Le Havre and Rouen. From stockpiles at the bases and at intermediate bases along the LOCs, supplies were forwarded by railroad to regulating stations where they were reconfigured for units and dispatched to railheads close to the battle zone. There the supplies were picked up by divisional transport and delivered to forward dumps and issued to units within three days after leaving the base.

American units adopted the British automatic supply and indent system in its entirety and American Quartermaster and Ordnance officers had to 'unlearn' much of the knowledge so painfully gained at home, but they did so quickly. Even before leaving the United States many American divisions had British instructors assigned to assist in their training. Once in France British logistical methods as well as tactical lore were included in the training program. Many American officers and men also attended the formal BEF schools established in rear areas. British liaison officers were also attached to each American division and proved invaluable in assisting the American commanders and staffs in learning and using the British logistical system. Not all problems could be solved by the liaison officers, but many could, and liaison officers played a key role in educating the eager but ignorant Americans.

To facilitate future accounting Walton had the British indent form reprinted on green paper and used by US troops for everything obtained directly from the British. Thus, US needs were not consolidated with those of British units served by the same railhead but were kept separate on paper. American battalion supply officers routed their indents through the Regimental Supply Officer to the Division Ordnance Officer or Division Quartermaster according to how the required item was classified under the American system. At division, however, the indents were dealt with according to the British system and forwarded through British Ordnance or Supply channels as necessary. In order to avoid confusion, elaborate instructions for the processing of indents were prepared and disseminated to all American units and requisitions for strictly American items were made on American forms and forwarded to the AEF Services of Supply.[47] Although elaborate instructions for the processing of indents were prepared and disseminated to all American units, considerable difficulty was experienced at times due to the failure of supply officers to know the procedures, but the same was true of units in the AEF and in the United States.

The results obtained from subordinating the American to the British system were very satisfactory. The Quartermaster of the US 78th Division found that ' . . . if we followed instructions, supplies were forthcoming. Not a requisition was sent to the base that was not promptly acknowledged, with a statement as to probability of supply . . . and shortage [in shipments] almost never occurred'.[48] Although routine supplies were usually received promptly, the large quantities required because of the larger size of American units ' . . . sometimes caused a questioning of the "indents" and this would cause delay. The most serious delays experienced were in the case of articles which would be classified as initial equipment, requisitions for which would be submitted to II Corps G–1'.[49]

When it came to discussing supply matters unusual acronyms and different British and American terminology caused considerable confusion. Despite their common language, the Anglophone partners in fact had some trouble communicating effectively until each was more familiar with the other's peculiarities of speech. Such difficulties in handling the common language were often humorous but occasionally caused real problems. The British custom of 'waging war by a seemingly endless array of mysterious initials' baffled many Americans.[50] Immediate steps were taken to familarize newly arrived Americans with the meaning of these abbreviations. A circular letter of instruction setting forth the principal differences which US officers would have to note in order to keep their troops supplied was provided to each division Quartermaster on landing in France. An important part of this letter was a glossary of British terms and a list of the principal British office titles and the initials therefore.[51] Americans quickly learned the British usage and even the extensive list of acronyms, so well in fact that on 19 June 1918, Headquarters, 27th Division issued a memorandum which instructed all personnel to refer to officers and departments in the American service only by the proper US designation rather than use the terms employed by the British army.[52]

Just as many American logisticians were becoming comfortable with the British procedures and terminology, their units were transferred to the AEF. Although the transfer posed little or no problem for the British, it did create problems for the American logisticians who had to forget the British system and learn from scratch the American supply system as practiced in France. For the much-travelled engineers the move to the AEF caused supply officers to realize that their 'free-wheeling' days were over and that they would have to learn to utilize the formal American system.[53] Sometimes that was easier said than done. The office force of the new Mobile Hospital No. 6, formed from the BEF-veteran Base Hospital No. 5, although expert in the British paperwork, was handicapped not only by its lack of knowledge of the AEF system but by an absolute lack of US Army forms and the possession of only one typewriter.[54] In several cases British methods, and probably certain beloved items of British equipment, were retained and used even after a unit was transferred to the AEF.[55]

Differences in Taste and National Custom

A multitude of problems arising from differences in taste and national custom provoked frequent complaint among the American soldiers supported by the British. These minor irritants were reduced by time and familiarity but were never entirely overcome. Although of little real significance in terms of the effective maintenance and employment of American combat power on the British front, such problems were indicative of the varied difficulties of achieving allied logistical cooperation at the lowest levels.

Many Americans received their first introduction to things Britannic either aboard ship or at the port of debarkation in France. The American divisions which began to arrive in April 1918 were processed into the BEF through rest camps at the ports of debarkation.[56] The processing system was both rapid and efficient. A British Military Landing Officer at each port received word when the ships left England and was told about how many troops were aboard. British rest camp commandants also received advance information as to the number of men and their estimated time of arrival. An American Port Officer was stationed at each place where US troops landed and was responsible for issuing instructions to the American units and co-ordinating all aspects of their processing.

On arrival the troops were disembarked as soon as possible, left a detail to unload the baggage, and were led by a British guide to the rest camp. Tents were allocated at once and the men were fed while their officers received instructions. After eating, one half of the unit stripped themselves down to just what they could carry on their backs, the officers being allowed 50 pounds of baggage in addition to what they were willing to carry.[57] Each man retained his best uniform, two suits of underwear, two pairs of shoes, three pairs of socks, two shirts, and the usual toilet articles and odds and ends. All government property was placed in one pile and private property was placed in a trunk or barracks bag and marked with the name and the unit of the owner.[58] While one half of the command thinned out its gear, the other half turned in their American rifles and drew British weapons, steel helmets, and gas masks.[59] The process was then reversed. Normally, the troops arrived, were billetted, and ate on the afternoon of the first day, processed the second day, and entrained for their training area on the morning of the third day, thus leaving their area free for the men who would arrive about noon that day.

The exchange of the accurate and well-balanced M-1903 Springfield for the stubby British Lee-Enfield, necessitated by considerations of ammunition supply on the British front, was the cause of much grumbling among the American troops, but they soon adapted and there were few complaints about the combat performance of the British rifle.[60] The Vickers machine-gun and the Lewis automatic rifle were generally received without complaint; in fact, one 27th Division soldier later noted that ' . . . [the Lewis gun] did not have to take a back seat to any gun'.[61] The normal allotment of weapons for the 1918 American division (less its field artillery brigade and ammunition train) was 15 313 rifles, 224 machine guns, 768 automatic rifles, and 24 trench mortars.[62] The Anglo-American support agreement required the British to supply 3-inch Stokes mortars and .303 caliber Lee-Enfield rifles at full American scale but only 168 Vickers machine-guns and 384 Lewis guns per division.[63] Ammunition for rifles, machine guns, and mortars as well as grenades and trench stores (pyrotchenics, and so on) were supplied to American units from British dumps in the normal manner.[64] The American units adopted the British ammunition system entirely and detailed instructions were provided to all the American units on how to obtain ammunition and other ordnance items. The ammunition system worked very well and there were few complaints but satisfaction with the arrangements for the repair of weapons was not as great. It was found that the system of replacement was poor and an armorer's shop, corresponding to the Equipment Section of the US Army Mobile Ordnance Repair Shop, had to be improvised for each division.[65]

The British were obliged by terms of the support agreements to provide the Americans with replacement clothing, except for distinctive American items, on the same scale as for their own soldiers. Many of the men in the newly arrived American divisions were not happy when they learned that they would have to turn in cherished extra items of uniform and equipment and make do with British issue replacements. The uproar came in part by reason of natural reluctance to appear in the uniform of another army, even that of an ally. In addition, the British issue scale was somewhat lean compared to the American.

Replacements for the distinctive American clothing items were issued from the stocks accumulated at Calais.[66] The American replacement items went only so far, however, and the units which remained with the British for any length of time finally had to rely almost entirely on the British Ordnance for replacement items including in some cases tunics and trousers and so went ' . . . to the business of war half American and half British in appearance'.[67] The men of the 11th Engineers soon found that the American shoes and canvas leggings were decidedly inferior to the heavy British field shoes and wrapped puttees for active service in the field. The regimental supply officer, Captain Hogan, obtained a pair of such shoes and puttees as well as three pairs of heavy socks for each man from the British Ordnance depot in Calais, and the next day the regiment appeared 'British from the knees down'.[68] The supply officer of the 14th Engineers also kept busy trying to complete the outfitting of his regiment through either American or British channels. Shoes, underclothing, fatigue uniforms, blankets, and overcoats were much needed. He obtained underclothing from the British but 'it was so coarse in quality that it resembled a suit of mail and caused considerable hard language'.[69] He also obtained overcoats, but unfortunately they were Canadian issue and still had the Imperial buttons attached, a fact which 'created a good deal of heart-burning in the recipients'.[70]

There were certain other difficulties associated with relying on the British for clothing and equipment. One problem was the difference in clothing and shoe issue tariffs. Generally speaking, the British soldier was smaller than his American counterpart, and this was reflected in the size distribution of bulk issues of clothing. Because the British tariff was short of larger sizes, American soldiers were not so easily able to trade around at the bath points until everyone was satisfied as did the British soldiers. One American veteran of the 27th Division later put it succinctly: 'Clothes didn't fit. Equipment was English which made it unfamiliar . . . We cussed the Huns and sometimes the English'.[71] The main difficulty, however, arose in connection with the British issue shirt which was grey and had no collar since it was never worn as an outer garment. The issue of British grey flannel shirts at bath points was unacceptable to American commanders because of the resultant mixed appearance of the troops at drill. An attempt was made to get by with the existing stocks of American shirts, but necessity forced the use of the British shirt. The solution of the US II Corps commander was simple: coats would be worn at all times.[72]

The men in organized American units were far better off than the doctors of 'the Lost Legion' who generally arrived with little more than the uniforms they wore. The individual medical officers serving with the British units and some other American officers in the BEF had frequent recourse to the British Ordnance stores for clothing, and they frequently appeared in very mixed uniform. Indeed, some may have made the transition too complete. In July 1918 the Commander,

Headquarters, US Army Troops on duty with the BEF, under whose administrative jurisdiction the medical personnel and engineers fell, was compelled to issue an official bulletin proscribing the wearing of 'slacks', uniform coats with bellows pockets, and the carrying of canes by American officers, all of which were commonplace in the British service.[73]

The American troops with the BEF were generally impressed by the British military transporation system in France. American soldiers in the British zone soon became accustomed to 'homming and chevauxing' in the tiny French box cars labelled for eight horses or 40 men and had few complaints except for the shortage of some vehicles. The British Army was a master of moving large bodies of men and supplies from one place to another and even at the far end of the supply chain the soldier in the line got his supplies regularly. American demands upon the rail transportation system in the British zone were significant; the daily supply of a full strength American division of over 28 000 men amounted to 18–23 French cars of ten tons each.[74] British logisticians were constantly amazed at the large number of 'trucks' required to move American units. When informed of the number of 'trucks' required to move the 11th Engineer Regiment from the BEF to the American zone in January 1918 one British officer exclaimed, 'My God man, are you going to move a division?'[75]

The medical and engineer units arriving in 1917 generally brought along whatever American motor transport they were authorized. These vehicles were maintained, and in some cases replaced, by the British on a catch-as-catch-can basis. The base hospitals were forever in need of motor vehicles and in fact received some from the American Red Cross.[76] Colonel Simonds was not impressed by the Rolls Royce he received from the British upon his arrival as II Corps Chief of Staff and quickly made out a requisition on the American depot system for American cars.[77]

The British intended to furnish all kinds of transport to the American division training in the BEF on the same or slightly larger scale provided to corresponding units in the British Army. However, the great losses in both motor and animal transport connected with the German offensive in March and April 1918 reduced available stocks to such a point that US units in training had to get along with much less than had been planned. The inability to provide motor transport on the agreed scale slowed the training progress of some units and generated criticism from GHQ AEF; however, the 27th and 30th divisions which stayed to fight with the British did receive their full allotments.[78]

On the other hand the British animal transport was generally adequate and was much admired by the Americans who served in the BEF, both for the condition of animals and the functionality of the wagons and carts. Remounts were supplied to American units according to the scale prescribed for the British units in the same area. All animal transport was retained when the divisions transferred to the AEF.

Although 'Sammy' was willing to use the Lee-Enfield, wear coarse British underwear, and ride in 'lorries' with only a minimum of grumbling, he was vociferous in his condemnation of the meagre and unpalatable British ration. He loudly and often '. . . cussed the lousy English cigarettes . . . , the lousy McConiche stew . . . , the goldfish (canned salmon), and the corned willy'.[79] Resistance to the British ration was eventually muted as the men became accustomed to it, the cooks learned how to handle it better, and some minor changes were made in the components, but no single aspect of American service with the BEF appears to have been remembered so vividly and so negatively as the rations.

Tea, mutton, cheese, orange marmalade, and other British delicacies cause 'first bewilderment, then hunger, and finally loud protests' from Americans accustomed to generous rations of good meat, potatoes, and vegetables.[80] Some Americans complained as much about the lack of quantity as about the type and quality of the British rations received en route to the training areas.[81] Private Joe Rizzi of Company A, 110th Engineers, 35th Division, found the rations at Camp St Martins in Le Havre 'an insult to a healthy man', and having seen some emaciated German POWs at work near Le Havre, Rizzi later recalled that: 'According to the breakfast we received, it would look like we were being considered prisoners, too'.[82] But not all reactions to the British ration were so negative. PFC Griffith L. Adams of Company C, 105th Machine-gun Battalion, 27th Division, recalled that 'when we reached France . . . we began to get English rations – OK!'[83] And William Clarke of the 27th Division recalled his 'first British Army breakfast' which consisted of hot Irish cracked oatmeal with a gob of jam in it, bacon, bread, and tea. He found it good, although there were howls of protest over the tea.[84]

The British used nine different rations for the various classes of foreign troops, line of communication units, and fighting organizations in France. A special scale of rations for the American troops serving with the British was worked out in detail and corresponded almost exactly to the standard British ration.[85] The main portion of the regular British ration included: 1 lb. of fresh or frozen meat (usually beef, sometimes mutton); 1 lb. of bread or 12 ounces of hardtack 'biscuits'; 8 oz. of fresh vegetables or 2 oz. of dried vegetables; 4 oz. of bacon; 3 oz. cheese; and tea, jam, tobacco, sugar, salt, and other condiments. Supplemental issues of tea, sugar, and some other items were provided for men in the trenches and in winter.[86] Frequently, a substitute for the separate meat and vegetable ration, called officially the 'Meat and Vegetable Ration', was issued. This was canned stew which included a variety of meat and vegetable ingredients of doubtful origin and which was best known as 'Maconochie stew' after the name of its manufacturer. It was a staple of the British ration and the British troops liked the mixture quite well.[87] American victims of Maconochie were not so easy to please; the 'inventor' of the infamous concoction was 'bitterly cussed by American soldiers' who saw his product frequently because it was so easy to prepare.[88] Harvey Cushing noted that ' . . . the hardest and most trying days of a soldier's existence in France with the B. E. F. [were] MACONOCHIE days with NO SECONDS'.[89]

The divisional troops who began to arrive in April 1918 objected so strenuously to the British ration that reports reached GHQ AEF, and Colonel Simonds therefore appointed a board to study the British ration. The members of the board reported that the food values of the British and American rations were nearly equivalent and that the principal items objected to were the smaller meat ration, tea, and cheese. They concluded, however, that the meat ration was sufficient and that the objections to the cheese would be overcome when the troops got used to it and the cooks learned to deal with it. They did note that the Americans soldiers were generally bigger and were used to both a greater variety and greater bulk in their diet than the British ration provided. Accordingly, they recommended that the vegetable component be increased and also that coffee be substituted for tea. After 'some dickering with British GHQ' Simonds succeeded in having coffee substituted for tea and achieved some other minor changes.[90]

Despite their reservations, the Americans with the BEF managed to survive on the British ration and what they could scrounge. No American starved to death, and such problems as did occur in the feeding of the men in active operations were the result of the usual confusions and difficulties of battle. Nearly two years of subsistence on the 'meagre and unpalatable' British ration were no doubt forgotten when Base Hospital No. 5 returned to Hoboken aboard the GRAF WALDERSEE on Easter Sunday, 20 April 1919, and eagerly attacked the dinner served by the American Red Cross: frankfurters, sauerkraut and apple pie.[91]

CONCLUSION

For over 18 months the British logistical system in France supported an ever-changing number of American soldiers and made possible their decisive employment against the common enemy. At the level of execution logistical cooperation proved workable in the short run, due in part to the urgency of the situation and the simplicity of the requirements. A more extended test might have revealed stresses which could ultimately have proven the concept unworkable, but despite problems arising from differences in organization, procedures, and national preference, the experiment in allied logistical cooperation was a decided success, proving the proposition that the military forces of one nation can break the cord to their own base of supply and throw themselves entirely on the facilities of another.

The key to success was the decision to avoid half measures and to completely subordinate the American supply system and American preferences to those of the British. Any attempt to combine the two systems or to have them operate on parallel lines would probably have been less successful. While it proved possible for the supported element to retain a few minor aspects of its own system, for example, the distinctive outer uniform, special ration items, and even a few special weapons and their ammunition, it was essential that full responsibility for the core of logistical support be entirely in the hands of the supporting entity.

Because both the British and the Americans clearly understood that cooperation was absolutely necessary if their common cause was to prosper, they developed an unusual degree of coordination and wholehearted cooperation. The British gave of what they had freely and without reservation. In a few cases they were not able to provide all that was agreed, not because they wished to hold back but because they simply did not have the wherewithal. Nor did they foist off on the Americans their cast-offs but provided on their own scale the best that they had available. For their part, the Americans proved unusually willing to put aside considerations of national prestige and preference and to adopt the logistical organization and procedures of their ally.

At lower echelons at least, the difference in organizations and procedure were quickly overcome. Problems arising from different tastes and customs were more difficult to resolve but tended to decrease as the two armies became better acquainted. No incident or controversy over matters of supply affected the final outcome to any appreciable degree. The usual logistical glitches and shortfalls were encountered, but they were problems common to all military operations and did not stem from any fundemental flaw in the concept of one army supporting another. Colonel Simond's own assessment of the results was that the British provided adequately for the Americans in their midst and that ' . . . the problems [were] difficult but not insurmountable. . . .'[92]

Colonel Walton, the US II Corps Quartermaster, and many other Americans found 'the Britishers most cordial and helpful, especially those in the supply end of the game . . . We had our troubles, of course, but none of them was caused by lack of cooperation . . .'[93] Indeed, for those Americans who remained for any length of time in the BEF, the thought of transfer to the AEF was most unappealling. They grew accustomed not only to the British character but also to the British methods and were most reluctant to surrender new-found friends or hard-won mastery of the British logistical system. One American officer expressed this feeling by saying: 'The first three months we were with the British, we were anxious to go to the American sector; the last three months, we were afraid we might be taken out of the British zone'.[94] In the end the British logistical support of those American units attached to the BEF proved to be very much like the infamous Maconochie stew – a decidedly mixed concoction, displeasing to some but sufficiently nourishing to ensure that the American combat units were sped into the fight at the critical moment.

APPENDIX I

Number of American Troops with the BEF by Month, April-November 1918

The number of American troops serving with the BEF on the beginning of each month from April to November 1918 is estimated to be as follows:

1 April 1918	31 000	1 August	109 200
1 May	42 300	1 September	59 900
1 June	174 400	1 October	58 000
1 July	111 200	1 November	46 900

This estimate is based on the general information available on non-divisional elements and the figures given in the charts on pages 319, 328, and 353–4 of USAWW, XII. The authorized strength of divisions as shown in *Equipment Manual for Service in Europe*, Series A, No. 15, *Infantry Division*, with changes to 26 June 1918 ([Chaumont?]: August 1918) has been adjusted for the known absence of elements as indicated in historical Section, Army War College, *Order of Battle of the United States Land Forces in the World War: American Expeditionary Forces: Divisions* (Washington: GPO, 1931). None of the American divisions which served with the BEF was at the full authorized strength of 28 059 officers and men. All of them lacked their Field Artillery Brigade (5055 men authorized), Ammunition Train (1333 men authorized), and half of their authorized Field Hospitals and Ambulance Companies (about 475 men authorized). Several divisions also served in the BEF without their Supply Train (501 men authorized) and/or Field Signal Battalion (488 men authorized). This table is intended only as an indicator of order of magnitude and does not represent actual morning report strength for the dates given.

APPENDIX II

ABBREVIATED TABLE OF US INFANTRY DIVISION STRENGTH AND EQUIPMENT, 1918*

Item	Div Hq	2 Inf Bdes	Mg Bn	Engr Regt	Fld Sig Bn	Tn Hq + MP	Sup Tn	Engr Tn	San Tn	Tot Tns	Agg
Officers	45	516	16	51	15	15	16	2	51	122	727
Enlisted Men	200	16422	377	1646	473	359	485	82	900	3121	20944
Total	245	16938	393	1697	488	374	501	84	951	1910	21671
Rifles	101	12914	—	1487	—	288	445	78	—	1825	15313
Auto Rifles	—	768	—	—	—	—	—	—	—	—	768
Heavy MGs	—	192	32	—	—	—	—	—	—	—	224
Trench Mortars	—	24	—	—	—	—	—	—	—	—	24
Animals	163	2078	—	354	26	349	—	110	205	1298	3285
Misc in Trans	7	720	—	58	14	11	—	26	23	107	859
Roll Kitchen	1	72	—	7	—	2	—	1	2	8	85
Mtr Ambulances	—	—	—	—	—	—	1	—	36	37	37
Truck, cargo	1	—	7	—	10	—	170	12	44	226	234
Truck, special	—	—	5	—	—	—	18	—	3	21	27
Misc Mtr Veh	35	22	84	17	22	6	16	3	28	53	231

*Less Field Artillery Brigade (5055 officers and men) and Ammunition Train (1333 officers and men)

SOURCE *Equipment Manual for Service in Europe*, Series A, No. 15, *Infantry Division* (corrected to 26 June 1918) ([Chaumont?]: August 1918), pp. 2–3.

APPENDIX III

COMPARISON OF BRITISH AND AMERICAN RATION SCALES, 1918

Authorized Ration Item	British Scale[1] Field	CHQ/LOC	American Scale[2]
Meat (Fresh or Frozen	16 oz	12 oz	20 oz
or			
Meat (preserved)	9 oz	6.75 oz	16 oz
Bread	16 oz	14 oz	16 oz
or			
Biscuit (Hardtack)	10 oz	8.75 oz	—
Bacon	4 oz	3 oz	Issued as meat
Cheese	2 oz	2 oz	—
Fresh Vegetable	8 oz	8 oz	20 oz[3]
or			
Dried Vegetables	2 oz	2 oz	—
Tea	0.5 oz	0.5 oz	—
or			
Coffee	—	—	1.12 oz
Jam	3 oz	3 oz	3 oz
Butter (thrice wkly)	2 oz	—	1.14 oz
Margarine	—	1 oz	—
Sugar[4]	3 oz	2 oz	3.2 oz
Oatmeal (thrice wkly)	2 oz	—	—
Rice	1 oz	2 oz	2 oz
Salt	0.25 oz	0.25 oz	0.64 oz
Mustard	0.01 oz	0.01 oz	—
Pepper	0.01 oz	0.01 oz	0.18 oz
Milk (condensed)	1 oz	1 oz	1 oz
Pickles (thrice wkly)	1 oz	1 oz	—
Tobacco (wkly; smokers)	2 oz	2 oz	28 oz
Matches (fortnightly)	1 box	1 box	—
Lime Juice (on M.O. order)	0.00625 gal	0.00625 gal	—
Candy	—	—	0.5 oz
Vinegar	—	—	0.16 gill
Beans, dry	—	—	4 oz
Cinnamon	—	—	0.14 oz
Flavoring Extract	—	—	0.14 oz
Calories	4193	3472	4714[5]

1. From 26 January 1918
2. The so-called Pershing Ration, 1918 (that is the Garrison Ration) authorized by G. O. No. 16, GHQ AEF, 1917.
3. Potatoes were issued as 80 per cent of vegetable ration; corn, peas or tomatoes comprised the other 20 per cent.
4. The sugar ration was reduced by 1/2 oz. when sweetened condensed milk was issued.
5. The caloric value given is for the US Field Ration which was seldom issued alone. In almost every case nearly all elements of the Garrison Ration were issued as supplements to the Field Ration.

SOURCES Great Britain, War Office, *Statistics of the Military Effort of the British Empire during the Great War* (London: 1922), pp. 584–6; *Report of the Military Board of Allied Supply* (Washington, 1924–25), I, pp. 546, 552, and 554; BG C. R. Krauthoff, 'Subsisting Troops', *The Quartermaster Review*, 1, no.2 (September-October 1921), p. 65.

NOTES

1. Historical Section, US Army War College, *The Genesis of the American First Army* (Washington: GPO, 1938), 15 [cited as *Genesis*]. About 150 000 troops were involved.
2. Letter, Chief of General Staff, BEF, to CINC, AEF, 9 February 18, in Department of the Army, *United States Army in the World War, 1917–1919*, 17 vols. (Washington: Historical Division, DA, 1948), III, 41–3 [cited as USAWW]; Memorandum for the Chief of Staff, AEF, 11 February 18, in USAWW. III, 44–6.
3. Cable 147, British War Office to General Bridges, 27 April 18, in USAWW, III, 91–2; *Genesis*, 27–8 and 67–8.
4. *Genesis*, pp. 29, 35–6, and 69; Johnson Hagood, 'Memoirs of the Great War', 2 volume typescript at US Army Military History Institute, Carlisle Barracks, Pennsylvania (USAMHI), II, pp. 572–3. The Hagood typescript contains some material not included in his published account, *The Services of Supply: A Memoir of the Great War* (Boston and New York: Houghton Mifflin, 1927).
5. Franklin H. Martin, *The Joy of Living: An Autobiography*, 2 vols. (Garden City, NY: Doubleday Doran, 1933), II, pp. 155–60. Martin was the chairman of the General Medical Board of the Advisory Commission of the Council of National Defense.
6. Marvin A. Kreidberg and Merton G. Henry, *History of Military Mobilization in the United States Army, 1775–1945*, DA Pamphlet No. 20-212 (Washington: DA, 1955), pp. 287–8. Equipped in part by the American Red Cross, each unit consisted of 23 doctors, two dentists, 65 nurses, and 150 soldiers and was designed to care for 500 patients.
7. Report of Activities of the [AEF] Chief Surgeon's Office, 28 February 18, in USAWW, XV, 370 and 404. The six base hospitals were loaned to the BEF for one year and the loan was later extended for the duration of the war.
8. [Members of Base Hospital No. 4, USA and Mobile Hospital No. 5, USA], *'Album de Guerre'* (Cleveland: Scientific Illustrating Studios, 1919), p. 15; Martin, II, pp. 174 and 248–9.
9. Martin II, p. 174; J. Phillip Hatch (ed.), *Concerning Base Hospital No. 5* (Boston: Barta Press, 1920), pp. 19 and 27. Base Hospital No. 5 was later transferred to Boulogne. The First American casualties of the war were from Base Hospital No. 5; one officer and three men were killed and three officers and six men were wounded during a German raid on Camiers on 4 September 1917. See Historical Branch, War Plans Division, US War Department General Staff, Monograph No. 7: *Organization of the Services of Supply, AEF* (Washington: GPO, 1921), p. 56; Harvey W. Cushing, *From a Surgeon's Journal, 1915–1918* (Boston: Little, Brown, 1936), pp. 200–2.
10. Base Hospital No. 2 to Entretat; Base Hospital No. 21 to Rouen; Base Hospital No. 10 to Le Treport; and Base Hospital No. 12 to Dannes-Camiers.
11. The most complete account of their service, although anecdotal, is that

of W. A. R. Chapin, *The Lost Legion* (Springfield, MA: Loring-Axtell, 1926).

12. The 6th and 16th Engineers as well as other US engineer elements also saw service with the BEF. See *Historical Report of the Chief Engineer, including all operations of the Engineer Department, AEF, 1917–1919* (Washington: GPO, 1919), pp. 158–63 and *passim*.
13. Van Tuyl Boughton, *History of the Eleventh Engineers United States Army* (New York: Trustees, Eleventh Engineer Fund, 1926), p. 82; Memorandum for Mr McCullum, Returns Section, Adjutant General's Office, from Historical Section, Army War College, 2 June 27, in Thomas File #3965, microfilm at USAMHI [cited as Thomas File. The 'Thomas File' includes documents collected or produced by the Historical Section, Army War College and its successors. Most of this material is in National Archives Record Group 165, but some is available on microfilm at USAMHI.]
14. John A. Laird and others, *History of the Twelfth Engineers, U. S. Army* (St. Louis: Buxton and Skinner, 1919), pp. 10 and 16–24; Robert G. Henderson, *History of the Fourteenth Engineers US Army, from May, 1917 to May, 1919* (Boston: Atlantic Printing, 1923), pp. 2–5 and 16; Thomas file #3965. See also: *History of the Sixth Engineers* (New York: Knickerbocker Press, 1920) and *History of the Sixteenth Engineers (Railway), American Expeditionary Forces, 1917–1919* (Detroit: La Salle Press, 1939).
15. Report . . . Chief Surgeon's Office, in USAWW, XV, p. 404.
16. *Historical Report of the Chief Engineer* . . . , p. 158.
17. Report, GHQ, AEF, 30 June 19, subj: 'Relations with Allied Governments and Armies', in USAWW, XII, p. 73.
18. Report, CHQ, AEF, 30 June 19, subj: 'Relations with Allied Governments and Armies, in USAWW, XII, p. 85. On the same date there were also 34 334 American combat troops training with the BEF. At various times in 1918, Headquarters, United States Army Troops on duty with the BEF, controlled six base hospital units, about 1400 Army doctors assigned directly to British units, elements of six engineer regiments and other engineer units, four aerosquadrons, and a miscellaneous collection of other troops. Elements of the 17th, 22nd, 28th, and 148th Aero Squadrons trained with the RAF. The 17th and 148th Aero Squadrons were reassembled in June 1918 and operated in the BEF under British control. A number of other American pilots flew with British pursuit squadrons and the Independent Air Force. See James J. Hudson, *Hostile Skies: A Combat History of the American Air Service in World War I* (Syracuse, NY: Syracuse University Press, 1968), pp. 250 and 254–5.
19. In terms of the additional burden on the already overworked British transportation system alone, the Six Division Plan meant an increase in daily movements of over 1100 tons. Each man in the BEF required each year about 2.5 tons of supplies or about 15 pounds per day exclusive of ammunition. See Cushing, p. 323.
20. Letter, Pershing to Robertson, 31 January 18, in USAWW, III, pp. 38–9.

21. Letter, Pershing to Haig, 31 January 18, in USAWW, III, p.39.
22. Letter, Chief of General Staff, GHQ, BEF, to [Chief to Staff?], GHQ, AEF, 9 February 18, in USAWW, III, pp. 41–3.
23. Letter, Pershing to Haig, 12 February 18, in USAWW, III, pp. 48–9.
24. On the basis of the secret letter of instructions from Chief of Staff, GHQ, AEF, to Lieutenant Colonel George S. Simonds, 20 February 18, in USAWW, III, pp. 49–50. See G. O. No. 1, HQ, US II Corps, 19 March 18, in USAWW, III, pp. 114–15.
25. On 15 June 1918, Headquarters, US II Corps, was formally organized and Major-General George W. Read, then commanding the 30th Division, was assigned as Corps Commander. See Historical Section, Army War College, *Order of Battle of the United States Land Forces in the World War: American Expeditionary Forces: General Headquarters, Armies, Army Corps, Services of Supply, and Separate Forces* (Washington: GPO, 1937), p. 220 [cited as OB II]; Ewen C. Macveagh and Lee D. Brown, *The Yankee in the British Zone* (New York and London: G. P. Putnam's Sons, 1920), pp. 149–50 [cited as *Yankee*].
26. Letter, Chief of Staff, AEF, to LTC Simonds, 20 February 18, in USAWW, III, pp. 49–50.
27. Brigadier General George S. Simonds, lecture given at the army War College, Washington, DC, 4 December 31, subj.: 'Problems of Service with Allies', page 1, in Thomas File #5436, microfilm at USAHMI [cited as Simonds lecture].
28. Elmer A. Murphy and Robert S. Thomas, *The Thirtieth Division in the World War* (Lepanto, AR: Old Hickory, 1936), p. 64.
29. Simonds lecture, p. 2.
30. Simonds lecture, p. 2.
31. Brigadier General George S. Simonds, informal talk at Historical Section, Army War College, Washington, DC, 14 October 31, p. 2, in Thomas File #5436, micofilm at USAMHI [cited as Simonds informal talk]. For sketches of all three men see *Yankee*, pp. 46–50. Other key logistical staff officers of the II Corps included: Lieutenant Colonel Richard K. Hale, G–1; Colonel C. C. Collins, Surgeon; and Lieutenant Colonel Mervyn A. Rice, Ordnance Officer.
32. Simonds lecture, pp. 2–3.
33. Captain C. A. Lidbury, the British Liaison Officer to HQ, US II Corps, and several other British staff officers subsequently worked with Lieutenant Colonel Hetrick to develop the tables. See *Yankee*, pp. 48–9; Simonds informal talk, p. 2.
34. Letter, Chief of Staff, II Corps, to Chief of Staff, AEF, 1 March 18, in USAWW, III, pp. 50–2.
35. Colonel E. S. Walton, 'Looked After by John Bull', *The Quartermaster Review*, 1, no. 2 (September-October 1921), p. 26. See also Letter, Chief of Staff, US II Corps, to Commanding General, AEF, SOS, 24 March 18, in USAWW, III, pp. 188–9.
36. Report of the II Corps Quartermaster, in US Army Quartermaster School, Monograph No. 9: *Notes on Army, Corps and Division Quartermaster Activities in the AEF, France* (Philadelphia: US Army Quartermaster School, Schuykill Arsenal, n.d.), p. 43 [cited as QM No.

9]. The Board of Contracts and Adjustments under the AEF General Purchasing Agent was created on 14 February 1918 to prepare and oversee agreements on supply matters between the US and the Allies.

37. Walton, p. 26; Report of II Corps Quartermaster in QM No. 9, p. 43.
38. US Army, AEF, Assistant Chief of Staff G–4, *Strategic Supply* (mimeograph, Chaumont: GHQ, AEF, 1919), p. 50. Appendix 'J' (not found) supposedly contains the text of the final agreement.
39. Walton, p. 26.
40. There is little evidence to suggest that the overall effectiveness of the British logistical system in France was impaired to any appreciable degree by the need to support over 200 000 American soldiers. However, the rapid fluctuation in American strength perhaps did complicate British logistical planning. The rapid build-up reached a peak on 4-6 June 1918, at which time the British were supporting ten American divisions, but even before the last division to arrive had competed its move into the British zone the size of the American force began to decline dramatically. The 4th, 28th, 35th, 77th and 82nd Divisions were transferred to the French front during the second week of June as were the 6th, 11th, and 16th Engineers. On 18 August Pershing visited Haig at Wiry-au-Mont to discuss the return of three of the remaining five divisions to the AEF in preparation for the St. Mihiel operation. Given his choice, Haig elected to retain the 27th and 30th Divisions, and between 20–23 August the 78th, 80th and 33rd Divisions left for the AEF. See Appendix 1 and Historical Branch, War Plans Division, US War Department General staff, Monograph No. 10: *Operations of the 2nd American Corps in the Somme Offensive, August 8 to November 11, 1918* (Washington: GPO, 1920), pp. 7–8 [cited as *Operation of II Corps*].
41. *Equipment Manual for Service in Europe*, Series A, No. 15 *Infantry Division*, with corrections to 26 June 1918 ([Chaumont?]: August 1918), pp. 2–3 [cited as *Equipment Manual*]; Report of the 78th Division Quartermaster in QM No. 9, p. 132. See also: Colonels Aultman and Anderson, subcommittee report, subj.: 'Organization of the Larger Units and the Replacement of Casualties', in Report of Baker Board, 26 July 17, in USAWW, I.
42. Simonds lecture, p. 3.
43. The British Supply Department took care of only rations, forage, fuel, POL, remounts, and pay. All other supplies, including clothing, weapons, and ammunition, were under the control of the Ordnance Department. The US Army Ordnance Department took care of rations, forage, animals, clothing, construction, billetting, and transport of all kinds as well as pay and other disbursements.
44. *Operations of II Corps*, p. 23; OB II, p. 220.
45. *Strategic Supply*, pp. 50–1. For example, officers were taken from the regimental supply company and detailed as Battalion Supply or Transport Officers.
46. Walton, pp. 24–6. American administrative systems were notorious for the volume and complexity of the paperwork required. British supply officers were repeatedly amazed at American 'indents' for stationery,

one 'indent' often taking the entire stock of a British depot. One British officer at Calais commented: 'I don't see when you blighters find time to fight'.

47. Walton, p. 25. Such items were delivered through the British supply system.
48. Report of 78th Division Quartermaster in QM No. 9, p. 133.
49. Idem.
50. John F. O'Ryan, *The Story of the 27th Division*, 2 vols (New York: Wynkoop Hallenbeck Crawford, 1929), I, p. 166.
51. Walton, pp. 22–3. I have been unable to find a copy of this document.
52. Memorandum, HQ, 27th Division, 19 June 18, found in Private Fred G. Schmidt (107 Infantry) folder, 27th Division File, World War I Questionnaires and Related Documents, Archives, USAMHI. Staff officers from GHQ, AEF were known to take the men of the 27th Division to task for calling things by their 'British name' rather than using the official US Army nomenclature.
53. *History of the Sixth Engineers*, p. 211.
54. *Concerning Base Hospital No. 5*, pp. 42–3.
55. The British system for ration dumps was one such set of procedures which worked so well that it was retained by some units after they left the British sector. See reports of the 28th, 77th, and 80th Division Quartermasters in QM No. 9, pp. 74, 114, and 144.
56. The early arrivals in 1917 were usually routed through camps in England to the ports in France. Although they generally arrived fully equipped, they were issued British helmets and gas masks and shortages of clothing and other equipment were made up by the British at the reception camps in France.
57. The enormous amount of baggage carried by American soldiers posed significant problems for logisticians in the AEF as well. Strong efforts were made to reduce the burden on the transport system, but excess baggage remained an important issue throughout the war.
58. Storehouses were established at Calais and Le Havre to receive and store the rifles and private property turned in by arriving American troops and to process the excess government property for reissue. The American depot at Calais was the principal source for replacing the distinctive items of American uniform and equipment for US troops serving with the BEF. The salvage and repair of clothing at Calais was accomplished by French and Belgian women under American supervision. American troops in the BEF turned in salvaged British items to the British and salvaged American items to the AEF salvage systems.
59. Although every effort was made to supply all the required personal equipment and weapons at the camps, it sometimes proved impossible and issue was completed in the divisional training area. Unit equipment, such as animals, wagons, and rolling kitchens, was also received at the training area.
60. Murphy and Thomas, p. 62. The 12th, 14th, and 16th Engineers were originally equipped with the Spanish-American War Krag-Jorgensen rifle and brought the necessary ammunition with them to France. The 12th Engineers were issued Springfields after the battle of Cambrai, and all of

the engineers turned in their American weapons for the British Lee-Enfield in April 1918 in anticipation of their use in the front line to counter the German offensive which began in late March.

61. Questionnaire #4330, Joseph J. Hoffman (108th Infantry) folder, 27th Division File, USAMHI.
62. See Appendix II.
63. Order O.B./2196, GHQ, BEF, 12 March 18, in USAWW, III, p. 65.
64. British ammunition supply dumps were established at various levels and the higher echelon delivered ammunition at predetermined rates (or on special indents) to the ammunition dump of the next lowest level. Ammunition for those American weapons which were retained (the .45 cal. pistol and 37-mm. gun) was supplied to the British in bulk by American authorities and then issued from British depots along with other ammunition.
65. 'Report of Activities of the Ordnance Dept., II Corps, American E. F.', 27 December 18, in decimal file 321.8, General Correspondence, II Army Corps, 1918–19, RG 120, National Archives, Washington, DC.
66. Walton, pp. 24–5. A small depot was also maintained at Le Havre but few calls were made on it until it was used to support the 37th and 91st Divisions with the French in Flanders late in the war. There was another small depot of clothing ordnance items at Dannes. The 27th and 30th Divisions drew heavily on the stocks at Calais, but Walton was able to meet all requirements until late in the summer when some new American clothing was made available.
67. William F. Clarke, *Over There with O'Ryan's Roughnecks* (Seattle: Superior Publishing, 1968), p. 92.
68. Boughton, p. 93.
69. Henderson, p. 33. The supply of underclothing was a persistent problem.
70. Henderson, p. 33. From time to time the British also provided items of clothing and equipment directly to the AEF for use in the American zone. The issue of British overcoats and tunics with British buttons caused some problems there as well.
71. Questionaire #6051, PFC George H. Monroe (HQ Company, 108th Infantry) folder, 27th Division File, USAMHI.
72. Report of the II Corps Quartermaster in QM No. 9, pp. 43–4; Walton, p. 25.
73. Bulletin No. 5, HQ, US Army troops on duty with the BEF, 29 July 18, in Correspondence of Headquarters of the American Troops on duty with the GHQ of the First Echelon of the BEF, 1917–19, RG 120, National Archives. While the American troops and their officers grew accustomed to being partially attired in British gear, General Pershing seems fully never to have accepted the necessity. As part of his effort to preserve the identity of the American Army in France he insisted that the Americans with the British must be kept in American uniforms even if other troops in the AEF had to use other than American clothing.
74. The Allied Armies under Marshal Foch in the Franco-Belgian Theater of Operations, *Report of the Military Board of Allied Supply*, 2 vols. (Washington: GPO, 1924–25), II, p. 486.

75. Boughton, p. 157.
76. Cushing, pp. 150–1.
77. Simonds informal talk, p. 3.
78. Walton, p. 24. British motor transport was allocated to subordinate formations on predetermined scales rather than being pooled under centralized control at higher levels. In general, the motor transport allocated to units was used only for carrying supplies and munitions and was never sufficient to carry organizational baggage and equipment. Furthermore, only a 10 per cent allowance was made for breakdowns when the actual rate of operations was likely to exceed 15 per cent.
79. Clarke, p. 43.
80. Murphy and Thomas, pp. 59 and 61.
81. There was a stark contrast between the American garrison ration and the reduced scale British LOC ration issued to troops in transit or training which was only 90 per cent of the regular British ration.
82. Joseph N. Rizzi, *Joe's War: Memoirs of a Doughboy* (Huntington, WVA: Der Angriff Publications, 1983), pp. 29–30.
83. Questionnaire, PFC Griffith L. Adams (Company C, 105th Machine-gun Battalion) folder, 27th Division File, USAMHI.
84. Clarke, p. 33: ' . . . whoever heard of drinking tea for breakfast . . .' Coffee was of more concern than any other item. The early arrivals resorted to a variety of methods to obtain their coffee. The 11th Engineers were blessed with an aggressive supply sergeant named Jones who approached the British colonel in charge of rationing at Albert directly. The sympathetic colonel acknowledged that he had earlier been able to get some coffee for some French troops and would try again. A few days later coffee began to be issued in place of part of the tea ration. It was rumored that the coffee was obtained by taking away the ration of the Portugese troops. See Boughton, p. 110.
85. 'Scale of Rations, Forage, Fuel and Light for U. S. Troops Serving with the British', HQ, 30th Division, 5 June 18, in decimal file 230–46.3, Records of Combat Divisions, 1917–19, RG 120, National Archives. For comparison with the standard American ration see Appendix III.
86. See Appendix III. British soldiers also received rum as an 'extra'. Presumably, American troops would have liked to have had rum, but General Pershing himself forbade it. See Letter, Pershing to Haig, 12 February 18, in USAWW, III, pp. 48–9.
87. Paul Fussell, *The Great War and Modern Memory* (New York and London: Oxford University Press, 1975), pp. 49–50. However, even the British soldiers admitted that the 'Pearl Biscuits' (hardtack) reminded one of dog biscuits. The name 'Maconochie' became synonymous with anything of mixed origin. For example, Non-Conformist chaplains in the BEF were sometimes called 'the Maconochie'.
88. Clarke, p. 34.
89. *Concerning Base Hospital No. 5*, p. 59.
90. Simonds lecture, p. 5; Simonds at informal talk, pp. 6–7. The British were not particularly sympathetic, pointing out that their troops got on quite well with the standard ration. Nevertheless, they did what they could to satisfy American tastes. Whenever possible American rations

items were obtained from American depots and sales commissaries in the AEF zone. On holidays even the most isolated American units could count on a special issue of real American food to supplement their British rations. For Thanksgiving 1917 the 11th Engineers drew from US Quartermaster depot at Nevers such American holiday staples as turkey, goose, sweet potatoes, cranberries, apples, lemons, raisins, and nuts. As soldiers are wont to do, the Americans also sought every means to supplement the rations received from the British. Packages from home and purchases from the British canteens or on the limited French market were common and some supplements were received through the American Red Cross, YMCA, and other welfare agencies.

91. *Concerning Base Hospital No. 5*, p. 38. Apparently, the same welcoming meal was served dockside to all returning American troops.
92. Simonds lecture, p. 10.
93. Walton, p. 26.
94. *Yankee*, p. 246.

7 Comment

T. H. E. Travers

Professor Morton's valuable chapter deals both with Home Front politics, and the sometimes painful evolution of the Candian forces on the Western Front from one inexperienced division in 1915 to the powerful, extra strength Canadian Corps of 1918. It also discusses the various battles engaged in along the way by the Canadians, especially the offensive at Vimy. In this context I would like to make a pitch for Canadian recognition of the role of 1st Canadian Division at Second Ypres in April 1915, which to my mind predates Vimy as marking the emergence of a Canadian style of tough, aggressive fighting. Thus, when Robert Graves and other officers at the instructors' mess at Harfleur in early 1916 discussed the merits of various divisions, they all agreed that the top fighting divisions in the BEF (British Expeditionary Force) were the 2nd, 7th, 29th, Guards and 1st Canadian.[1] Beyond this, as Professor Morton points out, more attention should also be paid to the Canadian role in the last 100 days of the war.

Turning to three of the significant points Professor Morton raises concerning Canadians in action, the *first* concerns Haig's decision to use the Canadians in late 1917 to take the village of Passchendaele, at a cost of nearly 16 000 casualties. When Haig told Currie that once the war was over, he could explain the necessity for this attack, Haig was being less than honest. While the ostensible reason was obviously the French mutiny, it seems fairly clear that Haig actually wanted to continue the Passchendaele offensive because he was optimistic that German morale might crack.[2] Then *secondly*, in March 1918 and following, the lucky exemption of the Canadian Corps from the German offensive was due partly to the Corps' location, but also to the fact that the Germans did not want to attack the extra size Canadian Corps. Furthermore, Haig felt that as long as he had the Canadian Corps available, then the defensive battle was not lost, despite the Corps' refusal to be split up to plug gaps. *Thirdly*, the surprising success of the Canadians and Australians in the Amiens offensive of 8 August 1918 was primarily due to just that factor – surprise – due to elaborate deception plans and the proper use of signals security. Hence, surprise, via deception and security, had once more returned to the battlefield in 1918.[3]

Professor Morton argues a certain style of Canadian warfare, of individual responsibility, aggression, useful amateurism, within set piece, fire-power oriented, deliberate preparations; and this I think is correct. Exceptions can be found, however, particularly in late 1918, when the slow, systematic style was sometimes replaced by a fluid and aggressive style. For example, as Private John McNab of 38 Battalion wrote in his diary on 15 September 1918, regarding his battalion's rapid advances: 'What is it – luck or pigheadedness, the latter I think, the way they go at any strong point is a shame'.[4] In fact, there may occasionally be a certain contradiction between arguing both for an aggressive Canadian style and a slow, deliberate Canadian tradition in the First World War.

One other point raised by Professor Morton is worth pursuing – when Currie insisted on his own tactics within Haig's strategic plans, he was safe in doing so because Army and Corps commanders within the BEF were encouraged to formulate their own tactics.[5] But when Currie protested at Lens, at Passchendaele, and in March 1918, he was on shaky ground. Yet because he was a Canadian it was unlikely that Currie would be *degummed* (lose his job). However, this sense of independence obviously rankled the British, as did Australian individualism, and there is an undercurrent of conflict between British officers and Canadian officers, which sometimes surfaced, for example when Lord Horne, commanding First Army, containing the Canadian Corps, complained that the 'Canadian Corps is perhaps rather apt to take all the credit it can for everything, and to consider that the BEF consists of the Canadian Corps and some other troops'. Or again, when the British Official Historian, Edmonds, made the very strange remark in 1926: 'As the [British] History proceeds, many and very serious difficulties with the Canadians will crop up – there was no limit to their lying as the war went on'.[6] Overall, however, the conclusion is that the Canadian forces on the Western Front showed remarkable adaptability in mastering what was a very complex manner of fighting.

Turning to Colonel Schrader's useful chapter, one finds little conflict between the AEF (American Expeditionary Force) and the BEF. Instead, at the level of logistical cooperation, the differences in organization, procedures and national values, were, rather surprisingly perhaps, overcome without serious difficulties. He suggests that the reason for this success was the short-term nature of the logistical commitment, the fact that the AEF did not try to run a mixed AEF and BEF supply system, and that the AEF and BEF worked positively together.

Colonel Shrader raises some interesting questions, for example, regarding training. The AEF Chief of Staff insisted that training was to be under American control and doctrine, and 40 AEF training centres were set up in France. Yet, even before leaving the US, many divisions had British or French instructors; and inevitably once in France, British and French tactical methods were central to American training, while AEF officers and men attended BEF and French training schools. The general idea was for the US infantry, and officers and staff, to train with the British, while the artillery trained with the French. What effect did this have? Apparently, there were complaints in the AEF that the Allies had in fact exerted too much influence on American tactical development. This is reflected, for example, in the very cautious statement of the semi-official history of the BEF Signals Service: 'It was to be expected that the [AEF] signal systems that resulted [from British and French training] should combine the best points of the British and French systems and this expectation was often realized to a great extent'.[7] Then it appears that the AEF Field Artillery Brigades got only half way through the program. There were also complaints from American troops trained by the French, who argued that the French instructors simply demonstrated set situations, while the American soldiers themselves were just spectators, and did not practice maneuvers, or how to react to such things as surprise attacks.[8]

In addition, Pershing himself confused AEF tactics by over-emphasizing open warfare training and the importance of the infantry rifleman. Small wonder then, that in the short time available – and partly as a result of training with the French and British – the AEF had the greatest difficulty in developing doctrinal uniformity, or a particular style of fighting, while the task of establishing tactics and training that were perceived to be different from British and French practices, was very frustrating. Therefore, in August, Pershing dispensed with British and French training, preferring to try to develop the AEF's own training methods.[9]

Another crucial area on which Colonel Shrader focuses is supply and transport procedures. Here the parameters of the situation are laid out by the fact the AEF really planned for a major effort with 80 or more Divisions in 1919 (in passing, one wonders how Fuller's 'Plan 1919' tank attack would have dovetailed with AEF plans), whereas the German offensive of March 1918 played havoc with US logistics, as is well known. Moreover, the imbalances of supply created by shipping problems, false expectations, and impractical demands by the Allies, created a critical supply shortage by November 1918.[10] But here again, one gets the impression that the influence of British and French supply systems, plus the lack of pre-war US training in supply and logistical procedures (there was no separate supply school at Fort Leavenworth) prevented the AEF, in the few months available, from developing an independent and fully workable US doctrine in logistical procedures. For example, in a footnote Colonel Shrader remarks that the British ration supply dump system was adopted by some US units, although it appears that when platoons of the US 2nd Division came to use these dumps, they found they were just that – wagons had deposited great heaps of bread and canned goods into a huge hole caused by the collapse of a dugout. There was no issue system: anyone carried away just what they wanted.[11] One wonders also about staff work – according to an AEF GHQ Report in 1919, many AEF officers could not understand the difference between an Army staff officer and a General Staff officer, and persisted in applying for the latter, which they understood to be the same as the former.[12]

Thus the general conclusion might be reached that the AEF had great difficulty, as might be expected, in developing doctrinal unity in several of the areas mentioned by Colonel Shrader, in particular training/tactics, and logistics/supply. But when all is said and done, as this chapter argues, the US achievement was remarkable, despite the necessity of going into, and then out of, the BEF and French training and logistical systems. Indeed few countries could have succeeded in putting those two million men into France by Armistice day, of whom over one million saw action.

A concluding comment on both chapters is that each deals with the arrival on the Western Front of two somewhat unprepared national forces – and the key to the success of both was the necessity of learning while doing. Some armies, like the British and French learned slowly, and suffered the consequences. Others, such as the German army, were a little quicker. Perhaps the Canadians and Americans (with the Australians) were quickest of all – reflecting their open-mindedness to innovation and change.

NOTES

1. Robert Graves, *Goodbye to all that* (Harmondsworth: Penguin, 1960). p. 152.
2. This argument is well supported by the correspondence between Pétain

and Haig in 1917, to be found in the file WO (War Office) 158/48, Public Record Office, Kew. See also Tim Travers, 'A Particular Style of Command: Haig and GHQ, 1916–1918', *The Journal of Strategic Studies* (September 1987, No. 3, vol. 10), p. 367.

3. John Robert Ferris, 'The British Army and Signals Intelligence in the Field During the First World War', *Intelligence and National Security*, (October 1988).
4. Private John McNab (38 Battalion, CEF), Diary, 15/9/1918, MG 30 E42, Public Archives, Ottawa.
5. Tim Travers, *The Killing Ground: the British Army, the Western Front, and the Emergence of Modern Warfare, 1900–1918* (London: 1987), pp. 86, 97.
6. Lord Horne to Currie, 27 March 1919, General Lord Horne Papers, 73/60/2, Imperial War Museum. Edmonds to Sir George Milne (CIGS), 30 April 1926, Cabint 45/155, Public Record Office, Kew.
7. R. E. Priestley, *The Signal Service in the European War of 1914 to 1918* (*France*). (Chatham: 1921), p. 301.
8. Timothy Nenninger, 'American Military Effectiveness in the First World War', and Douglas Porch, 'The French Army in the First World War', both in Alan Millett and Williamson Murray (eds) *Military Effectiveness: Volume I: The First World War* (Boston: 1988), pp. 143–4, 148–9, 153, 224.
9. Donald Smythe, *Pershing: General of the Armies* (Bloomington: 1986), pp. 73, 79, 159, 170, 196, 235–6.
10. *Ibid.*, p. 230.
11. Shrader, 'Maconochie's Stew: Logistical Support of American Forces with the BEF, 1917–18,' p. 128, fn. 55; Nennington, *op cit.*, p. 151.
12. General Staff Report, GHQ, AEF, 30 June 1919, *United States Army in the World War, 1917–1919*; Reports of C-in-C, AEF, Staff Sections and Services, Part I, 1948, Historical Division, Department of the Army, Vol. 12, Washington, DC, 1948, p. 95.

Part IV

Portrait of John J. Pershing. Reproduced courtesy of the National Archives of the United States of America.

8 The AEF Leaders' Education for War

Edward M. Coffman

On 3 August 1914, the day before the Germans invaded Belgium, a portly American lieutentant colonel set down his views on the coming war. Fort Ethan Allen, Vermont, was far removed from the battle that was about to erupt, but Joseph T. Dickman, a 56-year-old West Pointer, was known as a student. He had graduated from the Infantry and Cavalry School and the Army War College; had spent two tours as an instructor at the former; and had translated German military works as well as prepared assorted manuals. Recently, he had supplemented his professional reading with a tour of Europe where he had seen first-hand the armies of Germany, Russia, Italy, France and England.

Dickman foresaw a war of such great magnitude that it would make the Napoleonic Wars and the American Civil War seem small. He predicted: 'There will be fierce fighting in the air, underground in sieges, and beneath the waters of the ocean. The cheapness of human life is likely to be illustrated on an enormous scale'. As a dedicated cavalryman, he also anticipated large-scale cavalry actions and wondered if the lance would prove more crucial than the saber in these battles. When the United States entered this war in 1917, he quickly attained the rank of major-general and won distinction as a division and corps commander in combat.[1]

Dickman was an unusually well-prepared professional officer; yet, his contemporaries who commanded the divisions, corps, and armies of the American Expeditionary Forces and those who served as their chiefs of staff shared many of his educational experiences if not his particular enthusiasm for study. While few if any of them were as knowledgeable as he about the European military situation and the German theory of war, all had formed some assumption about war. As professional officers, they had to have some idea as to the shapes war would assume and the actions that they should take in order to deal with the situations and conditions which they might expect to face.

Few, if any, of these men, however, were articulate about such matters. One can, however, determine their educational preparation and thus ascertain the theoretical knowledge of war to which they were exposed. In most cases, a student could also readily find out if these officers had actually seen combat prior to the First World War. While it would be difficult to determine which officers were in what pre-war maneuvers, one can assume that most, perhaps all, participated in one or more. By examining the curricula of their schools and the relevant textbooks and describing the wars and maneuvers they experienced, one can isolate the influences on their views of war.

This approach is impressionistic. Anyone who has taught realizes that all students do not read all of the required books and may place different emphasis on what they do read. Then, those who saw the face of battle may have had very different experiences as well as attitudes while the maneuvers covered different problems and were on a varied scale. Finally, this study does not include all of the officers who occupied these key positions in the AEF but rather just those who were serving as commanders and chiefs of staff on 1 Novermber 1918.[2]

Information as to the schools attended and service in the Spanish-American War, Phillipine Insurrection, and Boxer Expedition is available for most regular officers in published sources. The *Official Army Register* which the War Department published annually is particularly valuable. There are also lists of graduates of the post-graduate schools while there is a wealth of information about West Pointers in the various Cullum's *Registers*. A final source which proved to be fruitful was *Who Was Who in American History: The Military* (Chicago: 1975).[3]

Of the 38 commmanders including Pershing, those who led the two armies and six corps as well as the 29 divisions (the 92d Division commander was also listed as commander, VI Corps), 31 were West Pointers from classes ranging from 1879 to 1894. Most of the commanders (25) graduated in the 1880s, with nine (including Pershing) from the Class of 1886.

The 40 chiefs of staff (the difference between this number and that of commanders is because there was no commander listed for VII Corps and one commander, as we have seen, was listed with both VI Corps and 92d Division) had, as a group, a significantly different undergraduate educational background. While 82 per cent of the commanders were West Point graduates, only 20 or half of the chiefs of staff had graduated from the Military Academy. Since most of the chiefs of staff were younger officers, their classes were later – ranging from 1888 (McAndrew, GHQ) to 1909 (Lee, 89th Div). Twelve did graduate in the 1890s, however, with seven in the class of 1899.

Since the authorities saw fit to celebrate the centennial of West Point by publishing a huge two-volume set which sketched the history of the academic departments, described courses, and listed textbooks, we know what cadets were supposed to study in the period in which most of the AEF leaders were there.[4]

The Tactical Department taught cadets to be soldiers. During his four years at West Point, the cadet learned not only the basic School of the Soldier but also the practical duties of privates, NCOs, and company grade officers in the Infantry, Cavalry, and Artillery. Near the end of their summer training, they ran small unit problems which encompassed an approach march and the attack and defense of a position. In 1900 the Department introduced some practical work in constructing shelter trenches and instruction about a machine-gun (the ten-barrel Gatling). In that instance, first and second classmen (seniors and juniors) had to learn the nomenclature and service of that gun as well as the 'maneuver of the horsed gun detachment' and spent some time firing blanks and ball ammunition with that weapon. Such classes might have been of some help when those cadets later had to cope with the trenches and machine-guns of the First World War. None of the commanders and only three of the chiefs of staff (Beck of the 32d Division, Sherrill of the 77th and Jewett of the 91st), however, went through those particular classes. It is possible that such classwork was continued so that the three later graduates (Herr of the 30th Division, Lee of the 89th, and Kingman of the 90th) would have had it. They may also have had the benefit of such lectures which the Tactical Department sponsored in 1900 as 'Defense of coast of United States, general plan and subdivision; classification of harbors and general methods of their defense' as well as 'Age of horse; bits and bitting'.[5]

Traditionally, the Department of Engineering offered the course in Military Art, a combination of military history and tactical theory. While none of these officers were at West Point in the days of Dennis Hart Mahan, as he had died in 1871, the one semester course they took in military engineering and the art and science of war continued to bear his stamp. His two successors who headed this department in the years during which all of the commanders who were graduates and four of the chiefs of staff (McAndrew of GHQ, Wells of IV Corps, Cloman of the 29th Division and Hawkins of the 35th) were cadets, were Junius B. Wheeler (1871–84) and James B. Mercur (1884–96). Both of these professors had taken Mahan's course as cadets and, in turn, both wrote the basic textbook on war which their students used.

When the torch passed in 1896 to the first department head who had not studied under Mahan, Gustav J. Fieberger, the semester course had five texts. A glance at the titles makes it clear that this was a course in the Department of Engineering and that it must have been heavy going for the cadets. The required books were J. B. Wheeler, *Elements of Field Fortifications*, and Mahan's *Permanent Fortifications* revised by James Mercur who also wrote *Attack of Fortified Places* and *Elements of the Art of War*. Although Mahan had been dead a quarter of a century and the efficacy of stone fortifications had come into question even earlier, cadets still had to study his *Fortifications and Stone Cutting*. In the first six years of his 26-year tenure as department head, Fieberger expanded the portion of the course devoted to the art of war by replacing Mercur's text with Arthur L. Wagner's *Organization and Tactics* and several pamphlets on specific campaigns. In 1902, he apparently inaugurated the annual trip to a Civil War battlefield by taking the first class to Gettysburg after they had made a special study of that battle. He also replaced several of the books on fortifications with his own versions.[6]

The basic books on warfare assigned to cadets from 1879 to 1902 were Wheeler's *A Course of Instruction in the Elements of the Art and Science of War for the use of the Cadets of the United States Military Academy*, from 1879 through 1888, and Mercur's *Elements of the Art of War prepared for the use of the Cadets of the United States Military Academy*, 1889 to 1896, with Arthur Wagner's *Organization and Tactics*, being used after 1899.[7] The first two are rather offputting in appearance as they march their facts in numbered paragraphs down the page. One can imagine the ambiguity with which a cadet faced the prospect of reading such a book. He must have asked himself: how much will I have to memorize? How much do I really have to know? How much can I safely skip? On the one hand, presumably he was eager to learn his trade as a soldier. After a full day's activities, there was not much in these books to excite a tired cadet's mind. But then Mahan's famed *Outpost* was of similar appearance albeit smaller than these two works. Mahan, however, had given a brief summary of military history through Napoleon at the beginning of his text while both Wheeler and Mercur merely used historical examples from time to time to support their points. Both authors devoted most of their books to definitions and descriptions of routine movements and operations.

Although Wheeler started out with a dutiful nod to Jomini, the great interpreter of Napoleonic warfare who had influenced Mahan so much, he wound up with a chapter on modern war in which he quoted William Tecumseh Sherman exclusively. He pointed out the great change that railroads made in war by giving commanders the capability of concentrating rapidly large bodies of troops and keeping them supplied to an extent which was impossible prior to that technological development. He also emphasized that modern arms forced troops to take cover at longer ranges and that battle should be avoided in open country. As for cavalry, he dismissed mounted charges as anachronisms and reflected a lesson of the Civil War when he said that cavalrymen would have to fight on foot.

General Sherman, who lived until 1891 and who visited the Academy on occasion, presumably made a large impression on cadets in the 1880s. Wheeler quoted him on the increased value of infantry in modern war and on the point that 'earth forts especially field-works, will hereafter play an important part in wars, because they enable a minor force to hold a superior one in check for a *time*, and time is a most valuable element in all wars'. A reader might wonder how many of the AEF paladins recalled that passage when they first saw the trenches on the Western Front.[8]

Although one would expect cadets in the 1880s to look back towards the Civil War as Grant, Sherman, and Sheridan visited West Point and the superintendents were army, corps or division commanders from that war (John M. Schofield, O. O. Howard, Wesley Merritt, and John G. Parke), there was one instance in which they looked prophetically ahead. The Hundreth Night show which the cadets staged a hundred days before graduation in February 1886 was a comic opera on the premise that there would be a war with Germany in 1908 in which West Pointers would play a large role. As it happened it was that class of 1886 on which 'the stars fell' in the war which took place ten years later than the play's prediction. Twenty-six of the 77 graduates became generals in that war.[9]

Professor Mercur's book also supplied the definitions and descriptions of strategy, tactics, and various operations such as the advance march, but he introduced examples from the Franco-Prussian War. He also took into consideration two new technological developments – breech-loading, rifled artillery pieces and machine guns – and differed with Wheeler as to the number of field guns needed for each thousand men. Mercur recommended four, twice as many as Wheeler had suggested. In regard to the breech-loading, rifled guns, he commented: 'Both the moral and physical effect of their shell fire *against troops*, bids fair to be much increased if it be found practicable to use dynamite or other high explosives for the bursting charge . . . .' He added that this would probably have little additional effect on earthworks. As for machine-guns, he noted the range, 1500 to 2000 yards, and the rapid exhaustion of ammunition supply because of their rapid rate of fire. He concluded: 'The full value of their fire will only be developed when it is directed against somewhat compact bodies of troops'. He urged that his readers not make full use of their machine-guns until enemy troops were at close range.[10] The five AEF commanders and three chiefs of staff who used Mercur's book in class thus had an introduction to the greater destructive capabilities of new weapons as well as an inkling of the corresponding increased logistical problem of ammunition supply.

The final book which 16 AEF chiefs of staffs had to read while at West Point was Wagner's. Those commanders and chiefs of staff who did not read it at the Academy must have become acquainted with it if they went to the Leavenworth school as it was used there. Whether they read it as cadets or junior officers, they probably found it more interesting than its predecessors. As Charles D. Herron (C/S 78th Division) who must have read it at West Point and then came into contact with it again at Leavenworth, commented: Wagner 'was the first of our military men to write anything readable on tactics . . . .'[11]

Wagner did not catalog definitions and descriptions in numbered paragraphs but rather gave more attention to style as he made his various points and cited copious historical examples. Wheeler had only listed Jomini and two other sources; Mercur expanded his bibliography to 49 works; but Wagner included 120 sources, ranging from Caesar's *Commentaries* through assorted Civil War memoirs to Clausewitz. He emphasized that experience was the best teacher, hence he would use history as a guide, but he warned that readers should not assume that there was an exact military science. He explained in his preface: 'the conditions vary in nearly every respect; no two battles are fought in the same way; and the most carefully matured plans have to be quickly altered to meet new and unforeseen circumstances. Human nature alone remains the same; all else is subject to many and great alterations'.[12] What a gust of fresh air through the classrooms his common sense approach must have been.

Wagner who, despite his West Point training, looked to Herron like a 'farmer dressed up in uniform', came up with an interesting observation about the Civil War but coupled it with a warning: 'Perhaps the most marked tactical feature of the War of Secession was the employment of hasty intrenchments'. He well knew that modern firepower forced men to take cover, but he alerted his officers to beware: 'Great as the use of intrenchments will be in future, they must not be invariably relied upon. The *morale* of the men will inevitably suffer if they be allowed to intrench at every step and under all circumstances, and intrenchment may thus prove a curse rather than a blessing'. One wonders how much this influenced Pershing and his subordinates to emphasize open warfare when they reached France.[13]

At the time he wrote in the 1890s, Wagner realized that he could not fully forecast the results of recent developments in artillery and machine-guns, but he did think that three or four artillery pieces (depending upon the terrain) per thousand men was the correct proportion. Both he and Mercur thus underestimated how many guns the AEF would consider necessary. The organizational table of the American division in World War I assigned 72 guns to the Artillery brigade which supported the two Infantry brigades which were supposed to have 16 938 officers and men. This came out to a proportion of 4.2 guns per thousand. Wagner recognized that artillery should be used in masses and that its fire should be concentrated. He acknowledged, however, that smokeless powder had introduced a variable, the effect of which no one could yet estimate as it had not yet been used in war. He also admitted that he really did not know what to do with machine-guns because of the lack of sufficient practical demonstration in wartime. He did recognize that it was a mistake to try to use machine-guns against artillery as the French had attempted during the Franco-Prussian War. On the basis of limited information, he concluded that: 'The machine-gun is undoubtedly a powerful weapon in the defense of positions, but its offensive value is probably very small'.[14]

Two excerpts from *Organization and Tactics* should serve to give a sense of Wagner and his writings and help us to understand why Herron and those others who heard him lecture or read his books appreciated him. The first has to do with staffs. Wagner quoted a German author, Bronsart von Schellendorf, to make his point: The staff of a commander should never be any larger than necessity absolutely demands

> . . . the most weighty argument against [a large staff] . . . [is] that *idleness is at the root of all mischief*. An unnecessarily numerous staff . . . can not always find duty and occupation sufficient for its mental and physical welfare; and its superfluous energies soon make themselves felt in every conceivable kind of objectionable way. Experience, at any rate, shows that whenever a staff is unnecessarily numerous, the ambitious before long take to intrigue, the litigious soon produce general friction, and the vain are never satisfied.

> These feelings, so common to human nature . . . are considerably counteracted if the persons to whom they apply have plenty of hard work.[15]

The second quotation is pure Wagner and must have drawn a chuckle from many of his readers who had struggled to make sense out of the books that he mentioned. In regard to the order of battle (the relative tactical positions of opposing forces), he wrote: 'The subject has been treated by some military writers with a wealth of diagrams and an infinitude of pedantic detail calculated to make a scientific matter out of a subject which really pertains to plain common sense'.[16]

Aside from whatever professional reading an officer might do or what he was forced to do in the garrison schools, the first opportunity he had after West Point, or in the case of those who did not attend the Academy, the very first chance for professional studies, was the school of Leavenworth. Founded in 1881 to give instruction to Infantry and Cavalry officers not only in military subjects but in reading, writing, and arithmetic for those who needed to fill gaps in their education, the Infantry and Cavalry School underwent a transformation and became more rigorous after the Spanish-American War.[17]

Thirty-one of the 40 chiefs of staff and five of the 38 commanders in Pershing's list attended Leavenworth in the period between the Spanish-American War and the First World War. Another six of the commanders had attended prior to 1898, but, given the difference which even those at the time ascribed to their education there as compared to that received by those who went in the later period, one can discount those who graduated before the Spanish War.[18]

For a year, student officers pored over Wagner's texts and assorted translations of German texts such as Griepenkerl's *Letters on Applied Tactics* and Albert Buddecke's *Tactical Decisions and Orders* as they worked on tactical problems for regiments, brigades, and divisions. Law, engineering, strategy, and military history completed the course load. Ironically, since these students would apply what they learned eventually against the Germans, the German influence was pervasive. They learned German techniques from German books and by the applicatory method of instruction which the Germans had popularized. In the process, they became thoroughly imbued with German tactical doctrine which emphasized the maintenance of cohesion and close control by commanders in the attack.[19] The best students continued for another year in the Staff College with appropriate advanced versions of what they had during their first year.

After 1907, the abolition of exams and grading made the Staff College much more enjoyable for those who made the cut-off at the end of their first year. An extensive staff ride, which in 1908 lasted eight days, gave them an opportunity to study the terrain of some of the great Civil War battles. Under the tutelage of such outstanding teachers as Eben Swift and John F. Morrison, new horizons opened up for these officers.

Two of Leavenworth's most distinguished graduates paid tribute to the contribution that Leavenworth graduates made in the AEF. Hugh A. Drum (School of the Line, 1911 and Staff College, 1912) was an important staff officer at Pershing's headquarters before he became chief of staff of the First Army. On 7 July 1918, just as the Americans were beginning to play a significant role on the Western Front, Drum wrote to his wife: 'Of course the Leavenworth teaching is the foundation of the whole system'.[20] Drum implied much in that 'Of course', namely that it was logical to rely on Leavenworth graduates to build the AEF staffs. For those staff officers who were not regulars and who had not been to Leavenworth, Pershing created a staff school at Langres modelled on that of Leavenworth.

The second tribute is from George C. Marshall (SOL, 1907; SC, 1908). Although he is not in this sample because he was not a chief of staff, he played a significant role as operations officer of the First Division and later of the First Army. In 1951 General of the Army Marshall said: 'The Command and General Staff College provided the men who played a determining part in the American military effort of 1918'. Later, he specified Leavenworth's crucial effect on him. Rather than remembering any particular book or school tuition, the most important result of his student years there was that he 'learned how to learn'.[21]

The next step in the Army's education system was the Army War College, founded in 1903. Originally conceived by Tasker H. Bliss as a place where relatively senior officers would work on plans and help conduct maneuvers, there were no courses offered the first year. This changed within three years as it became evident during the first class's tenure in the academic year of 1904–5 that they would benefit from some academic instruction. In 1906, when J. Franklin Bell, the officer who had presided over the renovation of the Leavenworth school, became Chief of Staff of the Army, he brought Leavenworth methods and even some of the instructors to the War College. For several years, incoming students who had not attended Leavenworth were required to take a brief (two month) version of the basic Leavenworth course prior to attending the War College.[22]

Seventeen of the 38 commanders (44 per cent) graduated from the

War College while a fourth (ten) of the chiefs of staff completed the course. It is perhaps a comment on how much this education came to be valued by those who saw the results during the war that the War Department sent nine of those chiefs of staff and two of the division commanders who had not been to the War College before the war to the first post-war class in 1919–20. Of course, this could also merely have been a place to put people between assignments that year. The fact that four more chiefs of staff and two division commanders who had graduated from the War College before the war were also detailed to this class reinforces that interpretation.[23]

By way of digression, that Class of 1920 was the most interesting one in the War College's history. As Harry P. Ball, the historian of the War College, pointed out, if it had convened in the spring of 1919 rather than the fall, it would have consisted of four major generals, 26 brigadier generals, 43 colonels, and two lieutentant colonels. After the demobilization and corresponding reduction in rank, it consisted of 19 colonels, 23 lieutentant colonels, 29 majors, and four captains.[24] It is easy to imagine the diffidence with which a faculty member introduced a First World War topic with four division commanders and 13 chiefs of staff not to mention others who had held important command and staff positions sitting in the class – waiting to air their versions of the war.

Before the war, students worked in two distinct areas. While they continued to do some planning for the General Staff and thus prepared for duty on that staff, they also learned the tasks of commanders and staff of 'larger troop formations'.[25] This was particularly crucial in a nation which possessed a relatively small army, since virtually all of this work had to be theoretical. Hunter Liggett, who graduated from the War College in 1910 and who then served as its president for nine months in 1913 and 1914, later, with the distinction as a division, corps, and army commander in the AEF gave startling evidence of this. Five months after the war, Liggett told his aide that he wanted to attend a review of the 81st Division because 'he had never seen a division together'.[26] Presumably many of the other commanders and chiefs of staff had the same experience in the series of post-war reviews.

The most striking feature of the education for command and staff work that the War College offered was the extensive study of the Civil War. In addition to whatever examples that were used to support other aspects of the course, students spent a month devoted to the study of military history with special emphasis on the Civil War: then five classes (1909–13) devoted the last month and a half of the course to a tour of the battlefields of Virginia, Maryland, and Pennsylvania. For that generation, to whom the Civil War seemed close, this must have been a most interesting period as they visited the several battlefields, examined the terrain, listened to lectures, and then worked out tactical problems. In 1913, they spent 47 days from 2 May to 18 June and rode horseback 637 miles on what turned out to be the last tour of this nature.[27]

Robert L. Bullard (AWC 1913) who commanded a division, corps, and army in the AEF, was exhilarated by the experience and credited the battlefield tour with giving him valuable insights including one that impressed him the most: 'how hard it was for a general to get his orders understood and executed by his subordinates'. Bullard, who had been very successful as a commander of small forces in the guerrilla war against the Moros, had been doubtful as to the value of the Leavenworth and War College education, but, after his year at the latter, he came away with the belief that: 'Clearly General Staff experience and formal schooling helped ease this "friction of war"'. He also acknowledged that the course 'forced officers to think about the duties they would have to perform in a mass wartime army rather than in terms of peacetime routine'.[28]

If the War College did nothing else but achieve the result to which Bullard referred, one could argue that it had served its purpose. But for what kind of warfare did it prepare its students? The fixation on the American Civil War gave them the model of a war of maneuver. Apparently they paid little attention to the siege of Petersburg which would have offered them the closest model to the trench war which they were to face in France. They focused their attention instead on First and Second Manassas, Fredericksburg, Chancellorsville, the Wilderness, Spottsylvania, the Peninsula Campaign, Antietam, and Gettysburg.[29]

While students apparently learned well the advantages of open warfare, the study of the Civil War generally combined with the inherent limitations of the applicatory method in which students solved tactical problems by acting out the roles of the various commanders and staff officers kept them from coming to terms with the capabilities of modern firepower. Because of the nature of theoretical problems, students stopped short of contact – actual combat. When they put themselves in the place of Civil War commanders, they came to understand the possibilities of rifle fire, but machine-guns and recently developed artillery were not present in the 1860s. If they had devoted more attention to the experience of the Russo-Japanese War, the destructive power of modern weapons might have been more apparent to them.[30]

Maneuvers offered another opportunity to study war in peacetime.

Presumably many officers who became AEF leaders took part in the several maneuvers prior to the First World War. There had been some large-scale exercises before the Spanish War, but the first one in the twentieth century was at Fort Riley in 1902. Arthur Wagner headed the board which planned this maneuver and served as the Chief Umpire. It is indicative of his recognized position as the nation's leading authority on tactics that he played a prominent role in maneuvers until his death in 1905. Not surprisingly, he chose the annual Prussian maneuvers as a model for this first maneuver which had some 6000 troops participating. A major purpose of the American maneuvers, however, was to provide the opportunity for militia and regular army units to work together in the tactical exercises. This led to the problem that one might expect of units not being at the same level of training when militia worked with regulars.[31]

Maneuvers became a part of army life over the next several years. In 1908 there was a particulary interesting exercise at Fort Riley. This is important, in part, because it was planned and conducted by one of the most brilliant officers of his time, Major Peyton C. March, who not only had made an excellent record in combat in the Spanish War and Philippine Insurrection but also had been an observer with the Japanese Army during the Russo-Japanese War. March introduced lessons of that war into the play and, moreover, made it much more realistic. In particular, he emphasized the effectiveness of modern artillery and rifle fire and tried to involve machine-guns much more in the maneuver. Although a machine-gun detachment had been introduced in another maneuver at Fort Riley five years earlier, apparently they had not played much of a role up to this time.

As a part of his effort to achieve greater realism, March eliminated lectures and critiques while the exercise was in progress and made the troops on defense dig in with trenches deep enough to kneel in. Such attempts were effective only up to a point. As March complained in his report, it was difficult to get across the effect of machine-guns when they were allowed only 100 blanks in the defensive problem, and, throughout the entire maneuver, each soldier only had 75 blanks. He also criticized the artillery's use of black powder which was anachronistic.[32]

Another noteworthy maneuver took place in 1911 when, because of Mexico's internal problems, the War Department formed a Maneuver Division at Fort Sam Houston. There was increased emphasis on communications as well as the first use of an airplane in the exercises carried out by these troops. Foreign observers who saw this division in the field were not impressed. A German officer flatly stated in an article published in a Berlin newspaper that the United States did not possess an army in the sense of those of the European powers or Japan. He considered the American regular army 'deficient in training and in everything else that is necessary for the constitution of an armed force'.[33] That certainly placed the Americans in perspective. Such a view also gave the German High Command, in the winter of 1916–17, reason to discount the possibility of the United States making an effective effort when the Germans decided to declare unrestricted submarine warfare. They knew that the Americans would enter the war, but they did not think that it would make a significant difference.

Certainly, the experience of operating with troops in the field and that of working with citizen soldiers who would make up the large majority of an American wartime army was valuable to those officers who took part in one or more of these various maneuvers. But peacetime maneuvers were not war, and the tactical exercises which they performed were those of open warfare, not of the siege variety with which they had to deal on the Western Front.

To be sure, many of the men who became AEF leaders were veterans of actual warfare. That experience must have made a more profound impression on them than any books, lectures, staff rides, or peacetime maneuvers. One of Pershing's West Point classmates, T. Bentley Mott, recognized that when he commented on the experience of the Spanish War in his memoir: 'Dating from this war, the American Army became slowly transformed, and its officers, however unconsciously, fitted themselves for the part they were to play in 1917'.[34]

All of the 38 commanders were in service during the Spanish War and Philippine Insurrection. Ten of them saw action in Cuba and two fought in the Philippines, while two more were in the Puerto Rican campaign. In addition, the one Marine in the group, John A. LeJeune, was on board a cruiser off Cuba and Puerto Rico. Twenty-six (including 11 who were combat veterans of the Spanish War) served in the Philippine Insurrection and four in the Boxer Expedition.[35]

The fact that chiefs of staff, as a group, were younger than the commanders makes a difference in their war experience. Of the 40 chiefs of staff, only 23 were in the service during the Spanish War. Seven, including Gordon Johnston (82d Division), who was one of Roosevelt's Rough Riders, and Charles D. Roberts (81st), who won the Medal of Honor at El Caney, fought in Cuba. Two others were in the Philippine campaign. Those nine and 15 others saw action in the Insurrection. Three of the Insurrection veterans (Heintzelman, 2nd

Army, Craig, I Corps, and Naylor, 33rd Division) also went to China during the Boxer Rebellion.[36]

Those who fought in those wars experienced, in the case of the Spanish War and the Boxer Rebellion, short wars in which the major tactic was a dash against the enemy, holed up in blockhouses in Cuba and in the battle of Manila and marches in a somewhat hostile country in Puerto Rico and China. Those who went to China also witnessed the difficulty of attacking fortified towns which a medieval warrior would have recognized.

The conventional stage of the Philippine Insurrection was also short-lived and consisted of a war of maneuver in which the Americans rather easily overcame the opposition. The guerrilla war which made up most of the Insurrection and, indeed, the several Moro wars and conflicts with bandits that lasted virtually until the First World War, gave these junior officers responsibility as commanders of small garrisons in hostile territory and in leading small units in pursuit of smaller guerrilla bands. One can only conjecture as to what lessons these officers carried over from their experience in the Philippines, but this unconventional warfare must have made them aware that the principal objective was defeat of the enemy force, not the holding of some key terrain feature.

Hugh Drum, who as Chief of Staff of 1st Army was one of the most important American staff officers in France, had won distinction in the fighting in Luzon and in Mindanao during the Insurrection. We do not know the degree to which those actions influenced him; however, it became apparent to him that the German army was the objective in the Meuse-Argonne Offensive. As he explained to his wife in late October 1918: 'The gaining of ground counts for little, it is the ruining of the army that will end the struggle'.[37]

In addition to whatever tactical knowledge they brought away from their earlier combat experience, these veterans learned how to control fear and how to lead men. They also learned, as one of the First World War division commanders, George B. Duncan (82d), said, that 'war as it's fit is quite different from war as it's writ'. Although Duncan would have agreed with the obvious point that participating in battle is different from reading about it, what he meant specifically was, in itself, another valuable lesson. He made the comment after reading a report written by a staff officer about a campaign in which he took part. He was astounded by the details as to locations, times, and places which that officer had obviously made up to make the commanding general and staff look much better than they actually were. When he reminisced after his retirement, Duncan added that this particular campaign in Luzon in June 1899 was 'typical of many a campaign that was to follow. There was no concrete, well-thought-out plan, no staff study or preparation made for coordinate effort. . . .' He was amazed at how well the poorly trained troops had done under such circumstances. He was also impressed by the Chief of Staff (Clarence Edwards) who wrote the report, and he let him know on the spot what he felt about it: 'The colossal nerve you show in getting up a report like that will probably get you far in the military service'. And it did as Edwards became a brigadier general in 1906, long before most of his contemporaries, and commanded the 26th Division in France. Eventually, a few weeks before the Armistice, Pershing did what he had wanted to do for some months, namely, relieve this controversial general.[38]

When Pershing led the AEF to war, he and his subordinates might accept their own combat experiences as being in wars which were aberrations; nevertheless, those unconventional wars and the ones they studied were wars of maneuver.[39] His dictate that the AEF should break the trench deadlock and engage in open warfare was based thus on study and experience. Essentially because of the age difference between the commanders and the chiefs of staff, the former had more experience while the latter had more professional education, although roughly similar proportions of both groups (68 per cent commanders and 60 per cent chiefs of staff) shared the experience of the Insurrection.

As these officers coped with the problems of planning and conducting battles with tens of thousands of men, two of them did note that their education, at least at Leavenworth and the War College, served them well. When John M. Palmer reported to take command of a brigade early in October 1918, Drum took him up to meet with three corps chiefs of staff. The five Leavenworth graduates felt at home, as Palmer recalled: 'Except for an ominous rumble to the north . . . It seemed just like a Staff College conference between the phases of one of the old map maneuvers. The technique and talk were just the same . . . .' What Hunter Liggett said of the War College presumably applied as well to the Leavenworth courses within the different level of their approach: 'The object of the course was to prepare a graduate to grasp the fundamentals of any conceivable war problem and to know how to go to work on it'.[40]

The AEF leaders almost did not have the chance to apply what they had learned. Allied leaders pressed for a mere token AEF with the great mass of American manpower being used as replacements within their depleted ranks. This made a lot of sense as they had already commanded and staffed large armies on the Western Front for almost three years before the first Americans arrived. Most of the French and British generals probably knew very little of peacetime establishments. Apparently, they did not take into consideration the effect of the professional military education system that had emerged in the United States since the turn of the century. One could argue that graduates of Leavenworth and the War College and those who had seen combat in the Spanish War and the Philippine Insurrection were as professionally prepared, if not more so, than their French and British counterparts had been, on the basis of their schooling and colonial war experience, in 1914.

Largely because of Pershing's obstinacy, the AEF did fight as an independent force, and those commanders and chiefs of staff surveyed in this chapter had units to command and staff. After the German offensives in the spring of 1918, talk of open warfare did not seem as naive as it had earlier. There were great problems as both officers and men had to learn how to fight on the Western Front against veteran German troops. There were failures among commanders and staff officers as the large turnover indicates. In the end, however, the AEF did make a break through German lines. On Armistice Day, Drum wrote his wife: 'All the hard hours of study at Leavenworth and those spent here have borne fruit. . . .' Be it Leavenworth, the War College, the Military Academy, or battle along a Luzon jungle trail, or more likely, the combination of two or more of these experiences, this background equipped the AEF leaders well enough to play the role they had to play in 1918.[41]

APPENDIX

AEF Commanders, 1 November 1918 (Pershing, II, pp. 401–8)

Unit	Officer	USMA	Leavenworth	AWC	SWar	PI
GHQ	John J. Pershing	1886	No	No	C	Yes
1st Army	Hunter Liggett	1879	No	1910	Yes	Yes
2d Army	Robert L. Bullard	1885	No	1912	Yes	Yes
I Corps	Joseph T. Dickman	1881	1883	1905	Yes	Yes*
II Corps	George W. Read	1883	No	1914	Yes	Yes
III Corps	John L. Hines	1891	No	No	C	Yes
IV Corps	Charles H. Muir	1885	1895	No	C	Yes*
V Corps	C. P. Summerall	1892	No	No	Yes	Yes*
VI Corps	C. C. Ballou	1886	No	1917	Yes	Yes

1st Div	Frank Parker	1894	No	No	Yes	No
2d Div	John A. LeJeune	No	No	1910	C	No
3d Div	Preston Brown	No	1913 & 1914	No	C	Yes
4th Div	Mark Hersey	1887	No	No	Yes	Yes
5th Div	Hanson E. Ely	1891	1905 & 1906	1916	Yes	Yes
6th Div	Walter H. Gordon	1886	No	1914	Yes	Yes
7th Div	Edmund Wittenmyer	1887	1895	No	Yes	Yes*
26th Div	Frank Bamford	No	1914 & 1915	No	Yes	?
27th Div	John F. O'Ryan	No	No	1914	Yes	No
28th Div	William H. Hay	1886	1891	1913	Yes	No
29th Div	Charles G. Morton	1883	No	1905	Yes	Yes
30th Div	Edward M. Lewis	1886	No	No	C	Yes
32d Div	William G. Haan	1889	No	1905	PI	Yes
33rd Div	George Bell	1880	No	No	Yes	Yes
35th Div	Peter E. Traub	1886	No	No	C	Yes
36th Div	William R. Smith	1892	No	No	Yes	?
37th Div	C. S. Farnsworth	1887	1909 & 1910	1916	Yes	No
42d Div	C. T. Menoher	1886	No	1907	Yes	Yes
77th Div	Robert Alexander	No	1909 & 1910	No	Yes	?
78th Div	James H. McRae	1886	No	1911	C	Yes
79th Div	Joseph E. Kuhn	1885	No	No	Yes	No
80th Div	Adelbert Cronkhite	1882	No	No	PR	No
81st Div	Chales J. Bailey	1881	No	No	Yes	No
82d Div	George B. Duncan	1886	No	1912	PR	Yes
87th Div	Samuel D. Sturgis	1884	No	No	PI	No
88th Div	William Weigel	1887	No	No	Yes	Yes
89th Div	William M. Wright	No	1891	No	C	Yes
90th Div	Henry T. Allen	1882	No	No	C	Yes
91st Div	Wm. H. Johnston	No	1887	1908	Yes	Yes

Two dates under Leavenworth indicate graduation from School of the Line and the Staff College.
Under Spanish War, C means wartime service in Cuba; PI = Philippines; PR = Puerto Rico.
Asterisk after Yes under PI means service in the Boxer Campaign.

AEF Chiefs of Staff, 1 November 1918 (Pershing, II, pp. 401–8)

Unit	Officer	USMA	Leavenworth	AWC	SpWar	PI
GHQ	James W. McAndrew	1888	1910 &1911	1913	C	Yes
1st Army	Hugh A. Drum	No	1911 & 1912	No	No	Yes
2d Army	Stuart Heintzelman	1899	1905 & 1906	No	No	Yes*
I Corps	Malin Craig	1898	1904 & 1905	1910	C	Yes*
II Corps	Geo. S. Simonds	1899	1904	No	No	Yes
III Corps	Campbell King	No	1905 & 1906	1911	Yes	Yes
IV Corps	Briant H. Wells	1894	No	No	C	Yes
V Corps	Wilson B. Burtt	1899	1911 &1912	No	No	Yes
VI Corps	Edgar T. Collins	1897	1910 &1911	1917	C	Yes
VII Corps	Herbert J. Brees	No	1903 & 1904	1907	Yes	Yes
1st Div	John N. Greely	No	No	No	No	No
2d Div	James C. Rhea	1899	1908 & 1909	No	No	No
3d Div	Robert McCleave	No	1910 & 1911	No	C	Yes
4th Div	Christian A. Bach	No	1916	No	Yes	Yes
5th Div	Clement A. Trott	1899	1905 & 1906	No	No	Yes

6th Div	Joseph W. Beacham	No	1915 & 1916	No	PI	Yes
7th Div	Wm. W. Taylor	No	1914 &1915	No	Yes	?
26th Div	Duncan K. Major	1899	1906 & 1907	1912	No	Yes
27th Div	Stanley H. Ford	No	1904	No	Yes	?
28th Div	Walter C. Sweeney	No	1912 &1913	No	Yes	Yes
29th Div	Sydney A. Cloman	1889	No	1905	PI	Yes
30th Div	John K. Herr	1902	No	No	No	No
32d Div	Robert M. Beck	1901	No	No	No	?
33rd Div	Wm. K. Naylor	No	1904 & 1905	1910	Yes	Yes*
35th Div	Hamilton S. Hawkins	1894	1911 &1912	No	Yes	Yes
36th Div	Ezekiah J. Williams	No	1909 & 1910	1912	Yes	?
37th Div	Dana T. Merrill	No	1908 & 1909	No	Yes	Yes
42d Div	Wm. N. Hughes	No	1904	No	?	?
77th Div	C. O. Sherrill	1901	1906 & 1907	No	No	Yes
78th Div	C. D. Herron	1899	1907 & 1908	No	No	Yes
79th Div	Tenney Ross	No	1904 & 1905	No	Yes	?
80th Div	Wm. H. Waldron	No	1905 & 1906	1911	Yes	?
81st Div	Chas. D. Roberts	1897	1912 &1913	No	C	Yes
82d Div	Gordon Johnston	No	1903	No	C	Yes
87th Div	Henry R. Richmond	No	No	No	Yes	?
88th Div	Fay W. Brabson	No	1907	No	No	?
89th Div	John C. H. Lee	1909	No	No	No	No
90th Div	John J. Kingman	1904	No	No	No	No
91st Div	Henry C. Jewett	1901	No	No	No	No
92d Div	Allan J. Greer	No	1912 & 1913	No	Yes	?

Two dates under Leavenworth indicate graduate from School of the Line and the Staff College.
Under Spanish War, C means wartime service in Cuba while PI = Philippines.
Asterisk after Yes under PI means service in the Boxer Campaign also.

NOTES

1. Joseph T. Dickman, *The Great Crusade* (New York: 1927), pp. 2–6 and James G. Harbord, *The American Army in France, 1917–1919* (Boston: 1936), p. 301. I want to express my appreciation to Timothy K. Nenninger who commented on an earlier draft.
2. In an Appendix, General Pershing published such a list. John J. Pershing, *My Experiences in the World War*, 2 vols (New York: 1931), II, pp. 401–8. I did not include in this study the several logistical commands, the staff officers other than chiefs of staff, or the commanders and chiefs of staff of depot and replacement divisions.
3. When I used an *Official Army Register*, I relied mainly on the one for 1924. Graduates of Leavenworth and the Army War College are listed, respectively, in *Commandants, Staff, Faculty, and Graduates of The General Service Schools, Fort Leavenworth, Kansas: 1881–1926* (Fort Leavenworth: 1927) and *Directory: Present and Former Staff and Faculty, Graduates and Students by Class: 1905–1987* (Carlisle Barracks, PA: 1987). The information about the West Pointers is in George W.

Cullum, *Biographical Register of the Officers and Graduates of the U.S. Military Academy at West Point, New York Since its Establishment in 1802*, Volume IV (1890–1900), Vol. V (1900–10), and Vol. VI A and B (1910–20).

4. *The Centennial of the United States Military Academy at West Point, New York, 1802–1902*, 2 vols (Washington, DC, 1904).
5. The Tactical Department entry is in *ibid*, pp. 374–415 in Vol. I. References to the trenches, machine-guns, and lectures are, respectively, on pages 402, 401, and 408.
6. *Ibid.*, pp. 274–90.
7. *Ibid.*, pp. 214, 459, 464. It is possible that Liggett, the 1st Army commander, who graduated in 1879 may have used Mahan's *Outpost*. The editions of the three books which I used are Wheeler (New York: 1879), third edition of Mercur (New York: 1898), and Wagner (London: 1895).
8. Wheeler, pp. 8, 53, 320, 323, with quotation from p. 324.
9. Edward M. Coffman, *The Hilt of the Sword: The Career of Peyton C. March* (Madison, WI: 1966), p. 8; Donald Smythe, *Guerrilla Warrior: The Early Life of John J. Pershing* (New York: 1973), p. 11.
10. Mercur, pp. 36–9, with quotations from 36 and 38; Wheeler, p. 53.
11. Herron was quoted in Forrest C. Pogue, *George C. Marchall: Education of a General* (New York: 1963), p. 94. There is a difference as to the date cadets were assigned Wagner. The notation in the textbook list indicates that it came into use in 1899 but Professor Fieberger wrote in his report that he replaced Mercur with it in 1896. I consider his report more reliable in this regard. *Centennial*, I, pp. 274, 459.
12. Wagner, vi.
13. The Herron quotation is from Pogue, p. 94. The Wagner quotations are from pages 93 and 159.
14. *Ibid.*, pp. 14–15, 66–67, 168, 387. The quotation is from page 67. The pertinent organizational charts for the Infantry division are on pages 343 and 351 in Vol. I of *United States Army in the World War: 1917–1919*, 17 vols (Washington, DC: 1948).
15. Wagner, pp. 31–2.
16. *Ibid.*, p. 395.
17. The basic monograph on the Leavenworth Schools is Timothy K. Nenninger, *The Leavenworth Schools and the Old Army: Education, Professionalism and the Officer Corps of the United States Army, 1881–1918* (Westport, CT: 1978).
18. I examined the difference between the Leavenworth experience of the commanders and chiefs of staff at length in 'The American Military Generation Gap in World War I: The Leavenworth Clique in the AEF', in William Geffen (ed.), *Command and Commanders in Modern Warfare* (USAFA, 1969: pp. 39–48. I should point out that I used a somewhat different data base in that article than I am using in this one; nevertheless I do not believe that makes any difference in the basic interpretation. See also Chapter 8 in Nenninger.
19. *Ibid.*, pp. 12, 85–6.
20. Drum to wife, 7 July 1918, Drum Papers, US Military History Institute.

21. Marshall Statement, 3 July 1951, Leavenworth Museum (xerox in author's possession); Pogue, p. 101.
22. Harry P. Ball, *Of Responsible Command: A History of the U.S. Army War college* (Carlisle Barracks, PA: 1983) is the best monograph on this subject. See pages 101, 107, 117.
23. Those who had graduated prior to the war and then took the course again were division commanders Preston Brown (3rd) and William H. Johnston (91st) and chiefs of staff Malin Craig (I Corps), Edgar T. Collins (VI Corps), Campbell King (III Corps), and Ezekiah J. Williams (36th Division). Those division commanders who took the course for the first time after the war were Hanson E. Ely (5th) and Mark Hersey (4th) while the chiefs of staff in this category included Stanley H. Ford (27th), Stuart Heintzelman (2d Army), Charles D. Herron (78th), Dana T. Merrill (37th), Charles D. Roberts (81st), Tenney Ross (79th), George S. Simonds (II Corps), Walter C. Sweeney (28th), and Clement A. Trott (5th).
24. Ball, p. 158.
25. *Ibid.*, 139.
26. 9 April 1919 entry, Pierpont L. Stackpole Diary in the George C. Marshall Research Library.
27. The class of 1908 spent four days at Antietam, but it was not until 1909 that the full scale tour started. Although one was scheduled for 1914, the Secretary of War cancelled it. George P. Ahern, 'A Chronicle of the Army War college: 1899–1919' (Mimeograph copy of typescript in US Army Military History Institute), pp. 63–4, 115, 153–5, 188–91, 224.
28. Allan R. Millett, *The General: Robert L. Bullard and Officership in the United States Army, 1881–1925* (Westport, CT: 1975), pp. 231–2.
29. Ahern, *op cit.*, p. 142. Hunter Liggett commented on the study of the Civil War in his *A.E.F.: Ten Years Ago in France* (New York: 1928), pp. 292–6.
30. Ball, pp. 141–2. Several returned observers lectured the Class of 1905 about what they saw of the Russo-Japanese War but evidently succeeding classes were not exposed to this instruction. Ahern, p. 41.
31. Charles D. McKenna, 'The Forgotton Reform: Field Maneuvers in the Development of the United States Army, 1902–1920' (Duke University: PhD Dissertation, 1981), pp. 44, 59–60, 75.
32. *Ibid.*, pp. 73, 116–18. *Report of Major Peyton C. March, Chief Umpire, Camp of Instruction and Maneuver, Fort Riley, Kansas, 1908* (Np: nd), pp. 3–4, 10, 21, 29, 106.
33. McKenna, pp. 116–17. The quotation is from page 136. In Chapter VII of his biography of George C. Marshall, Forrest Pogue recounts Marshall's experiences in the Maneuver Division and other maneuvers.
34. T. Bently Mott, *Twenty Years As Military Attache* (New York: 1937), p. 51.
35. Those commanders and chiefs of staff who fought in the several Moro wars and other guerrilla wars between 1902 and 1917 are not included under the category of the Philippine Insurrection. The type of action they saw, however, was probably similar to that of many of the Insurrection campaigns. I could not find where Bamford (26th

Division), Alexander (77th), and Johnston (91st) served during the Spanish War. Of those who went to China to fight the Boxers in 1900, Muir (IV Corps) also fought in Cuba and in the Insurrection while Dickman (I Corps), Summerall (V Corps), and Wittenmyer (7th Division) also served in the Insurrection.

36. I had more difficulty finding information about the chiefs of staff. I could not determine where 14 of the 23 Spanish War veterans served in that war. Nor could I find out whether or not ten of this group served in either the Insurrection or China Relief Expedition.
37. Drum to wife, 26 October 1918, Drum Papers.
38. Duncan, 'Reminiscences, 1882–1905', pp. 157–8. Xerox copy in author's possession.
39. According to Ball (p. 142), they did not study the Insurrection at the War College.
40. An interesting coincidence which Palmer also mentions is that the Leavenworth graduates had worked on maps of the Moselle region of France and hence had to fight over some of the terrain that they had studied. John M. Palmer, *Washington, Lincoln, Wilson: Three War Statesmen* (Garden City, New York: 1930), pp. 299, 340; Liggett, p. 289.
41. Drum to wife, 11 November 1918, Drum Papers.

Josephus Daniels U.S. Secretary of the Navy. Reproduced courtesy of the National Archives of the United States of America.

9 The American Naval Leaders' Preparations for War

Paolo E. Coletta

For the period from August 1914 to April 1917, this chapter will center upon four topics: Woodrow Wilson's policies towards the Great War and their effects upon the Navy; changes in Navy Department organization and on the national defense level; the contrasting approaches to preparedness by the top naval leaders of the period, Rear Admiral Bradley A. Fiske, Aide for Operations to 11 May 1915, and of the first Chief of Naval Operations, Admiral William S. Benson; and an evaluation of the status of the Navy in August 1914 and in April 1917.

Wilson's attitude until the nation went to war was that Army and Navy personnel should speak only when asked and should be denied a voice in the determination of national policy. The very few communications he received from naval officers dealt with the war scare with Japan in 1913 and the American interventions in Mexico, Haiti, and Santo Domingo in 1914–15. Despite the outbreak of war, he saw no need to strengthen the Army or Navy or to create agencies that would enhance the coordination of foreign policy, military policy, and logistics requirements for war. In these matters he had the support of a Democratic 'small navy' faction that held the balance of power in Congress and from Republicans in general. On the other hand, with the great decrease in merchant shipping activity of the belligerents, he would build or buy more merchant ships and scrap the law that prohibited the transfer of foreign ships to American registry. He also toyed with the idea of using his warships for commercial purposes and taking over the Austrian and German ships interned in American ports. On these matters he was blocked by non-interventionists and by the Allies. The result was that the British, who ruled the waves, controlled American trade with Europe.[1]

A newspaperman ignorant about naval matters but a 'deserving Democrat', Secretary of the Navy Josephus Daniels agreed with Wilson's policies, stood to lose his position if he did not support them and staunchly supported civil control over his department. The purely advisory General Board of the Navy, in existence since 1900, had already prepared Atlantic and Asiatic war plans, the former concluding that when at war the US fleet would fight a European fleet somewhere in the Caribbean. In 1911 the president of the board, and the only admiral, George Dewey, had told President Taft's Secretary of the Navy, George von Lengerke Meyer, that war plans were current and that 'The General Board designates Germany as the next country against which a naval war should be formulated'.[2] However, after President Wilson announced the nation's neutrality in the war, Daniels told Dewey that he could continue to draft war plans only on condition that he not have a specific potential enemy in mind.[3]

Daniels inherited from Meyer an aide system in which four high-ranking officers coordinated the work of the naval bureaus in the areas of personnel, operations, material, and inspections and together served as an advisory board. These officers served Daniels in an advisory capacity only, and had no direct access to the President. As members of the General Board, the Aides for Operations and for Material provided liaison between it and the Secretary. Instead of relying upon his senior officer, the Aide for Operations, Bradley A. Fiske, Daniels called the aide system a 'fifth wheel' and substituted for it a navy-wide council comprised of the Assistant Secretary, bureau chiefs, and Commandant of the Marine Corps. Yet he leaned mostly upon the Aide for Material, Captain Albert G. Winterhalter, and some favored bureau chiefs. Eventually, by refusing to replace aides when they went to sea, Daniels killed the aide system. Fiske was dissuaded from resigning his billet only at the Secretary's request.[4] While hanging on for two more years, he strove mightily to convince the administration to prepare the navy for war.

Fiske applauded Daniel's improving certain conditions under which naval personnel served and lived but felt that he saw the navy as merely a department of the government, not as a fighting machine.[5] Especially objectionable was his refusal to legalize the aide system or adopt a naval general staff, hold realistic fleet war games, approve an administrative plan by which the bureaus would report quarterly on their preparedness, seek a continuous, rather than an annual, building program, and demand the establishment of a council of national defense. To no avail did he counsel Daniels that naval power was relative, that the US Navy was inferior to other great navies, and that getting the navy ready for war was his paramount duty.

On the ground of finding the 'golden mean' between what the navy needed and what the nation could afford, in March 1913 Daniels advocated an annual two-battleship program and other ships that would move the Navy into a position 'second to none'; in 1914 and 1915 he cut in half the building programs recommended by Fiske and the General Board. Two battleships a year would not fulfil the board's recommendation of 1903 that 48 capital ships be built by 1920 nor, obviously, keep pace with the mad European naval armaments race. Yet Daniels's record remains unique, for Congress accepted every building recommendation he made during his eight years except for completing a large program after 1918.[6] On the other hand, by personally deciding how many ships of what types to recommend to Congress, all he let the General Board do was to prescribe their characteristics.[7]

Daniels rejected Fiske's suggestions of January 1914 to add various officers and 7000 men to the fleet by 1916 and that senior captains be promoted sooner to admiral so that they could serve longer as fleet commanders. However, he forwarded to Congress Fiske's recommendation that fleet commanders be made admirals and their seconds in command, vice admirals. Thereafter American fleet commanders had rank commensurate with those of foreign navies.[8]

In August 1914 the US Navy ranked third in the world, after Britain and Germany. The British Grand Fleet was about 60 per cent stronger than the German High Seas Fleet. With the completion of current building programs, the British would have 49 battleships to Germany's 33, but complete mobilization would raise the number to 65 and 38, respectively. To these could be added the 28 French battleships and, after May 1915, those of the Italian Navy.

The 12 British battleships on the way in 1914 had 12- or 13.5-inch guns (most German ships 11- and 12-inch) and more steaming range than German ones. In 1915 the British produced five *Queen Elizabeths*. These carried 15-inch guns, and their oil rather than coal plants and turbine drive gave them a speed of 25 knots and more. They could therefore cross the T of any other ship. The United States had but 19 battleships less than ten years old.

Although responsible for war plans and the efficient operation of the fleet, Fiske also worked to invent equipment that would permit ships to engage in director-controlled continuous-aim fire at long range and to improve naval aviation.[9] By mid-1914 an aeronautic station had been established at Pensacola, Florida; and, by obtaining an officer to serve as the Director of Naval Aviation, Fiske began American naval aviation administration. The aircraft he had shipped to Veracruz,

Mexico, in April 1914 convinced Daniels of their worth.[10] Yet with the outbreak of war in Europe Fiske parted company with Daniels on aviation because the latter did not give it the support he demanded. For example, the Department did nothing to produce the torpedo plane Fiske had patented in 1912.

In 1914 as in 1913, Fiske obtained Daniels's permission to spend the month of August with the General Board, which during the summer met in Newport, instead of taking annual leave. On 1 August he told the board that despite the critical situation developing in Europe President Wilson had blocked him from assembling the fleet and preparing it for service. The board thereupon wrote a letter to Daniels that a European war might endanger America's neutrality and that battleships not needed in Mexican or Caribbean waters should be returned home 'to be docked and gotten ready'.[11] In his memoirs, published in 1919, Fiske noted that 'I think this was the first step toward preparedness that was taken in the United States'.[12]

In 1910 President Taft sent four battleships to Mexico's east coast and some cruisers to its west coast to protect American lives and property during the Mexican civil war. Fiske wanted the battleships returned and prepared for possible action in the European war he predicted would soon ensue. Instead, President Wilson in October 1914 ordered four more battleships sent to Mexico, and Daniels rejected Fiske's suggestion that they be replaced by merchant ships or by a special service squadron. Fiske's fleet was further dispersed when he was ordered to send four more battleships to Mexico and still other ships to Santo Domingo and to Haiti during the summer of 1914. Clearly Wilson and Daniels rather than he were managing naval operations.[13]

In consequence of the beginning of the Great War, on 5 August 1914 President Wilson forbade the transmission of non-neutral messages from the United States. On the sixth he announced national neutrality, meaning that he would as scrupulously demand that the United States live up to its duties as a neutral as that the belligerents respect a neutral's rights. On the eighteenth, by prohibiting both active and retired officers from commenting publicly on the war he may have denied himself some expert opinion, as from the retired pro-British Alfred T. Mahan and active Rear Admiral Austin M. Knight.[14] However, Germanophiles were few. One example must suffice. Retired Rear Admiral French Ensor Chadwick, though of British ancestry, on 22 August 1914 told Daniels and later told Wilson that if Germany lost the war Britain would dominate the Western and Russia the Eastern world. Britain had defeated every maritime opponent –

Spanish, Dutch, and French. After defeating Germany she would move against the United States. Britain sought conquest; France, revenge; Germany, merely self-preservation. Chadwick added a most cogent point: if Wilson embargoed the sale of arms the United States could improve its own defenses, reduce Britain's war-making capacity, and bring Germany to a reasonable view of peace.[15] In contrast, most American naval officers and most of the public feared German naval ambitions in the Caribbean, abhorred the German breach of treaty pledges and her reported atrocities while violating Belgian neutrality, and viewed the Allies as upholding constitutional government against German autocracy and imperialism. Nonetheless, this conculsion did not mean that the nation would enter a war in which it had no stake.

Fiske, however, held that Germany was responsible for the war and was a threat to the United States, and envied her superior staff methods. He believed that Wilson should have declared war on Germany rather than adopting neutrality, 'and there would be no real risk, because the British fleet can control the Seas'.[16] At his suggestion, on 4 August the General Board left Newport for Washington in order to be readily accessible to Daniels. Fiske was upset when Daniels conferred not with him but with the Assistant Secretary of the Navy, Franklin D. Roosevelt, and Wilson with his Cabinet secretaries rather than his leading servicemen. He was also piqued because neither Wilson nor Daniels kept him fully informed of their policies.[17]

His recommendations rejected by Wilson and Daniels, Fiske determined to improve the status of the navy by increments, starting with a recommendation to Daniels of 17 August that the Atlantic Fleet be concentrated and hold tactical and gunnery drills and realistic war games. Daniels disapproved. On 9 September Fiske asked Wilson to order home the 12 battleships off Mexico because their target practice and personnel training suffered greatly, their material condition was poor, and personnel morale was low. Wilson permitted only ship replacements.[18] Meanwhile Fiske detailed two captains to serve on the Joint State, War, and Navy Neutrality Board. It had been established in mid-August and was to coordinate naval and foreign affairs with Robert Lansing, Counselor of the State Department.[19]

On 14 September Fiske arranged for the semi-annual fleet exercises. On the eighteenth Daniels rejected the General Board's recommendations for the naval estimates for fiscal year 1916, saying that he saw no need to augment the fleet. While the board reconsidered, Fiske told Daniels that the fleet would fail inspection. He added, correctly, that the United States would have trouble with her if Britain made foodstuffs contraband or the United States built a large merchant marine.[20]

In early October, with support from the like-minded officers and from a number of new – and mainly Republican – preparedness societies, Fiske again sought to convince Wilson and Daniels that the navy was too weak to support national interests. They instead believed that even the victor in the Great War would be too exhausted to challenge the United States. In his annual message of December 1914 Wilson deemed 'nervous and excited' those who demanded a preparedness program, adding that we had been 'thrown off balance by a war with which we have nothing to do'. He would rely for defense upon 'a citizenry trained and accustomed to arms' rather than upon a standing or reserve army, and upon a 'powerful navy'.[21] He therefore kept the service estimates for 1916 close to those of 1915. But by the fall of 1914 Democrats as well as Republicans had introduced resolutions requesting that Congress investigate, as one put it, 'the question of the preparedness of the United States for war, defensive or offensive'. Lemuel P. Padgett, chairman of the House Naval Affairs Committee, agreed to hold hearings on a resolution offered by Republican Representative Augustus P. Gardner beginning 3 November. Wilson opposed an investigation, telling Gardner that 'it was an unwise way to handle a question which might create a very unfavorable international impression'.[22] Fiske explained his predicament not only to Gardner and to Senator George Clements Perkins, of California, a member of the Senate Naval Affairs Committee, but to the editors of the *Army and Navy Journal* and of the *New York Herald*. In addition he had his staff prepare a plan by which the Navy could be readied for war and directed during wartime. When Gardner and Perkins told him that he must go through Daniels or ruin his career, Fiske stuck by his demand for a naval general staff. Such a staff would merely gather intelligence on other navies and prepare contingency war plans. Daniels rejected it, saying on 24 October that it was a Prussian idea, hence not consonant with the principles of a republic. At the suggestion of one of his staff, Fiske summarized his preparedness recommendations for the official files. If the Navy was unprepared if it went to war, the responsibility would rest with Daniels.[23]

After failing on 5 November to get Daniels to demand increased naval appropriations or to permit him to hold realistic war games, Fiske handed Daniels his preparedness paper, in which he noted that the Navy was unprepared for war. First, a naval general staff was needed to prepare for and to conduct war. Second, the Navy was deficient in training because of insufficient personnel, poor departmental organization, and lack of small ships. Were his recommendations not adopted and war came, he concluded, disaster would result. Daniels read the paper, made no comment, and returned it. Fiske then filed it.[24]

Daniels told the General Board that he would speak with it on 11 November about the 1916 estimates. However, the board sent its conclusions to him on the tenth while he was talking with Winterhalter and Victor Blue, Chief of the Bureau of Navigation. The latter had assured Daniels that by obtaining men from certain ships and stations he could provide more men than were needed in 1916. Daniels told Fiske to leave and return in two hours. When he did so, the three men ganged up on him. As he recalled, Daniels said that the board should not ask for more men than President Wilson or he wanted. Nor should the board concern itself with whether war was probable or should be declared. Fiske demurred, and no agreement was reached. When Daniels visited the board on the eleventh, the members agreed not to publish their recommendation that 19 600 men be added to the fleet in an emergency and that Daniels should seek to obtain at least 15 000 of them. Feeling that Daniels had gotten the message, Fiske also agreed to the deletion of the matter from Daniels's annual report.[25]

So bad was the personnel situation that on 22 November Fiske decided to take some ships out of commission.[26] By 3 December he believed that 'I am liable to be bounced any day'.[27] On 10 December Daniels told the House Naval Affairs Committee that no emergency existed and countered all of Fiske's suggestions for strengthening and improving the Navy.[28] On the seventeenth Fiske parted company with Daniels by telling the committee all of his differences with him.[29] With Daniels deaf to his importunities, he must go over his head to Congress and to the people.[30] To bolster his case, he arranged to have himself recalled by the committee and planted questions with one of its Republican members.[31] In answer to these questions he offered data showing how weak the Navy was on the surface, below it, and over it. His bombshell came in his declaring that it would take five years to prepare the navy for war – and that with the help of a naval general staff.[32]

Instead of firing him when he called him to his office on the morning of 18 December, Daniels merely asked Fiske for a copy of his testimony. Since Fiske had gone over his head to Congress, Daniels overlooked him henceforth.

While Fiske believed that he had aroused at least a powerful minority to realize the nation's peril, Wilson and Daniels saw no challenge to American security and refused to strengthen their military arms. Indeed, because of a decrease in federal revenues Wilson in January 1915 considered reducing rather than increasing the military budgets.[33]

Fiske again resorted to politics, this time by turning to Representative Richmond P. Hobson, a big navyite who favored a general staff. Fiske violated law and risked a court martial on the evening of 3 January 1915 by secretly taking five officers with him to Hobson's home. There they drafted legislation to create an Office of Naval Operations whose head would be 'responsible for the readiness of the navy for war and be charged with its general direction'. Fifteen assistants would draft war plans. Asked who would fill such an office, Fiske retorted that it would not be he. On 6 January Hobson took the bill to Daniels, who said that he would go home if it passed because 'it left the Secretary little power except to draw his breath and draw his salary'.[34] Hobson then won unanimous approval for the bill from a subcommittee of the House Naval Affairs Committee and asked Fiske to prepare a supporting brief. Admiral Dewey, president of the General Board, was 'delighted', and, despite a long talk with Daniels whose tenor remains unknown, chairman Padgett said that he would incorporate Hobson's bill into the naval appropriations bill.

Daniels opposed the Fiske-Hobson bill even though he had ascertained that Dewey and all fleet commanders applauded it. To Fiske's great joy, on 24 January 1915 Daniels said that he would help get the bill through the House – but he failed to assess Daniels's resourcefulness. While Daniels played on Dewey's fear that the bill would wipe out the General Board, the House struck the plan from the appropriations bill, saying that no new business could be added to it. Fiske alerted Hobson, who rushed to get the Senate Naval Affairs Committee to add his bill to its appropriations bill. On 19 February Daniels asked the latter to substitute for the wording of the Fiske-Hobson plan the statement that there would be 'a Chief of Naval Operations . . . who would be charged . . . with the operations of the fleet, and with the preparations and readiness of plans for its use in time of war'. In this way, he said, civilian control would be maintained.[35] Fiske argued the matter in vain with Daniels on 22 February. On the twenty-fifth, the full Senate agreed to Daniels's version of the bill. Fiske got a promise from two of the House members of the conference committee to support his original plan, but on 3 March, the day before it adjourned, Congress passed the appropriations bill including Daniels's version of the Office of CNO but without the 15 assistants to draft war plans. Fiske thought that the bill provided 'a greater advance than any other naval legislation had accomplished in many years'. He was too sanguine. His plan made the CNO responsible for preparing the navy for war and for directing its management including power to coordinate the bureaus. Since Daniels's version made the CNO responsible only for operating the fleet and providing war plans, the Secretary retained management control and the bureaus remained uncoordinated.[36]

Although Daniels cut to 20 the 48 new ships recommended by the General Board for 1916, other provisions of the Naval Act of 1915 were quite important. In addition to the Office of CNO, it provided that selected officers could engage in engineering duty only, established an advisory committee on aeronautics and a naval reserve, and approved promotion by selection of officers to the upper grades.

Fiske hoped to show from the realistic war games held between 10 May and 15 June 'what would really happen if a hostile [that is, German] fleet attacked the east coast' and do so before a CNO was chosen.[37] He acknowledged that Dewey and Cameron MacRae Winslow, commanding the Pacific Fleet, were superior to him as strategists. He knew that Dewey's advanced age and illness prevented his selection as CNO and that he himself would not be named. On 25 March he asked Daniels to relieve him yet continued to fight him. For example, he got the House to provide 15 assistants to help the CNO draft war plans – but Daniels took the credit.[38] When Daniels persisted in bypassing him and dealing with his subordinates, on 2 April Fiske proffered his letter of resignation. Daniels accepted it, saying that he would set the date later. While naval reformers saw Fiske as a martyr, Daniels rejected him as CNO because 'his consuming passion was to confer all power on the head of operations'. Instead he sought 'an officer of practical judgement who believed in the American system'.[39]

After canvassing his rear admirals, Daniels asked Winslow to serve as CNO. Winslow declined on the ground that the office lacked the necessary powers and that he preferred a general staff – as did the other 12 rear admirals. President Wilson 'enlightened' Daniels by asking why he did not select a suitable captain.[40]

To the amazement of Fiske, the Navy, and the nation, on 28 April Daniels announced that he had chosen Capt. William Shepherd Benson as the CNO. Benson was a good shiphandler and educator but he was no strategist. Further, he was such a stickler for detail that he refused to delegate responsibility. Most naval officers sneered at his selection,[41] and Fiske decided to leave the Department as soon as possible. After Benson relieved him on 11 May, Daniels ordered Fiske to rusticate at the Naval War College for the year prior to his being retired on account of age.

From the war games of May 1915 observers concluded that an enemy fleet could easily reach the east coast of the United States. Daniels confessed outside of Fiske's hearing that he found the fleet's condition 'very painful' – and Benson wanted its commander replaced.[42] Meanwhile, Fiske, who believed that war would soon come, publicly and privately demanded additional preparedness and characterized Daniels as 'a mill-stone about the neck of the navy' who should be replaced by a 'prepared' secretary rather than a mere politician. On 24 December 1915 Daniels throttled him, saying, 'You cannot write or talk any more; your can't even say that two and two make four'.[43]

Soon after Fiske resigned, many of his preparedness demands were echoed by an administration caught between Allied and German methods for ruling the seas regardless of a neutral's rights.

Upon the outbreak of hostilities, Wilson offered his good offices as a mediator and urged the belligerents to adopt the unratified Declaration of London, 1909, which included principles for conducting naval warfare. To be legal, a blockade must be effective, that is, strong enough to prevent the entry and departure of ships from a port. Contact mines must be made inoperable an hour after being laid. Contraband was termed absolute or conditional, the remainder being free goods. All a belligerent could do to a neutral ship was to search it and allow it to proceed if it contained no contraband. If it contained contraband, it would be taken to a prize court. Moreover, a neutral ship could not be sunk without warning or giving its passengers and crew time to seek safety.

Alleging German violations of international law, as by mining international waters, the British made their own rules, many of them also violating international law. They undertook an extensive mine campaign, made contraband of everything Germany sought to import, and conducted a distant rather than close blockade of German ports. While at Wilson's request Col. Edward H. House in January 1915 sought peace terms from Britain, France, and Germany, Germany on 4 February retaliated with a U-boat blockade against Britain.

The British promised to make reparation for improper injury inflicted upon American shipping. But how could Germany repay if U-boats caused the loss of American lives in neutral ships? Was war the only solution? On 10 February Wilson warned Germany that he would hold her to a 'strict accountability' if American lives were lost on American ships, but he did not make it clear whether Germany was to spare just neutral ships or *all* ships carrying American passengers. To balance matters, he asked Britain to stop her ships from using neutral flags and suggested that she give up her 'hunger blockade' and Germany abandon her submarine blockade. Both nations refused the compromise. Devoted to the freedom of the seas, Wilson vetoed Secretary of State W. J. Bryan's advice that he warn Americans against sailing in belligerent ships. On 28 March an American was killed when a U-boat torpedoed the British passenger liner *Falaba* without giving its crew and passengers time to escape. On 29 April a German seaplane bombed the American ship *Cushing* in the North Sea without causing loss of life. On 1 May, the same day that the German ambassador in Washington, Johann von Bernstorff, warned Americans not to travel in belligerent ships, the tanker *Gulflight* was torpedoed. Two crewmen drowned, and her captain died of a heart attack from the excitement. Most important, on 7 May the U-boat that sank the British liner *Lusitania* caused the death of 785 of its 1257 passengers, of whom 124 were Americans. Wilson saw 'red' whenever he thought about the *Lusitania*. Britain challenged America's neutral rights, Germany its sovereign rights. Forced to choose between the British and German techniques of maritime control, he favored the British, for the *Lusitania* sinking showed that he could not risk America's defense to an Allied victory over Germany. But he refrained from telling either belligerent side to cease its violations of America's neutral rights on pain of his supporting her enemy.

From a report about it dated 18 May 1915, Wilson knew that the Atlantic Fleet was in poor shape. On 21 July he told Daniels that he had been giving much thought to an 'adequate naval program' to present to Congress when it met in December and would like to speak with him about it. Now, for the first time, he wanted professional naval advice. As he told Daniels:

> I would be very much obliged if you would get the best minds in the department to work on the subject: I mean the men who have been most directly in contact with actual modern conditions, who have most thoroughly comprehended the altered conditions of naval warfare, and who best comprehend what the Navy must be in the future in order to stand upon an equality with the most efficient and

most practically serviceable. I want their advice, a program formulated in the most definite terms. . . .[44]

While Wilson asked Berlin to give assurances that the *Lusitania* tragedy would not be repeated – or he would sever diplomatic relations – on 26 May a U-boat torpedoed the American steamer *Nebraskan* near Land's End. On 19 August two Americans were killed when a U-boat attacked the British liner *Arabic* off the Fastnet. Germany promised Wilson satisfaction for the latter if the U-boat captain had exceeded his instructions to spare passenger liners. Moreover, on 1 September von Bernstorff promised that liners would not be sunk without warning and with safety of life assured provided they did not try to escape or offer resistance. Still unresolved was the question of the safety of merchantmen carrying passengers – and Wilson's patience with Germany was ebbing.[45]

Early in October, when his navy ranked fourth in the world, Wilson asked Daniels to prepare plans for a five-year building program to cost $500 million. Included were ten battleships, six battle cruisers, ten cruisers, 50 destroyers, 100 submarines, and lesser craft. On 12 October he approved a plan the General Board sent Daniels; on the fifteenth he submitted it to Congress. In addition, Daniels asked Congress for a 20 per cent increase in personnel, $5 million for an experimental laboratory to be used by the Naval Consulting Board created on 13 July and headed by Thomas A. Edison, and for funds to augment naval aviation and ammunition stockpiles. When the 64th Congress rejected Wilson's demands, he took them and a reiterated demand for an enlarged merchant marine to the country in a speech of 4 November, repeated these in his annual message to Congress of December, and sought popular support for them during a tour during late January and February 1916. By the plan he submitted to Congress on 7 December 1915, the Navy by 1921 would have built or be building 27 battleships of the first line, 25 battleships of the second class, six battle cruisers, 41 cruisers of various classes, 108 destroyers, 18 fleet and 157 coastal submarines, and numerous auxiliaries. Among the last, however, were only four transports. Yet he spoke of preparing not for war but for defense, adding that 'No thoughtful man feels any panic haste in the matter'.[46]

In January 1916 Daniels urged the House Naval Affairs Committee to adopt Wilson's naval program and, in addition, many items Fiske had recommended and he had rejected. Among others, Admirals Frank F. Fletcher, William S. Sims, Knight, and Winslow echoed

Fiske's demands for a naval general staff, and Benson admitted the need for 15 000 more men and for officers to work on war plans. Yet Benson revealed great ignorance about the capabilities of naval aviation, and he would build only prototype ships until Congress declared war and provided funds.[47] The difference between Fiske's relations with Daniels and Benson's was made clear in Benson's stating that 'I know that any order I sign is accepted without question'. For his utter loyalty to Daniels, Fiske's supporters labelled him a 'yes' man.[48]

Fiske stuck to his having stated that it would take five years to prepare the fleet for war. Asked what would make the fleet more effective, he replied, in order of priority: the development of naval aviation, a naval general staff, adding 20 000 men to the fleet, and battle cruisers – the last proven useful in the naval battles thus far fought in the European war – and blamed the ineffectiveness of the fleet upon poor civilian administration. Republicans on the committee approved while Democrats opposed his ideas. Daniels at first denied that he had received and read Fiske's preparedness letter of 9 November 1914 until, under pressure from President Wilson, he admitted that he had – and had done nothing about it.[49]

In an address of 1 June 1916, Benson slashed at Fiske. It was unthinkable, he began, to give a CNO 'authority independent of the Secretary'. Upon entering office, he had found only 'the fragment of organization'. He had reorganized the fleet into three divisions of three battleships each, given special attention to naval aviation (which turned out to be disastrous), and won approval for an administrative plan by which the bureaus would report quarterly on their status of preparedness for war. Further, he had taken an inventory of merchant ships available as auxiliaries in time of emergency, reorganized the naval districts that administered the shore establishments, and selected new men to head the Office of Target Practice and Engineering and the submarine service. Lastly, he had had ships overhauled as needed, and acquired an effective Naval Communications Service.[50] Most of these steps were pure Fiske, others defensive compared with the offensive steps Fiske had recommended.

At his request for recommendations, the General Board on 30 July 1915 told Daniels that the Navy should be expanded by 1925 until it was 'equal to the most powerful maintained by any other nation in the world'. For $1.6 billion over six years, the Navy could be furnished 48 dreadnoughts, it being understood that the aim was to obtain parity with Britain in this class rather than to produce antisubmarine ships.[51] Concurrently, there should be an increase in personnel and in the shore establishment. In September Daniels adopted Fiske's continuous building plan when he asked the board to report on a five-year program to cost $100 million annually. On 15 October he forwarded to Congress the first annual increment – 56 ships to be built at a cost of $502.5 million. Wilson and Daniels put pressure on Congress to adopt the measure, only to learn that the Republicans wanted more ships built more quickly and would strengthen the Office of CNO. Benson supported the building program but, alleging that it was tantamount to a general staff, spurned changing his office.[52]

With small-Navy Democrats opposed to the larger and continuous building program favored by Republicans, on 2 June 1916 the House voted for merely a one-year program including no dreadnoughts, five battle cruisers, four scout cruisers, ten destroyers, 20 submarines, and three auxiliaries. News then arrived of the Battle of Jutland, 31 May–1 June, in which battleships particularly had shown their worth. With Republican help, Wilson was able on 21 July to get the Senate to revive the five-year program and on 15 August got the House to go along.

The Naval Act Wilson signed on 29 August 1916 called for 148 combatants out of 157 ships and for starting construction on four battleships and four battle cruisers that would be the most powerful and speediest in the world, and 48 other ships within six months, all to be completed in three rather than five years. Naval aviation was given $3.5 million. Enlisted personnel would increase from 51 000 to 74 000, a number Wilson could raise to 87 000 in an emergency. The act also gave the CNO 15 assistants to write war plans and authorized government armor-making and projectile plants and a naval experiment laboratory. To provide officers for the program, the Naval Academy class would grow from 900 in 1916 to 1200 in 1917, the course would be reduced from four to three years, the class of 1917 would be graduated in February 1918, and the classes of 1918 and 1919 would be graduated a year early. Lastly, a Council of National Defense, a War Industries Board, and a National Research Council were created. The first would coordinate industry and war needs; the second could authorize the military services to requisition or withhold materials.[53] On 16 November non-interventionists, who since 1914 had opposed Wilson's demands for an enlarged merchant marine, finally relented. On 18 December Wilson asked the belligerents to state their war aims as a basis for possible peace negotiations. Rebuffed, on 22 January 1917 he appealed to the peoples of the warring nations to adopt a 'peace without victory'. Meanwhile, on 14 December 1916 Wilson's alter ego, Colonel House, told his diary that in speaking to Daniels 'my worst fears about our unpreparedness were confirmed'. For example, Daniels thought that he would have enough mines in a year to protect the East coast 'fairly well'. House also noted that Wilson had performed magnificently in domestic legislation but that he was a failure as an administrator. More importantly, he concluded that Wilson 'had had nearly three years in which to get the United States into a reasonable state of preparedness and we have not done it'.[54]

Under pressure from the United States, Germany had abandoned its first submarine campaign in September 1915. The torpedoing of the unarmed French Channel steamer *Sussex* on 24 March 1916 provoked a threat by Wilson that he would sever diplomatic relations unless Germany stopped attacking unresisting merchant ships. Germany said she would comply on the impossible condition that Wilson get the British to abide by international law. On 9 January 1917, with the land war still stalemated, lacking food and materials in consequence of the Allied blockade, and believing that the U-boat would win the war before the United States intervened, the Kaiser had ordered unrestricted U-boat warfare resumed on 1 February, meaning that neutral as well as belligerent ships would be sunk. Moreover, the United States could send only one ship to Europe weekly on humiliating stipulated terms. On 3 February he ordered his military departments to prepare plans for full mobilization, and on the nineteenth he directed all Navy bureau chiefs to report on their status of preparedness. Meanwhile Congress increased appropriations for the services and empowered the President to commandeer shipyards and munitions factories in the event of war or national emergency. In addition, Daniels made joint plans with the Army for the air defense of the Atlantic and Gulf coasts.

On 24 February 1917 the General Board forwarded to Daniels the 'Steps to be taken to meet a possible condition of war with a Central European Power'. These would among other things bring the fleet up to a status of war readiness, arm American merchant ships defensively, 'And as most important, arrange, as soon as possible, plans and cooperation with the naval forces of the Allies for the joint protection of trans-Atlantic commerce and for offensive naval operations against the common enemy'. On 5 April, further, the board alerted Daniels to the 'Assistance that United States can give Allies upon declaration of war'. The Navy's mission at war would 'best be determined by arrangement with the Allied Powers . . . There is no doubt that, if desired by the Allies, sending immediately a number of destroyers to cooperate with the Allied powers in the barred zones would greatly add to the moral effect, at home and abroad'. Finally, to cover the possibility that the United States might be compelled to fight Germany alone, large as well as small war vessels should be built.[55]

Because of U-boats, American commercial ships hugged their harbors. Demands arose that they be armed and furnished escorts so they could sail overseas. Wilson authorized guns but not gun crews. By 26 February he had won Congressional approval to arm merchant ships for defensive purposes. On 18 March, however, news came that three American ships had been torpedoed by U-boats. Wilson thereupon decided to go to war rather than continue an armed neutrality and adopted some of the advice the General Board had given Daniels. When he mentioned the adoption of convoy, however, Daniels said that its use might lead to war with Germany.[56]

On 20 March Wilson called Congress into session for 2 April and directed that the Navy be built to full personnel strength and asked Daniels to immediately establish confidential liaison with Britain. Daniels stopped work on battle cruisers and put all workers instead on building destroyers and smaller anti-submarine craft, finally recalled to Chesapeake Bay the ships in southern waters, and ordered Sims, President of the Naval War College, to Washington to be briefed for a journey to London. On 6 April, aided in reaching his decision by Germany's Zimmermann telegram and the Russian Revolution, Wilson approved a joint Congressional resolution of war against Germany, and Daniels ordered the fleet to mobilize.[57]

During his 22 months as Aide for Operations, Fiske had failed to get Daniels to adopt elementary principles that would make the Navy an effective fighting machine or to accept the technical advice necessary to have the Navy carry out national policy. Rather than concentrating upon fleet readiness and war plans, Daniels stressed democracy, education, temperance, parsimony, and humanitarianism.[58] With respect to naval policy, however, Wilson supported Daniels's insistence that military men have nothing to do with it.

In addition to publicizing naval needs and preventing a lowering of the navy's efficiency, Fiske had established by law an Office of CNO that could not be changed by a secretary. He had created a Division of Aeronautics and Naval Radio System and instituted realistic war games, created a state naval militia and a departmental agency to recognize and develop new inventions, and drafted an administrative war plan. Because Daniels signed the last soon after Benson was installed, Fiske could later crow that '*the plan and the office of chief of naval operations are the means by which the Navy Department got ready for war, and by which it operated during the war and has operated since*'.[59]

On 6 April, when Congress approved Wilson's declaration of war, Daniels ordered the fleet to mobilize. Its commander, Rear Admiral Henry T. Mayo, said that 'I did not have to give a signal of any kind or description to pass the fleet from a peace to a war basis'.[60] He was wrong, for the Navy was unprepared for the kind of war it would fight. No anti-submarine warfare plan had been prepared. The shore establishment was not ready to support a war effort, and the merchant marine was only beginning to grow. Benson lacked authority to give orders to the bureaus or even move a ship without Daniels's approval. Daniels had acted only upon six of the 45 preparedness suggestions the General Board had offered him. No arrangements had been made with the Allies to receive American aid, to cooperate with them, or to obtain overseas bases and troop transports. Fiske was upheld when a post-war investigation revealed that only one-third of the Navy's ships were materially fit, and only 10 per cent were adequately manned on 6 April 1917. Further, the Navy was woefully short of anti-submarine ships, minelayers, mines, and auxiliaries, and had only an infant aviation service. With the German High Seas Fleet immobilized, the battleships the United States had concentrated upon building were not needed overseas.[61]

From the outbreak of the Great War to the summer of 1915 Wilson followed a neutrality policy. Democrats who had campaigned in 1916 on the theme that he had kept the nation out of war would not sanction warlike activity against a particular belligerent as long as he supported that policy. Fiske appeared militaristic by predicting war, demanding war preparations, and wanting military men rather than civilians to direct war. Benson would as soon fight Britain as Germany for their violations of America's neutral rights. While he never favored intervention, he believed that the British could not win without America's help, yet he would prepare for war only *after* Germany defeated the Allies. He therefore concentrated on building capital ships rather than anti-submarine types. Only after the war did he acknowledge that he would have augmented the preparedness of the fleet had he known that the nation would go to war, in other words, that he should have been kept informed of national policy. Further, although still under civilian authority, he should have been empowered to prepare the navy as a whole and to coordinate the bureaus.[62] He therefore belatedly agreed with Fiske on these important points. However, Daniels refused on the eve of America's entry into the war either to admit the possibility of that entry or to ready his navy for war. He had done too little too late.

Several lessons suggest themselves from the experience of the

American naval leaders' preparations for the First World War: (1) administration leaders should seek the advice of their service heads in determining national policy. This President Wilson did not do, and not until July 1915 did he ask for professional advice about an 'adequate' naval program; (2) with policy announced, service leaders should devise ways to support it in accordance with their professional expertise; (3) it would help if a naval secretary is familiar with the technology and traditions of the Navy as well as being a political figure; (4) in emergencies, proper arrangements should be made with possible allies; (5) lacking policy direction, service leaders must draft their own policies. If these disagree with those of the administration, the leaders' options are to keep quiet or, in the rare case of a Fiske, to state their differences and resign; (6) perhaps the greatest lesson was that taught by Fiske – that foreign policy, military policy, and logistic requirements for war should be coordinated.

NOTES

1. Josephus Daniels, Diary, 16 January 1915, Josephus Daniels Papers, Manuscript Division, Library of Congress (hereafter MDLC); among others, Woodrow Wilson to the Secretary of the Treasury, William G. McAdoo, 8 March 1915, Woodrow Wilson Papers, MDLC; Josephus Daniels, *The Wilson Era: Years of Peace, 1910–1917* (Chapel Hill: University of North Carolina Press, 1944); Paolo E. Coletta, *Admiral Bradley A. Fiske and the American Navy* (Lawrence: The Regents Press of Kansas, 1979), pp. 117, 131, 133, 147; Arthur S. Link, *Woodrow Wilson and the Progressive Era, 1910–1917* (New York: Harper, 1954), pp. 145 n9, 160–2.
2. President General Board (GB) to Secretary of the Navy (SECNAV), 13 March 1911, GB Letters, 7: Serial 420–2. Washington: Naval Historical Center, Operational Archives.
3. Coletta, *Fiske*, p. 139.
4. For the conflicting attitudes of Daniels and Fiske, see Daniels, *The Wilson Era*, pp. 239–43, and Coletta, *Fiske*, pp. 102–9.
5. Among Daniels's improvements were his provision that officers be promoted by selection rather than by seniority, prohibiting Naval Academy graduates from resigning at will, restricting bureau chiefs to four-year rather than indeterminate terms, sending officers to attend the 18-month 'long' course at the Naval War College, offering enlisted men an off-duty academic course, and making life for the men easier, as by having mechanical laundries fitted in ships. On the other hand, he refused to promote officers lacking sufficient sea service in grade even if

they had been ordered to shore duty and caused naval aviators to lessen their proficiency by requiring them to have alternate sea tours.

6. Daniels, Diary, 5 January 1915; Daniels, *Wilson Era*, p. 337.
7. Bradley A. Fiske, *From Midshipman to Rear-Admiral* (New York: Century, 1919), pp. 513–15.
8. Feeling that the commanders of the Pacific and of the Asiatic fleets did not warrant the rank because of the few ships they commanded, Daniels gave it only to the commander of the Atlantic fleet.
9. Coletta, *Fiske*, Chapters 7 and 16, and 'Bradley A. Fiske: Naval Inventor', in Richard von Doenhoff (ed.), *Versatile Guardian: Research in Naval History* (Washington: Howard University Press, 1979), pp. 87–98.
10. Among other accounts, see that in Paolo E. Coletta, *P. N. L. Bellinger and U.S. Naval Aviation* (Lanham, Md.: University Press of America, 1987), pp. 76–9.
11. Bradley A. Fiske, Diary, 1 August 1914, Bradley A. Fiske Papers, MDLC; GB Proceedings, 1 August 1914, 6:147–8.
12. Fiske, *From Midshipman*, p. 545.
13. Fiske, Diary, 19 October 1914; Coletta, *Fiske*, pp. 120–5, 130. In fairness to Daniels it must be noted that at the request of the General Board as early as 7 March 1913 he asked Wilson to return home the battleships off Mexico. Wilson vetoed the move because Mexico might conclude that their removal meant that he was satisfied with his relations with Mexico. Daniels, Diary, 7, 9 March, 9 April 1913. Unfortunately, Daniels's diaries for 1914 and 1916 are missing.
14. At Wilson's order, Daniels chastized Knight for publicly advocating the adoption of a naval general staff and told him to reserve his comments for Congressional committees. Daniels saw Knight 'as obsessed by the belief that the Navy Department should be organized on the German system and in order to bring that plan about is guilty of doing injustice to the service and criticizing administration policy'. Daniels, Diary, 16 January 1915.
15. Paolo E. Coletta, *French Ensor Chadwick: Scholarly Warrior* (Lanham, Md.: University Press of America, 1980), pp. 155–9. The sale of munitions by a neutral like the United States, approved by international law, aided the Allies, who ruled the seas, and injured the Central Powers. While an embargo might have coerced the belligerents to respect America's neutral rights, it probably would have damaged Allied war-making capacity and resulted in an economic depression that would have hurt the United States as a whole and the Democratic Party in particular. Wilson upheld the principle that neutrality laws could not be changed during the progress of the war, and Congress refused to enact an embargo. The United States thus seemed to acquiesce to the British maritime system.
16. Fiske, Diary, 5 August 1914.
17. Coletta, *Fiske*, pp. 131–4.
18. Fiske, Diary, 29 September 1914.
19. Coletta, *Fiske*, p. 134.
20. Fiske, Diary, 29 September 1914.

21. Ray Stannard Baker, *Woodrow Wilson: Life and Letters*, 8 vols (New York: Doubleday Page and Doubleday Doran, 1927–39), 6:37; Charles Seymour (ed.), *The Intimate Papers of Colonel House*, 4 vols (Boston: Houghton Mifflin, 1926–28), 1:434–35; 2:1, 13.
22. 'Our Naval Preparedness for War', *Literary Digest* 49 (31 October 1914) : 835–6; 'A News Report and a Statement', 7 December 1914, Wilson Papers.
23. Fiske, Diary, 21–23 October 1914, and *From Midshipman*, p. 553.
24. Fiske, Diary, 3 November 1914, and *From Midshipman*, pp. 556–60.
25. Dewey to SECNAV, 10–17 November 1914, GB 420–2; Fiske, Diary, 10 November 1914.
26. Fiske, Memorandum for the General Board, 25 November 1914, GB 420–2.
27. Fiske, *From Midshipman*, p. 571.
28. US Congress, House, Committee on Naval Affairs. *Hearings before the Committee on Naval Affairs of the House of Representatives, on Estimates Submitted by the Secretary of the Navy, 1915* (Washington: GPO, 1915), pp. 34–7, 282, 288.
29. Ibid., pp. 482, 554, 560–1, 572–722.
30. Fiske, *From Midshipman*, p. 571.
31. Fiske, Diary, 16 December 1914.
32. *Hearings . . . 1915*, pp. 1059–83.
33. Daniels, Diary, 22, 23 January 1915; Wilson to Jules J. Jusserand, with enclosures, 1 April 1915, Wilson Papers; Link, *Wilson and the Progressive Era*, p. 178.
34. Daniels, *Wilson Era*, pp. 242–3.
35. Daniels to Swanson and Padgett, 9 February 1915, Papers of the Secretary of the Navy, Naval Archives Record Group 80.
36. Coletta, *Fiske*, pp. 152–4.
37. Fiske, *From Midshipman*, p. 577.
38. *Annual Report of the Secretary (ARSN), 1915* (Washington: GPO, 1915), pp. 9–11.
39. Daniels, *Fiske*, p. 243.
40. Ibid.
41. Albert Gleaves, Diary, Albert Gleaves papers, MDLC; Ernest J. King and Walter Muir Whitehill, *Fleet Admiral King: A Naval Record* (New York: W. W. Norton, 1952), p. 103; Mary Klachko with David Trask, *Admiral William Shepherd Benson: First Chief of Naval Operations* (Annapolis, Md.: Naval Institute Press, 1987), pp. 32–3; David F. Trask, 'William Shepherd Benson, 11 May 1915–25 September 1919', in Robert William Love, Jr. (ed.), *The Chiefs of Naval Operations* (Annapolis, Md.: Naval Institute Press, 1980), pp. 3, 5–7.
42. William S. Sims to Mrs Sims, 21 October 1915. William S. Sims Papers, MDLC.
43. Coletta, *Fiske*, pp. 163–6; Fiske, *From Midshipman*, p. 616.
44. Wilson to Daniels, 21 July 1915, Wilson Papers.
45. Paolo E. Coletta, *William Jennings Bryan, II: Progressive Politician and Moral Statesman, 1909–1915* (Lincoln: University of Nebraska Press, 1969), Chapters 9–12, and 'A Question of Alternatives: Wilson, Bryan,

Lansing, and America's Intervention in World War I', *Nebraska History* 63 (Spring 1982) pp. 33–57; Arthur S. Link, *Wilson: Confusion and Crises, 1915–1916* (Princeton, N.J.: Princeton University Press, 1964), pp. 165–289.

46. Daniels to GB, 7 October 1915, President to SECNAV, 12 October 1915, GB 420–2; Woodrow Wilson, 'Address on Preparedness to the Manhattan Club, Nov. 4, 1915', and 'Annual Message to Congress, Dec. 7, 1915', both in Wilson Papers; Daniels, *Wilson Era*, pp. 490–500.
47. US Congress, House, Committee on Naval Affairs. *Hearings before the Committee on Naval Affairs, House of Representatives, Sixty-fourth Congress, First Session, on Estimates Submitted by the Secretary of the Navy*, 3 vols (Washington: GPO, 1916), 1:356–402, 943–7, 2282–2418; 2:602–60; 3:3136–56; Matthew Josephson, *Edison* (New York: McGraw-Hill, 1959), pp. 446–55; Lloyd N. Scott, *Naval Consulting Board of the United States* (Washington: GPO, 1920).
48. Klachko and Trask, *Benson*, p. 36.
49. Coletta, *Fiske*, pp. 170–5.
50. Ibid., p. 175; Daniels, *Wilson Era*, pp. 244–5; Klachko and Trask, *Benson*, pp. 42–5. On the poor status of naval aviation, see the report of the Commander in Chief, Atlantic Fleet, Henry T. Mayo, ARSN, 1916. On 8 November 1916, Henry C. Mustin, commanding the naval aeronautic center at Pensacola, wrote his wife that 'The aviation situation is too disgusting for words'. Henry C. Mustin Papers, MDLC. His conclusion is borne out in Coletta, *Bellinger*, Chapters 5 and 6.
51. On 25 October 1915, Colonel House had written to Wilson: 'I wonder whether we did not make a mistake in not preparing actively when this war first broke loose. If we had, by now we would have been in a position to enforce peace'. Klachko and Trask, *Benson*, p. 46.
52. *New York Times*, 18, 19 November 1916.
53. Ibid., 25 December 1915; Daniels, Diary, 27 February, 6, 8, 9, 10, 12, 13, 18, 19 March, 2, 7 April 1917; ARSN, 1916, pp. 4–5, 11, 75–6; Arthur S. Link, *Wilson: Campaigns for Progressivism and Peace, 1916–1917* (Princeton, N.J.: Princeton University Press, 1965), pp. 588–93, and *Wilson: The Struggle for Neutrality, 1914–1915* (Princeton, N.J.: Princeton University Press, 1960), pp. 15, 35–6.
54. Edward M. House, Diary, New Haven, Conn., Sterling Memorial Library, Yale University, 14 December 1916.
55. Senior Member Present, GB, to SECNAV, 27 February, 5 April 1917, GB., No. 425.
56. Daniels, Diary, 6, 7 March 1917.
57. Ibid., 25, 26 March 1917, and *Wilson Era*, pp. 580–96; Link, *Wilson: Campaigns for Progressivism and Peace*, pp. 165–437. The Zimmermann telegram invited Mexico to join the war against the United States and as a reward regain the territory lost to the United States in the war of 1846–48. Mexico was also to invite Japan to enter the war against the United States. It appeared to Wilson that with the overthrow of the Russian Tsar all nations fighting Germany were democracies.
58. On these matters see Daniels, *Wilson Era*, pp. 253–78, 386–403.
59. Fiske, *From Midshipman*, p. 588.

60. Josephus Daniels, *The Wilson Era: Years of War and After, 1917–1923* (Chapel Hill: University of North Carolina Press, 1946), p. 39.
61. US, Congress, Senate. *Naval investigation Hearings Before the Subcommittee of the Committee on Naval Affairs, United States Senate, 66th Congress, 2d Sess.*, 2 vols (Washington: GPO, 1921).
62. Trask, 'Benson', in Love (ed.), *Chiefs of Naval Operations*, pp. 7–9.

10 Comments
Joseph G. Dawson

In his chapter, Edward Coffman helps counteract the view (advanced by Ronald Spector[1] and others) that 'Neither the Army nor the Navy was at all prepared for the kind of war they would have to fight' in 1917–18. Coffman argues instead that most of the top US Army officers were well prepared for the major European war in which they participated. His thesis is supported by appropriate examples. Of particular value is his excellent description and analysis of the books and readings that were assigned to American officers who attended the Staff College at Fort Leavenworth and the Army War College. These reading assignments can be seen as part of the growing pattern in the US Army to rely on formal schooling of its officers, who came into the service from several sources – West Point, other military colleges, and by direct commission – in order to lay a common foundation among the officer corps. This common foundation, especially the schooling at Leavenworth, clearly improved the professionalism of American officers between 1903 and 1917.[2]

A clear example of that improved professionalism can be seen by briefly contrasting the number of West Pointers (most with post-graduate education) in 1917–18 with some selected top officers of the period 1898–1900. My own impressionistic look at these officers shows the following:

In the Spanish War the top American officers (in actual positions of responsibility or high-profile commands) were all originally volunteers. These included Nelson Miles as commanding general of the Army and leader of the expedition into Puerto Rico, who had enlisted in the Union Army in 1861; William Shafter, another Civil War Union volunteer, who acted as commander of the V Corps invading Cuba in 1898; Henry Corbin, a Union volunteer infantry lieutenant who held the influential position of Adjutant General of the Army during the War with Spain, a position that might be seen as counterpart to the Chief of Staff in the Great War; and finally, two sentimental choices, Leonard Wood and Theodore Roosevelt of the 1st US Volunteer Cavalry Regiment, an outfit made famous at the San Juan fight. By the time of the Spanish War, Miles, Shafter, Corbin, and Wood were all regulars, with only Roosevelt coming on duty recently. Command of one of America's major overseas forces, however, went to a West Pointer: Wesley Merritt, the initial leader of the US ground forces in the Philippines. The command examples were mixed later for the US contingent in the China Relief Expedition to suppress the 'Boxer Rebellion'. Adna R. Chaffee was another officer who had entered the service by volunteering for the Union in the Civil War; one of his chief subordinates was James H. Wilson, a West Pointer who had been out of the Army for 28 years before returning to duty in 1898.[3]

Now, to contrast these men with a selected list of top officers during the Great War: in place of Miles, there is John J. Pershing (USMA 1886), commander of the American Expeditionary Forces. Instead of Shafter one might select Robert L. Bullard (USMA 1885; Army War College), commander, successively of the 1st Infantry Division, III Corps, and Second Army. Peyton C. March as Chief of Staff of the Army did an excellent job; he was USMA, Class of 1888. Balancing Wood and Roosevelt, we can look to one of the officers featured by Professor Coffman: Joseph T. Dickman (USMA, 1881; Staff College and Army War College), who led the 3rd Division and later commanded the IV Corps and then the I Corps; and Hunter Liggett (USMA 1879, Army War College), I Corps and First Army commander. For officers to compare with Merritt, Chaffee, and Wilson, we can choose Mason Patrick (USMA, 1886) who headed the Air Service of Pershing's AEF; William S. Graves (USMA, 1889 and member of the General Staff, 1914–18) who commanded the extraordinary American Siberian Expedition, 1918–20.[4]

Therefore, in contrast to the Spanish War era, the top leadership of American forces in the Great War and after were mostly West Pointers with advanced education or technical expertise. The AEF was fortunate *not* to have a Miles or a Shafter, both of whom would have been inadequate leaders in the Great War. The Army had made a clear shift away from the volunteer tradition of the nineteenth century and had entrusted its top commands to professionals who benefited from the Army's improved educational system.

While few would argue against the benefits of education at the Staff College, the practical 'field' education (combat experience) of American officers might be another matter. Combat experience for US Army officers might be seen from two perspectives: what did it do for the officers themselves, and what did other nations' officers think of the experience the Americans brought to their tasks in the Great War?

One might agree with the saying that 'some combat experience is better than no combat experience'. According to most of the descriptions left by those who lived through it, combat presents personal and professional challenges that cannot be equalled even in the best maneuvers or training exercises. But one might question if the experiences of some of the American officers in Cuba or Puerto Rico in the War with Spain were of much benefit or, more particularly, if the experience of the guerrilla warfare in the Philippines was of much help in understanding the standard European war that was fought on the Western Front in 1917 and 1918. The challenges of the European War probably were best simulated and anticipated by exercises at Leavenworth, as Professor Coffman indicates in his chapter.

And what of European officers' views of Americans' combat experience? It appears that most British and French officers were not much impressed with either the War with Spain or the fighting in the Philippines. Would actions of American units in France and the education of American officers be able to overcome the negative views of the Europeans toward the US Army?

With some exceptions, the Europeans had a general lack of respect towards the American forces. One of Pershing's main tasks was to create 'a respectable army'. The phrase has a familiar ring to it: it comes from George Washington's objective in the American Revolution, to form and train an army that would be respectable in the eyes of the British.[5]

The requirement to create a 'respectable army' is one of the main themes of American military history. The theme begins with Washington's decision to establish his army on the standard European model, and carries into the Second War with Britain in 1812, when officers such as Winfield Scott and Jacob Brown put soldiers in the field whom British commanders complimented by saying, 'Those are Regulars, by God!'[6] It extends to the war with Mexico, in which Scott led an unappreciated campaign that captured Mexico City[7]; to the American Civil War, which offered for study major campaigns of large armies over broad geographical areas but prompted little close analysis by Europeans, as Jay Luvaas has described so well[8]; up through the Trans-Mississippi Indian Wars and the War with Spain and the Philippine Insurrection. Although G. F. R. Henderson highlighted Stonewall Jackson's career, when had the US Army fought a war or developed commanders or campaigns worthy of deep study by Europeans? The bizarre antics of General Shafter's forces in Cuba hardly qualified as campaigning to be held up to Napoleonic standards.

The guerrilla fighting in the Philippines was similar to colonial wars elsewhere around the world.

By 1914, even with the Root Reforms and quadrupling its size from 1898, the US Army was laughably tiny by Continental measurements. Three years later America's force of about 200 000 could be shattered in a week of fighting on the Western Front. As Coffman points out, it is small wonder that the Germans discounted the weight that the Americans could bring to bear on the Western Front. And small wonder that the British and French held out little promise for the Americans to make much of an impact until late 1918 or 1919.

So Europeans on both sides of 'No Man's Land' in France in 1917 had little respect for America's army, its equipment, its training, or its state of readiness.[10] The US Army was far from what Secretary of War Elihu Root had wanted in 1903: an army that would be 'an instrument of national power'.[11]

Coffman shows that US Army leadership was prepared to take on the daunting tasks of fighting a major war in Europe. But the American performance was not enough to overcome the many doubts that skeptical Europeans had in 1914 or 1917. And those doubts carried over all the way into the 1940s.

Only spectacular American victories in a smashing wide-front campaign of 1919 – a campaign that was not fought – would have gained deep respect for the US Army, and persuaded the Europeans to agree with the opinion of Pershing: that America had an excellent citizen army led by high-quality professional officers.[12]

In one of the 'bibles' of naval history, *The Rise of American Naval Power, 1776–1918*, Harold and Margaret Sprout concluded that Secretary of the Navy Josephus Daniels adopted a 'policy of inaction' and 'enforced it as strictly as he could from the outbreak of war in 1914 right down to [American] entry in 1917'. Furthermore, the Sprouts argued, Daniels 'persistently ignored the recommendations of his professional advisors and obstructed their individual efforts to put the Navy in readiness for war'.[13] Paolo Coletta, through his research and writing on naval history, has added much to the Sprouts' account.

His chapter here and his other deep research indicate that Daniels and President Wilson began making some change in their outlook in 1915, but confirms that Daniels did not encourage advice from top naval officers if it included recommendations for action, such as maneuvers, or a buildup, such as increasing personnel and adding ships.[14]

Coletta points out the need for civilian leaders of an administration – especially an administration in office during time of war – to seek the advice of service heads and then determine national policy. Wilson concluded on neutrality, and announced that policy emphatically to the nation. Secretary Daniels opposed the suggestions of Admiral Fiske because Wilson had given no signal that he wanted a military buildup.[15]

National views on a great expansion of the Navy only began to change when Wilson decided, about a year after the Great War began, to pursue a policy that came close to what Fiske already had advocated for several months. Earlier, Fiske could not get the program adopted because it was not politically acceptable – to Wilson, Daniels, the Congress, or the nation. By late 1915 Wilson began working on the Congress and the country effectively to change their minds about the need for naval growth. These actions indicate one of the continuing features of American history: military officers fail to recognize that some steps cannot be taken at certain times for political reasons or, on the other hand, that other steps must be taken for political reasons.

Secretary Daniels can be faulted for not accepting the need for a Naval General Staff, and for not helping Fiske gradually to bring the President and the Congress to support such a staff. Given Daniels's lack of familiarity with America's military forces and the Navy in particular, such opposition is understandable. He was reluctant to condone a Prussian-style system and self-consciously tried to maintain the age-old maxim of civilian control of the military establishment.[16]

Daniels reflects the typical American Cabinet member. Most of them are accustomed to having long lead-times for thinking about military changes and expansions, debating military development programs, considering which companies might get military construction contracts, and expecting comfortable margins of time for testing ships and equipment and training soldiers and sailors. Daniels and Wilson can also be faulted, as Coletta points out, for not understanding that the nation needed to have ships in existence, and that national leaders must be thinking ahead – 10 or 15 years ahead – as to what ships will be needed, not just thinking in annual increments.

Wilson and Daniels fell into the familiar pit of thinking mostly of political constraints of the *immediate* cost of ships and equipment while filtering out any sense of urgency expressed by naval officers for building new ships and procuring new equipment. Perhaps, as James Abrahamson argues, Daniels showed 'distrust for his admirals'.[17] The civilians had some reasons for being skeptical of the demands made by the navy brass. The Navy's reputation stood high as a result of its excellent showing against the Spanish. Moreover, the Navy was much larger than the Army, and in a better state of modernization, training, and general readiness than the land forces. Admittedly, the Navy was weak in anti-submarine vessels, but that did not seem to be an urgent matter for several months, well into the war. By the time of American entry into the war, the need would be evident, even to Daniels.[18]

But Coletta's assessment of Daniels holds up: although he worked hard, was patriotic and competent, at heart Daniels was, as Coletta calls him, a 'mere politician'. Franklin D. Roosevelt, Daniels's assistant secretary of the navy, was less generous, concluding that the Secretary was 'bewildered by it all, very sweet, but very sad'.[19] Daniels's appointment was typical in American history of Presidents playing politics with the War Department and the Navy Department. For most presidents it is more important to have a party loyalist in the Cabinet than someone made appropriate for his post by education or experience. Daniels's ignorance on naval matters meant that he could reject Fiske's recommendation to bring the number of enlisted men up to a full complement for each ship. With a major war raging in Europe, increasing the number of enlisted men was in the national interest, and Daniels should not have opposed it. Time and again, as Coletta shows, Daniels's lack of knowledge made him doubtful about what steps the Navy should take.

As for Admiral Fiske, he was not above 'playing politics' himself, as evidenced by his willingness to use Congressional hearings or to go to Congressman Richmond Hobson with special inside information in order to gain support for naval improvement programs. The irony came in January 1916 when Daniels had to admit that Fiske had been right on almost every score.

The National Defense Act of 1916 and the Naval Act of the same year signaled a sharp change in policy for the Wilson Administration. While emphasizing 'defense', both laws put in motion a sequence of steps that would considerably strengthen America's military forces. The office of Chief of Naval Operations was strengthened by the Naval Act, and it was ironic that Admiral William Benson should have been in the chair rather than Fiske. The two men had not seen eye-to-eye for months, but Benson would be charged with developing many of the preparedness programs that Fiske had promoted.[20]

Only slowly did Wilson and Daniels reach the point where they saw the need to prepare the Navy for war.[21] And Bradley Fiske deserves much of the credit for proposing the programs and actions that the

Navy had to take. In the meantime, as Coletta shows, Fiske publicized the Navy's needs, helped to pave the way to the Naval Act of 1916, and kept the Navy operating as efficiently as Daniels would allow. It is unfortunate, but politically understandable, that in such matters as naval aviation Daniels lacked Fiske's visionary outlook. Once again, Daniels's lack of technical knowledge let him down, and thus he let the nation down in the opening months of the Great War.

NOTES

1. Ronald Spector, 'You're Not Going to Send Sailors Over There Are You?': The American Search for An Alternative to the Western Front, 1916–1917', *Military Affairs*, 36 (February 1972), p. 1.
2. Timothy K. Nenninger, *The Leavenworth Schools and the Old Army: Education, Professionalism, and the Officer Corps of the United States Army, 1881–1918* (Westport, CT: Greenwood Press, 1978), pp. 53–133.
3. Convenient summaries of the careers of these officers are found alphabetically, in *Dictionary of American Military Biography*, 3 vols, (Westport, CT: Greenwood Press, 1984), ed. by Roger J. Spiller and Joseph G. Dawson III.
4. Ibid.
5. James Kirby Martin and Mark Edward Lender, *A Respectable Army: The Military Origins of the Republic, 1763–1789* (Arlington Heights, IL: Harlan Davidson, 1982), p. 47.
6. Harry L. Coles, *The War of 1812* (Chicago: University of Chicago Press, 1965), p. 157.
7. James W. Pohl, 'The Influence of Antoine Henri de Jomini on Winfield Scott's Campaign in the Mexican War', *Southwestern Historical Quarterly*, LXXVII (July 1973), pp. 85–110.
8. Jay Luvaas, *The Military Legacy of the Civil War: The European Inheritance* (Chicago: University of Chicago Press, 1959).
9. G. F. R. Henderson, *Stonewall Jackson and the American Civil War* (London: Longmans, Green, 1898).
10. James L. Stokesbury, *A Short History of World War I* (New York: William Morrow, 1981), p. 218; Donald Smythe, *Pershing: General of the Armies* (Bloomington: Indiana University Press, 1986), pp. 69, 111, 112; Russell F. Weigley, *History of the United States Army* (New York: Macmillan, 1967), pp. 387, 393; Harvey DeWeed, *President Wilson Fights His War* (New York: Macmillan, 1968), p. 202; Allan R. Millett, 'Cantigny', in C. E. Hiller and W. A. Stofft, (eds), *America's First Battles* (Lawrence: University Press of Kansas, 1986), p. 160; Lee Kennett, 'The A.E.F. Through French Eyes', *Military Review*, 52 (November 1972), pp. 5–7, 11.

11. Maurice Matloff (ed.), *American Military History* (Washington: Office of the Chief of Military History/U.S. Government Printing Office, 1969), p. 347.
12. Smythe, *Pershing, General of the Armies*, p. 142.
13. Harold and Margaret Sprout, *The Rise of American Naval Power, 1776–1918* (Princeton: Princeton University Press, 1967), pp. 357–8.
14. Paolo E. Coletta, 'Josephus Daniels', in Coletta (ed.), *American Secretaries of the Navy*, 2 vols (Annapolis, MD: Naval Institute Press, 1980), II, pp. 525–81.
15. David F. Trask, *Captains and Cabinets: Anglo-American Naval Relations, 1917–1918* (Colombia: University of Missouri Press, 1972), p. 46.
16. Paolo E. Coletta, *Admiral Bradley A. Fiske and the American Navy* (Lawrence: The Regents Press of Kansas, 1979), pp. 104, 116.
17. James L. Abrahamson, *American Arms for a New Century: The Making of a Great Military Power* (New York: Free Press, 1981), p. 160.
18. Trask, *Captains and Cabinets*, p. 64.
19. Franklin D. Roosevelt to Eleanor Roosevelt, 5 August 1914, in Elliot Roosevelt (ed.), *FDR: His Personal Letters* (4 vols, New York: Duell, Sloan & Pierce, 1947–50), II, p. 243.
20. Mary Klachko and David F. Trask, *Admiral William Shepherd Benson: First Chief of Naval Operations* (Annapolis, MD: Naval Institute Press, 1987), pp. 27–62. See also David F. Trask, 'William S. Benson', in Robert Love (ed.), *The Chiefs of Naval Operations* (Annapolis, MD: Naval Institute Press, 1980), pp. 3–22.
21. John Patrick Finnegan, *Against the Spector of a Dragon: The Campaign for American Preparedness, 1914–1917* (Westport, CT: Greenwood Press, 1974), pp. 162–3.

Index